CELEBRATING The Anglican WAY

Edited by

Ian Bunting

Hodder & Stoughton
LONDON SYDNEY AUCKLAND

First published in Great Britain 1996

10 9 8 7 6 5 4 3 2 1

British Library Cataloguing in Publication Data
A record for this book is available from the British Library

ISBN 0 340 64268 8

Designed and typeset by
Kenneth Burnley at Typograph, Irby, Wirral, Cheshire.

Printed and bound in Great Britain by
Mackays of Chatham PLC, Chatham, Kent

Hodder & Stoughton
A Division of Hodder Headline PLC
338 Euston Road
London NW1 3BH

Contents

	Introduction	9
	Celebrating the Anglican way *George Carey*	13
Part 1	**Believing the Anglican way**	
1	The Anglican character *Stephen Sykes*	21
2	Church and society *John Habgood*	33
3	Anglican belief *Bruce Kaye*	42
4	A worldwide communion *Michael Nazir-Ali*	53
Part 2	**Belonging in the Anglican Church**	
5	Anglican origins and ethos *Elizabeth Culling*	69
6	The Anglican way of worship *Michael Vasey*	82
7	Word and sacrament *Philip Seddon*	97
8	Churchmanship *Jonathan Baker*	110
Part 3	**Following the Anglican way**	
9	Praying our way through life *Graham Pigott*	127
10	Sharing our faith in the world *Amiel Osmaston & Alison White*	143
11	Care and change in our society *Lawrence Osborn*	161

Part 4 Appreciating Anglican structures

12 Orders and officers of the church — 179
David Sceats

13 Church government — 199
Michael Botting

14 Church buildings — 215
Richard & Sarah Burton

Part 5 The way ahead

15 The Anglican future — 229
Ian Bunting

16 Praying with the church — 244

Further reading — 247

Acknowledgments — 248

Index — 249

Authors

George Carey *Archbishop of Canterbury*

John Habgood *formerly Archbishop of York*

Stephen Sykes *Bishop of Ely*

Michael Nazir-Ali *Bishop of Rochester*

Bruce Kaye *General Secretary, Anglican Church of Australia*

Jonathan Baker *Assistant Curate, Sanderstead Team Ministry, Surrey*

Michael Botting *formerly Joint Director of Training, Diocese of Chester and Member of General Synod*

Ian Bunting *Director of Ordinands, Diocese of Southwell*

Richard & Sarah Burton *Richard is Vicar of Tadcaster, York*

Elizabeth Culling *Priest-in-charge of Cherry Burton, York and Senior Adviser in Rural Affairs*

Lawrence Osborn *Templeton Research Fellow, Ridley Hall, Cambridge*

Amiel Osmaston *Director of Mission and Pastoral Studies, Ridley Hall, Cambridge*

Graham Pigott *Vicar, St Paul's, Wilford Hill, Nottingham*

David Sceats *Director of Local Ministry Development and Warden of Readers, Diocese of Lichfield*

Philip Seddon *Lecturer in Biblical Studies, School of Mission and World Christianity, Selly Oak Colleges, Birmingham*

Michael Vasey *Tutor, St John's College, Durham, and Member of the Liturgical Commission*

Alison White *Director of Mission and Pastoral Studies, St John's College, Durham*

Introduction

Who is the book for?

As this book was being written, we had in mind the intelligent enquirer who wants to learn about the faith and life of the Anglican Church. We belong to a worldwide communion of churches which share common roots. We have some characteristics which are those of the family of all Christian churches. There are also some identifiable features which mark us out as having a particular contribution to make.

First, our book is written for the person who is thinking of joining an Anglican church. While some try to be Christians on their own, or in informal fellowships of believers, it is important sooner or later to join a church. Christians down the centuries have emphasised the point and the Bible has been witness to the importance of it. To follow Jesus Christ is to belong to his Church. This book could be part of someone's personal journey to faith or could form the basis of a course leading to baptism and confirmation. It could be a resource for religious studies or lay training.

Second, many find that after their early experiences of Christian life and fellowship, they want to explore their roots. At first there can seem to be a big black hole between the exciting life of the Church in the New Testament and the developing life of the churches today. Then the question arises: How has God been at work in the intervening period? The Anglican Church witnesses to God at work in history as well as God revealed in Bible times and in our own day.

Third, we have in mind those who already belong to Anglican churches, perhaps are even contemplating ordination or some other form of ministry, but want to find out more about the church in which they have been nurtured and now belong. Someone has said, 'Anglicans are very good at being nice to people and hoping they will guess why.' We need to do better than that. We hope our readers will recognise this contribution as an authoritative and, for its size, a comprehensive celebration of Anglican faith and practice which will serve as a stimulating introduction to our church and what we believe. We will be pleased if it prompts further study, maybe through group discussion of the questions we have included in each chapter.

The shape of the book

The book covers three themes: Anglican believing, belonging and behaving. The chapters follow roughly in that order and end with a confident look forward to the future. The title suggests that we have in mind a celebration of the Anglican way. We do not deliberately ignore or avoid the hard issues which divide Christians, Anglicans among them. The way we try to face controversy is by offering open-ended questions. By their nature they suggest a belief that committed Anglicans may with integrity hold different views on different subjects. The fact that we have included questions at all reflects an Anglican conviction that it is important Anglicans do not duck hard debate or jump too quickly to easy solutions to complex problems. We do, however, have an Anglican approach to the discussion process. We try to integrate what the Bible says with the conclusions of the Christian tradition, and human wisdom enlightened by the Holy Spirit who is with us now in the setting in which we find ourselves.

The book differs in another way from traditional introductions to the Anglican way. It attempts to escape from the Englishness of much Anglican self-understanding. We have tried to do this by including frequent references to churches in the Anglican Communion other than the Church of England. For example, we talk about the resolutions of Lambeth Conferences which for more than a hundred years have drawn together Anglican bishops from all over the world in consultation. We are a global communion. The majority of faithful Anglicans now live in the developing world. Many believe that the mother churches have to learn from the newer churches much that will revitalise and renew our Anglican faith and practice in the developed world. In this way, reviewing our historic roots and our worldwide mission and communion, we hope the book will contribute to the renewal of the Anglican Church in a changing world as we move into a new millennium.

Who wrote the book?

At the time of the publication in England of the *Alternative Service Book* (1980), I was one of a group of authors who wrote an illustrated guide to it called *Anglican Worship Today*. We planned to produce a follow-up publication but it never got beyond the drawing board. Fifteen years later the idea has borne fruit in the form of this book. I decided to ask two groups of people with whom I had warm working relationships to co-operate in the project.

The first group was, with one exception, made up of colleagues I worked with during the 1970s and 1980s in Durham. Although they are enormously busy people, they have seen the value of the project and have willingly contributed from their recognised wisdom, authority and experience of the Anglican Church worldwide.

The other group was the Grove Spirituality Group of which I have been a member since it first met in 1980. This group of writers, the membership of which has changed over the years, produces four booklets each year. We have become a group of friends as well as authors, and each one able to do so has accepted the responsibility of contributing to this book. I am particularly grateful to Graham Pigott and Michael Vasey who have helped in the editing. My thanks also go to James Rosenthal (editor of *Anglican World*) who supplied many of the photographs.

Ian Bunting

Celebrating the Anglican way

George Carey

'Celebrating the Anglican way' – that title does indeed sum up my own experience of the Anglican Church and my appreciation of it. What began as an almost accidental encounter with the Church of England has developed over the years into a deep love for the variety and breadth of the traditions of the Anglican Church worldwide.

Others will describe the origins and development of those traditions during the course of this book; but in writing this keynote I hope I will be forgiven for being autobiographical.

I have chosen to write in this way for two main reasons – the first theological and the second personal.

Theologically I do so because I believe at the heart of our faith lies an experiential encounter with God. Christ's earliest followers came to know him first and then, out of that experience, did their theological reflection. That same pattern should be repeated in our theological thinking today. Too often we have treated experience as in some way separate from real theology. Of course it must not be used as an excuse for the avoidance of tough rational debate but neither must it be treated as being irrelevant to that debate. The experience of God lies close to the heart of true theology.

The personal reason for choosing to write autobiographically is linked to those theological reflections. I suspect that many of those reading this book will, in their own way, be exploring the Anglican way. The exploration will, of course, be different for every person. Yet, as we hear the stories of a wide variety of people, we find common strands linking them to ours and that sharing of experience can often be a source of strength and encouragement. It is in that spirit that I offer a few reflections on my own story in the hope that it will be of help to others.

My choice of a church in my teens was not dictated by theological conviction or carefully weighed-up considerations. Instead, it came as a result of a personal invitation from my younger brother, Bob, who was the first member of our family to start attending the local church regularly. At that stage my Anglican roots were very shallow indeed. I had been baptised in a London parish but was not brought up as a churchgoer.

Yet, at another level, it was far less accidental than might appear at first sight. The parish in Dagenham represented one small part of a church which was then, and still is, committed to serving the spiritual needs of the whole nation, regardless of background, colour, wealth, sex or age. As I was later to discover, although I was not a practising Christian and my knowledge was scanty, I was still a member of a church that counted me in. This is one part of the Anglican way which I came to value then and still rejoice in.

That church I joined at the age of 17 was thoroughly *evangelical* in its preaching and teaching. Of course, I did not know what the word 'evangelical' meant then. I was later to discover that it represented a tradition in the life of our church which valued the teaching of the Reformation and in particular the twin doctrines of 'grace' and 'justification by faith'. Preaching in Dagenham parish church focused on an appeal to respond to Christ whilst its teaching was rooted firmly in seeking to make the Bible relevant to everyday life. My vicar instilled in us all the sense that Christianity was not something to be treated lightly. The call from our Lord was one to whole-hearted discipleship, and those of us in the youth group were left in no doubt about that.

I owe a great deal to those who encouraged me in those early years. My own spirituality is still grounded in the regular personal Bible study we were encouraged to make central to our Christian discipleship. Indeed, for me, one of the long-term attractions of the Anglican way has been the fact that it is rooted in Scripture as the foundation for our understanding of the faith.

But in those years I also encountered a narrow biblicism which to my mind failed to do justice to the rich diversity of the biblical record. I have always wanted to ask questions of anything I read, and I became increasingly dissatisfied with those who seemed to be avoiding some of the obvious difficulties in the biblical text. Words like 'inerrancy' have never really appealed to me and certainly my own belief in the Bible's authority with regard to its revelation of God does not depend on having a text free of minor contradictions.

This desire to explore and to question I also discovered to be a part of the Anglican way. It is something I treasure. The great *liberal* tradition, with its stress on taking the world in which we are set very seriously indeed and using our reason to try to discern the mind of God was, when I look back, something I yearned for, but had not discovered in my early years as a Christian. Later I was to discover that the word 'liberal' is one of those portmanteau words which can be used to describe on the one hand someone who is open to discovering the truth wherever it may be found or, on the other hand, the root and branch radical who is eager to demolish every structure of tradition or authority. Within mainstream Anglican thought the word 'liberal' is best understood as a commitment to orthodoxy which is open to new thought, new knowledge and to the challenges of our culture. To my delight I found on my journey as a Christian that the tradition I had embraced did not encourage me to cast my mind away or to feel guilty if I was challenged by concepts that questioned my faith. To this day I remain proud of a tradition that is broad enough to include great diversity and the questioning spirit which is not content with narrowness of thought.

My encounters with the *Catholic* tradition within the Church of England were much more limited at that stage. Intellectually I was first introduced to it by my studies in Patristic Theology during my time as a curate in Islington. Professor Eric Mascall, then teaching at King's College, London, and a number of others, showed me that 2,000 years of Christian history should never be overlooked in seeking to understand the ways of God. It was simply not good enough to assume that nothing had happened between the writing of the New Testament and today! This, I have to say, was initially a great challenge to the nurturing of my faith as an evangelical Christian. God, I realised, had not been absent for 1,900 years but had been working unceasingly in the development of Christian doctrine and thought, and the Catholic tradition was a witness to this powerful source of faith and life. Through

St Augustine of Canterbury established the first church in 597. All Anglicans are in communion with, and recognise the leadership of, the Archbishop and see (from the bishop's 'seat' or 'throne') of Canterbury.

those studies, too, I began to realise how much the Anglican tradition owed to men and women steeped in the Catholic tradition. The importance of the sacrament of the Holy Communion, the use of silence, the practice of making retreats – all these I came to appreciate more fully and they now provide a richness to my life which I would be loath to be without.

Indeed, since becoming Archbishop my appreciation of the Catholic heritage of our church has developed still further. My fellowship with my colleagues in the House of Bishops has been one aspect of this, but I have also benefited greatly both through ecumenical encounters and through my visits to the Anglican Communion. On many occasions, particularly in Africa, I have been struck by the way in which many of these churches manage to combine a depth of Catholic devotion with an evangelical zeal for the Gospel. They have left me in no doubt that the Church of England still has a great deal to learn from the other Provinces of the Communion.

The evangelical, liberal and Catholic traditions have, then, all had a distinctive role to play in my own development as a Christian and to them I would add a fourth, the *charismatic*. Whilst I have never been what some would term a 'card-carrying charismatic' I have greatly benefited from many of its insights. In particular its theology of the Spirit as active in the church and a power for living changed my perspective on the way God works in the world. Theologically the contribution of the charismatic movement to my development as a Christian enlarged my understanding of the Holy Trinity and gave me an experiential understanding of God as Father, Son and Holy Spirit. But the contribution of this movement to lay ministry and its yearning for greater freedom in worship have proved to be formative in the church as well as in my own spiritual development. My time as Vicar of St Nicholas, Durham was a very exciting one indeed, not least because of the ways in which the charismatic movement affected us during those years.

Historians will, no doubt, argue in the days to come about its significance for the life of the church, but I am in no doubt that it is one of the distinctive works of the Spirit this century. I rejoice too that many who have been deeply affected by it have also remained firmly committed to the Anglican Church. This I see as a mark both of

Opposite:
The Archbishop of Canterbury travels widely throughout the Anglican Communion.

the maturity of their own spirituality and of the Anglican Church's capacity to absorb new influences. Indeed the Anglican way should never be described merely in static terms. At its best it is like a growing plant, constantly pushing out new shoots in a variety of directions, but always relating back to the roots from which it springs.

The Anglican Church is, of course, just one part of the greater tapestry of worldwide Christianity. 'Celebrating the Anglican way' should never be done in a spirit of triumphalism. Indeed, when any church or denomination begins to look as if it is claiming the right to be viewed as the only true church then misunderstandings can easily result. Rather we should acknowledge the provisional nature of all institutional churches. But what divides us from our fellow Christians is, after all, of far less significance than what unites us in Christ, and within this variety the Anglican way has often proved to be a bridge between the Catholic, Orthodox and Reformed wings of the church. As such it has come to perform a vital ecumenical function, as some of our recent dialogues with other churches have shown.

However, because it is neither simply Catholic nor simply Reformed, it has been characterised by some as falling between two stools and ending up being neither one thing nor the other. Such an accusation is false and for this reason, if no other, I believe the publication of this book to be a timely one. It is simply not true, as these chapters show, that to be an Anglican means that you can believe anything you want provided that you do not do so too strongly! Rather, the Anglican Church has its own distinctive tradition and one that it is well worth celebrating. It is a tradition in all its richness and variety that I have come to appreciate greatly over the years. My hope, therefore, is that this book will help many people to join together with others in 'Celebrating the Anglican way'.

Part 1

Believing the Anglican way

1

The Anglican character

Stephen Sykes

It is very well known that there are different kinds of Anglicans. What is it that holds them all together? This question is all the more important because the breadth and variety of the Anglican family is actually increasing in the modern world.

Local difference is completely consistent with traditional Anglican self-understanding. From the sixteenth century onwards, Anglicans have seen themselves as the local embodiment of the catholic or universal Church, not as the best church for all the peoples of the earth. English Anglicans expected there to be other reformed catholic churches in other places. They spoke of God's 'harmonious dissimilitude' (Richard Hooker) of types of church. For example, Wales acquired its own Bible and Prayer Book in Welsh in the sixteenth century. The readiness to acknowledge and enjoy cultural variety has grown in the nineteenth and twentieth centuries. This frequently is a source of enrichment.

Variety is also increased for Anglicans by the deliberate attempt to be an inclusive type of church. The main continental sixteenth-century reformers came to disagree with each other about a number of theological and practical matters. In England, under Elizabeth I, many Anglican leaders tried to avoid controversy, and to keep people of different convictions within a common framework. Arguments between 'puritans' who wanted more radical changes, and 'conservatives' who emphasised continuity with the pre-Reformation church, have continued in Anglican churches to the present day. In the early 1950s, for example, the Archbishop of Canterbury commissioned studies of the differences between 'Catholicity' and 'Protestantism' from different English Anglican schools of thought. The impact of historical critical study of the Bible and of varying schools of philosophical thought has also tended to increase variety.

In this chapter an account will be given of the 'spirit' or character which unifies the different tendencies within this world communion. This attempt has been quite frequently made, especially since the early nineteenth century when people began to speak about 'Anglican-ism'. But an '-ism' may easily suggest something too static to be true to the variety. Another model or analogy might be that of a *family likeness*. Within families, A will share some characteristics with B, and B will share other characteristics with C. But there need be nothing which A, B and C all have in common. Yet the degree of overlap may be sufficient for the idea of family likeness to be coherent.

Or again, one may speak of a *common language* for Anglicans. Denominations are a bit like language groups, who share a particular way of communicating. In the case of Christian faith, by 'language' we should not simply mean words, but also common assumptions, ways of relating, tone and colouring, attitudes towards and use of common structures, and so forth. People learn by participation to speak with one another in the idiom of their own churches.

Or thirdly, one could use the helpful analogy of *a frame to a picture or window*. One of the important things about the Anglican character or spirit is that one should remember not to focus on it, but on the picture or view itself. But just as frames can be so ornate that they overpower the subject, or again so shoddy and inadequate that they detract from the picture, so we should aim for a frame which enables us to focus appropriately on the real subject matter to be seen.

The variety of these analogies helps us to appreciate the fact that there is no one way of giving an account of what holds Anglicans of different kinds together. And in fact Anglicans have traditionally been reluctant to claim too much distinctiveness for themselves. This is partly because of their original attempt to be as inclusive as possible, and partly because of the history of growing toleration of religious diversity characteristic of English culture. But there is another important reason for this reticence. It is also quite possible for the Anglican family to have characteristics without having any distinctive features. After all a cricket ball may be *characteristically* round, without being *distinctively* round. It may be a *characteristic* of Anglicans to enjoy liturgically ordered worship and to recite the creeds, without it being *distinctive* of them. No Anglican should want or need to claim absolute distinctiveness for the various features of the Anglican way.

This is important, of course, if it is the function of a church tradition to help believers focus on the substance of the faith, which, thank God, most Christian churches have in common. The heart of the matter may be spoken of as the paschal mystery ('Christ our Passover is sacrificed for us; therefore let us keep the feast': 1 Corinthians 5:7, Anthem for Easter Day, *BCP*). It is spoken of in Scripture in a variety of ways, which correspond to the analogies we have used. Christ is our brother, and we are to grow into his likeness (Romans 8:29). Jesus is the one who speaks the words of eternal life (John 6:68). What we see, we see through a glass darkly, but with the expectation of seeing face to face (1 Corinthians 13:12). But all of this is carried by a tradition which has certain characteristic features. The Anglican character may be described collectively as a particular way of interrelating Scripture, common worship and doctrine in the service of the unity of the Church. There is wide and admitted internal variety in the use of each of these features by Anglicans, none of which is distinctive of itself. But the interrelation tends to give a certain kind of pattern to the Anglican way, and thus to generate a sort of spirit or ethos, tending to unite Anglicans, even of discernibly different kinds.

In what follows, frequent reference will be made to the *Book of Common Prayer* (*BCP*), the Thirty-nine Articles and the Ordering of Bishops, Priests and Deacons (Ordinal). These constitute what in the Church of England is spoken of as its 'inheritance of faith' (see Canon C. 15 of the Church of England). These sources have been and are variously interpreted, and occupy no unified position in the constitutions and canons of the many Anglican Provinces. But insofar as they define the faith inheritance of the See of Canterbury, and insofar as communion with that See defines what it means to belong to the Anglican Communion, these documents have a significant authority among Anglicans throughout the world.

Thirty-nine Articles

At the time of the Reformation several attempts were made to set out the Anglican view of key points of doctrine. Archbishop Thomas Cranmer drafted forty-two Articles, which were published on Royal Authority in 1553 and all clergy, schoolmasters and members of the universities were to subscribe to them.

They were not enforced under Queen Mary (1553–8), but they became the basis of the Thirty-nine Articles of 1662, having been further modified in 1571. The final form of the Articles was approved by convocation – the assemblies of clergy and bishops.

The Articles were an attempt to state key doctrines of the faith and also to declare the Anglican view on certain matters of controversy. These related mainly to either medieval Roman Catholicism or extreme Protestant views.

The Chicago–Lambeth Quadrilateral

The conservatism and openness in the Anglican way has been expressed in a variety of ways throughout history. In modern times one of the most famous formulations is the so-called Chicago–Lambeth Quadrilateral. This formulation was agreed to at the Lambeth Conference in 1888. It is a somewhat broader version of articles agreed to by the General Convention of the Protestant Episcopal Church in the United States meeting in Chicago in 1886. The four points are laid down as a basis for approaching church reunion. The points refer to Scripture, creeds, sacraments and the historic episcopate. While the Chicago–Lambeth Quadrilateral is often quoted and the ecumenical movement has developed a great deal, Anglicans have not found it easy to enter into reunion schemes once the quadrilateral has not provided the basis that had been hoped for.

'That, in the opinion of this Conference, the following articles supply a basis on which approach may be by God's blessing made towards home reunion:

a) The Holy Scriptures of the Old and New Testaments as 'containing all things necessary to salvation', and as being the rule and ultimate standard of faith.
b) The Apostles' Creed, as the baptismal symbol; and the Nicene Creed, as the sufficient statement of the Christian faith.
c) The two sacraments ordained by Christ himself – Baptism and the Supper of the Lord – ministered with unfailing use of Christ's words of institution, and of the elements ordained by him.
d) The historic episcopate, locally adapted in the methods of its administration to the varying needs of the nations and peoples called of God into the unity of his Church.'

Lambeth Conference 1888, Resolution 11

The Anglican way of receiving the Scriptures

The *BCP* makes clear that one of the major aspects of public worship is the audible reading of the Scriptures in the language of the people. This was believed to be consistent with the practice of the early Church. In the reformed Church of England the public reading of Scripture took place according to carefully revised rules, the reader 'so standing and turning himself as he may best be heard by all such as are present'. A new collect was composed for the Second Sunday in Advent which expressed the intention of this practice:

> Blessed Lord, who hast caused all Holy Scriptures to be written for our learning, grant that we may in such wise hear them, read, mark, learn and inwardly digest them, that by patience and comfort of thy holy word we may embrace and ever hold fast the blessed hope of everlasting life.

Most Christians in the history of the world have been illiterate, so the public reading of the Scriptures is of great importance. The reason for reading the Scriptures was twofold. First, it was in this way that people were to hear of the offer of everlasting life to humanity by the life and work of Jesus Christ (Article 7). Secondly, people were enabled, from their knowledge of the Scriptures, to confirm for themselves that what they were being taught in the church was indeed consistent with the Scriptures. Faced with the sheer variety of teaching in the sixteenth (as in earlier) centuries, it was held that the knowledge of the Scriptures was sufficient for salvation (Article 6). If your priest or bishop insisted that you believed something not taught in the Scriptures, that person could properly be resisted. In the sixteenth century there were those who did resist, and paid for it with their lives.

That Anglicans have continued to insist on this feature of Christian faith is illustrated by the first item of the Chicago–Lambeth Quadrilateral of 1888, which reads, 'The Holy Scriptures of the Old and New Testaments, as "containing all things necessary to salvation" [a quotation of Article 6], and as being the rule and ultimate standard of faith.' In other words, every aspect of the teaching of the church has to be justified by reference to a publicly accessible criterion, the Scriptures. In the Ordinal, bishops, priests and deacons are each presented with the Scriptures, as a sign of their authority. In this way they are implicitly reminded to conform their teaching to the standard of Scripture.

Characteristic of Anglicans, but again not distinctive of them, is their use of the Book of Psalms, Jesus' own book of devotion, in their liturgical prayer. In this respect Anglicans find themselves connected to a long, Benedictine tradition of worship, which is discovering renewed vitality in our own times.

Finally, a word needs to be said about the use of reason in the interpretation of Scripture. Against certain radical puritans (it was possible to be both a puritan and an Anglican!) it was argued that only reason could enable you to differentiate between various kinds of material in the Scriptures. Discovery and rational argument were necessary in establishing what could and should be defended as the right way for the contemporary Church. In more modern times the critical study of the Bible has been vigorously defended as 'essential to the maintenance in the Church of a healthy faith' (Lambeth Conference of 1897). In this way theology is bound to include lively exploration and debate.

The Anglican way of common prayer and sacraments

The Scriptures have, however, never stood on their own. Their use, as we have seen, has always been related to common prayer and the administration of the sacraments, as well as to preaching. In the earliest *Books of Common Prayer* it was stated clearly that one of the purposes of *common* prayer was to promote a decent order and a godly discipline for the whole people of God. Part of the justification for insisting on a common order was to protect the ordinary Christian from the whims and fancies of their local minister. Reformed churches very soon discovered that people mistook their own enthusiasms for divine inspiration (as they still do). The deliverance of the people from the tyranny of a pastor who insisted on spontaneity, which soon enough settled into predictable grooves, was helped by the use of a common order of worship.

The first *Book of Common Prayer* was published in 1549.

The *BCP* (and later prayer books) have functioned in another important way. Together with the Articles and the

Ordinal, the three documents constitute a sort of confessional statement of Anglican belief. If you compare the Thirty-nine Articles with the Confessions of the Lutheran and Reformed churches, there are both similarities and differences. But in other reformed communions there is nothing precisely to correspond with the status of the *BCP*, which is one of the most important ways in which Anglicans are nourished in, and define, the Christian faith.

The *BCP* transmits the sacramental life of the church. It identifies the sacraments of baptism and the Lord's Supper or Holy Communion as definitive of what the term 'sacrament' means ('certain sure witnesses, and effectual signs of grace, and God's good will towards us, by the which he doth work invisibly in us', Article 25). Other rites are also celebrated: confirmation, ordination and matrimony for example, without having exactly the status of the 'two sacraments ordained of Christ our Lord in the Gospel'.

The Anglican Church receives the classic Christian tradition that these sacraments are performed in Christ's name and with his authority, and that their effect is not diminished in any way by the unworthiness of the priest or minister (Article 26). In an emergency, a baptism may be performed by a lay person. Infant baptism is carried out on the traditional basis of Christ's welcome of little children (Mark 10:13f) and in response to promises, made on behalf of the child by godparents, that he or she renounces evil, believes the Christian faith and intends to obey God's commandments.

In this way the child is brought into a faith-community shaped by baptism. Baptism 'doth represent unto us our profession; which is, to follow the example of our Saviour Christ, and to be made like unto him; that, as he died and rose again for us, so should we, who are baptised, die from sin, and rise again unto righteousness'. Baptisms ought to be public and celebrated when the largest congregations come together in order to remind as many people as possible of this 'profession'.

After infant baptism, it is envisaged that the child, growing in understanding, is taught the content of the faith and becomes ready to be admitted to the Holy Communion. Confirmation by the bishop is provided at the age of discretion, explicitly timed to coincide with the added temptations of adolescence, to strengthen the young person in the life of faith, by asking for the further blessing of the Holy Spirit. The purpose of the once-for-all baptism is brought to completion in admission to the Eucharist, which provides the 'spiritual food and sustenance' for the life of faith. Eucharist means 'Thanksgiving' and has become a common Anglican term to describe what the first *Book of Common Prayer* (1549) described as the Lord's Supper or Holy Communion or the Mass.

Eucharistic theology lay at the very heart of the debates of the Reformation. The Anglican reformers wanted worshippers to be in no doubt that they truly received the body and blood of Christ, but to avoid grossly physical misinterpretations and superstitions added the word 'spiritual'. With the witness of the early Church they taught the necessity of faith in the worthy reception of the sacrament. There was a conscious unwillingness to enter into the 'how' and 'why' of sacramental theology, combined with wholehearted gratitude for the reality of participation. It was of the essence of the sacrament that worshippers should be partakers at the heavenly banquet. Cranmer spoke of 'flying up into heaven in our hearts'.

Of course debates about sacramental theology continued within the Anglican Church, and remain lively today. Celebration of the Holy Communion, which Cranmer intended should be weekly, became more important to Anglican life in the nineteenth and twentieth centuries in response to the Oxford Movement. Incarnational and sacramental religion, which sees the physical world as indwelt by the gracious divine presence, has become an instinctive way of seeing things for very many Anglicans.

Feed on him in your hearts by faith

His was the Word that spake it,
He took the Bread and brake it,
And what his Word does make it,
That I believe and take it.

Queen Elizabeth I (1533–1603)

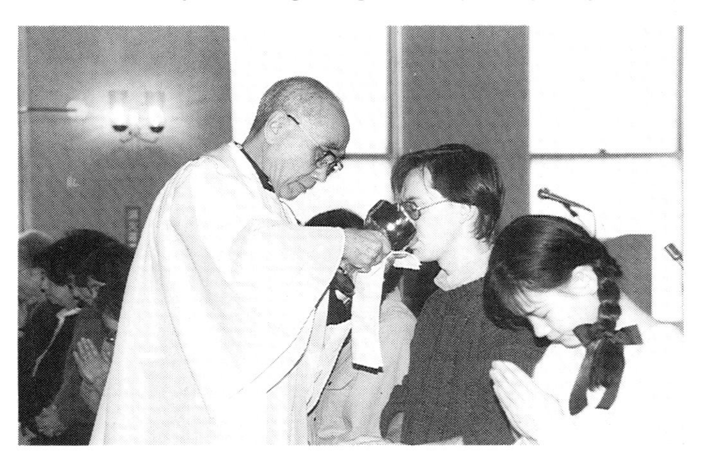

Japanese Anglicans receive communion in the YMCA in Fukuoko, Diocese of Kyushu.

Others, again, are more focused upon the hearing of the Word. The tension is creative. But it is clear that all Anglican clergy are required both to 'set forth [God's] true and lively word' and also 'rightly and duly' to 'administer [God's] holy Sacraments'.

It is, thus, the task of the priest to use the authorised services, together with all his or her loving persuasion and pastoral skill, to help the congregation into a 'ripeness and perfectness of age in Christ' (Ordinal, Ordination of Priests). Priests are never to forget that the church and congregation they serve is 'the spouse and body of Christ', 'the sheep of Christ which he bought with his death'. The Ordinal, based on the Pastoral Letters (1 & 2 Timothy and Titus) has given the office of priest in Anglican churches a strongly pastoral character.

In the modern world this needs to be supplemented with an equal emphasis upon evangelism, if the paganism of our day is to be confronted and challenged. There is no reason, however, to be anything other than grateful for the pastoral context in which liturgical and sacramental ministry has been handed on to us.

The Anglican way of teaching doctrine

The Anglican Church is, by definition, a teaching church. That is to say, there could not be a Christian church which was not a teaching church, and the churches of the Anglican Communion are no exception. But to be a teacher of sound doctrine one must first be a student of it, and the clergy are especially admonished in the Ordinal to be diligent in daily 'reading and weighing' of the Scriptures, so that their own lives are fashioned 'after the Rule and Doctrine of Christ'. They are bound also to get involved in controversy about true doctrine, since they are required to intervene, both in public and private, when false doctrine is promulgated. The church is also said to have authority in controversies of faith (Article 20).

The content of the faith which is to be taught is contained in the three Creeds, the Nicene, the (so-called) Athanasian Creed, and the Apostles' Creed (Article 8). After prolonged controversy the Quadrilateral dropped the reference to the Athanasian Creed. But the public commitment of the Anglican is to the full doctrine of the Holy Trinity, as Articles 1 to 5 of the Thirty-nine Articles make plain. The *Te Deum Laudamus*, set for use at Morning Prayer, is a great outpouring of praise to the Triune God.

The incarnation and atonement are likewise taught within this trinitarian context. The centrality of the atoning work of Christ becomes evident in the *BCP* Order of Holy Communion. God is addressed as follows:

> . . . who of thy tender mercy didst give thine only Son Jesus Christ to suffer death upon the cross for our redemption; who made there (by his one oblation of himself once offered) a full, perfect, and sufficient sacrifice, oblation, and satisfaction, for the sins of the whole world.

Sacrifice has remained central to Anglican understanding of the death of Christ. The action of the Eucharist is understood as the offering of a 'sacrifice of praise and thanksgiving', including prayer that 'through faith in his blood we and all thy whole Church may obtain remission of our sins and all other benefits of his passion'.

By doctrine one must also include moral teaching. Together with an inherited stress upon God's gracious gift as preceding all moral endeavour ('God, of whose only gift it cometh that this faithful people do unto thee true and laudable service', Collect for Trinity 13), goes a strong teaching about good works ('that we may . . . do all such good works as thou hast prepared for us to walk in', Holy Communion *BCP*). The relationship of good works and justification is treated briefly in Articles 9–14, in (for the time) a consciously moderate kind of way. To deny that human beings have an inherent natural strength to turn to God in faith (Article 10) or that people can be saved by the conscientious following of their own convictions (Article 18) is to abandon any facile optimism about salvation. There is a trinitarian understanding of human beings, however, which has a place for natural human goodness and a positive evaluation of at least some aspects of other religions. Anglicans have generally treated these matters as deserving serious and careful consideration. There has also been from the first a firm teaching about the importance of morality in the social and political order, and the necessity of an impartial and upright administration of justice.

Together with these elements of doctrine has gone a

George Herbert (1593–1633), poet and parish priest, was vicar of Bemerton near Salisbury.

realisation that the heart of the matter concerns openness to the transforming power of the love of God. This is frequently expressed in the *BCP*, for example in the Collect for the Seventh Sunday after Trinity:

> Lord of all power and might,
> who art the author and giver of all good things:
> Graft in our hearts the love of thy Name,
> increase in us true religion,
> nourish us with all goodness,
> and of thy great mercy keep us in the same.

It is characteristic (but again not distinctive) of the Anglican way to invest much effort in the maturing of personal lives of discipleship, within the secure framework of a trinitarian theology. Doctrine and life, said George Herbert, are related in the way in which colours and light blend in a stained glass window. Convictions about God, convictions about humanity and society, and the practice of the spiritual life belong together, and should not be separated.

The Windows

Lord, how can man preach
thy eternal word:
He is a brittle crazy glass:
Yet in thy Temple thou dost him
afford
This glorious and transcendent
place,
To be a window, through thy
grace.

But when thou dost anneal in
glass thy story,
Making thy life to shine
within
The holy Preachers, then the
light and glory
More rev'rend grow, and more
doth win;
Which else show wat'rish, bleak,
and thin.

Doctrine and life, colours and
light, in one
When they combine and
mingle, bring
A strong regard and awe: but
speech alone
Doth vanish like a flaring
thing,
And in the ear, not conscience
ring.

George Herbert (1593–1633)

Scripture, worship and doctrine in the service of unity

The task of the Church is that of the reconciliation of all things in Christ. Its apostolic mission is to unify all that Christ has gathered together in his own, catholic person, in lives of true holiness. So the purpose or end which the Anglican way serves is unification or reconciliation; again this is no distinctive feature of the Anglican spirit, but it is characteristic.

In the first place, a strong Anglican tradition sees this reconciliation as embracing *the whole created order*. The *BCP* canticle, *Benedicite,* suggested for use at Morning Prayer, indicates that the whole of creation – sun, moon, stars, fish, animals, birds, all 'green things' on the earth – join together with human beings to praise God. George Herbert saw humankind as the 'secretary of God's praise', making articulate what the creation longed to utter. Similarly the *Te Deum*, also used at Morning Prayer, asserts that all creation is implicated in the worship of God, their creator, together with angels, archangels, heavens and all the powers in it, cherubim and seraphim.

The *BCP* also clearly teaches *the unity of the Church*, 'built upon the foundation of the apostles and prophets,

Jesus Christ himself being the head cornerstone' (Collect for St Simon and St Jude). In another prayer, specially composed for the *BCP*, a deliberately inclusive reference is made to the whole or catholic Church 'that it may be so guided and governed by [God's] good spirit that all who profess and call themselves Christians may be led into the way of truth, and hold the faith in unity of spirit, in the bond of peace and in righteousness of life' (Prayer for All Sorts and Conditions of Men).

Of that church the bishop is to be the servant and to set forth quietness, love and peace in the diocese of which he is the chief pastor. He is to teach and uphold sound doctrine, to banish erroneous opinion, and to be an example of righteous and godly living. Because the bishop is directly responsible for ordaining, licensing or instituting priests in his diocese, every Eucharist, the celebration and memorial of God's own reconciling action, is directly connected to the bishop's own mission and task.

For this reason, the fourth of the four elements of the Chicago–Lambeth Quadrilateral reads: 'This Historic Episcopate, locally adapted in the methods of its administration to the varying needs of the nations and peoples called of God into the Unity of His Church.'

The mission of the whole people of God, clergy and laity alike, is to be kept faithful to its unity in Christ by the discipline of a common, ordained ministry. Anglicans believe that they transmit not their own rules and regulations, but the ministerial orders given by God to his Church. Deacons, priests and bishops are asked publicly to state whether they believed themselves called to their office 'in the Church of God'. In this way they are practically reminded of a unity of the whole Church which is not yet evident in history, but which is guaranteed in Christ's atoning ministry.

What is it then that holds Anglicans together? First and primarily, we must focus on the gracious, reconciling and unifying act of God in Jesus Christ. But Anglicans have received the fruit of that work through a tradition which has kept Scripture, common worship and doctrine in a dynamic interrelationship, serving the unity of the church. Each of the elements, taken by themselves, have been received by Anglicans in somewhat different ways. Common worship, especially sacramental worship, for example, has varied widely, so that the liturgical action of a service may be full of ceremony and ritual, or comparatively plain with elements of spontaneity. Scripture is interpreted differently by different Anglicans. Common doctrine, likewise, sometimes varies, within a framework of general agreement. But in almost all forms and expressions of the Anglican way, a certain character or spirit is evident which is the result of interconnecting Scripture, common worship and doctrine, and tending to make the whole serve the unity of the church.

Questions

1. What are the foundations of the Anglican Church?
2. What do you think is the Anglican character or spirit?
3. How may we build the unity of the Church which is the will of God?

2

Church and society

John Habgood

In Old Testament times it would have been difficult to draw any clear distinction between religion and society. Faith in God touched the lives of people at every point, from international politics to the tilling of the soil. So the books of the Old Testament tell the story of wars and migrations, family quarrels, the building of cities and the destruction of them, sickness and health, disaster and rescue – in fact all that is involved in the business of living and dying. And it is through such events that the hand of God is revealed.

Towards the end of the Old Testament period, after centuries of rule by various foreign powers, things had become much more complicated. Different parties within Judaism had different ideas about the relation between religious observance and political and social involvement. The best-known radical group, a tiny sect called the Essenes, lived an almost monastic life in the desert. In fact the idea of return to the desert was a constant theme of the late prophets as they recalled the heroic days of the nation during the Exodus. And the fact that people flocked to the desert to hear John the Baptist was no doubt all part of this same sense that it was necessary to escape from society to find God, in addition to finding him within it.

The Church in the world

Christianity inherited this duality. A faith based on God's incarnation in Jesus Christ, that is, God revealed in human life, cannot ignore the world in which he was incarnate, and which he loved so much that he died for it. But neither can a faith based on the death and resurrection of Christ ignore the fact that it was the powers of this world which rejected and crucified him. Jesus was concerned about the ordinary life of ordinary people, particularly those who were despised or rejected. But it is a misreading of the gospels to see him as some kind of social or political activist. St Paul likewise took the political order of his day for granted, and was content to work within it as the context in which a new kind of community could be built. Neither would have recognised, though, the purely personal and private kind of religion which has now become common in the Western world. When Jesus preached about the coming of the kingdom of God he certainly did not mean just an internal spiritual experience for a few individuals.

This inherent duality within Christianity has worked itself out in history in a wide variety of ways. Starting as a small sect within Judaism the early Church had no political power. As the Church grew, questions about how to build a Christian society without being corrupted by worldly power, became more and more difficult to answer. Some have seen the Emperor Constantine's decision in AD 312 to make Christianity the official religion of the Roman Empire as a disaster from which the Church has never recovered. Others have seen this as the Church accepting an inescapable responsibility, one fraught with danger maybe, but which could only be refused by contracting out of society. The story since then has provided evidence for both interpretations.

Sects

A sect may simply be a religious body which stands outside the mainstream of religious life in a particular culture.

In the context of social ethics the word has a more particular meaning. It describes a small, close-knit, generally exclusive body, which deliberately tries to cut itself off from compromise with 'the world', and to live out a pure uncontaminated form of Christian life, available only to true believers. Sectarian social policies thus either involve complete withdrawal from the mainstream culture, or revolutionary attempts to overthrow it. 2 Corinthians 6:14–18, where Paul says 'Do not team up with unbelievers' (REB), is frequently quoted as a justification for sectarianism, but St Paul makes it clear elsewhere in his letters that in urging separation his main concern is with the dangers of idolatry. He is not advocating rejection of the world as such.

No sooner was the Church in a position of power in the Roman Empire than it began to divide into contending groups over differences in doctrine. But as the Empire itself began to crumble in the following centuries, it was the Church which managed to preserve the remnants of the ancient world of Greece and Rome, and build a new civilisation. Medieval Europe became a remarkable fusion of church and society, an attempt to create an all-embracing Christian culture. But inevitably this led to a powerful reaction from within.

Since then the duality has expressed itself in many different ways. At one end of the spectrum there has been a continuous formation of new sects, each trying to escape from what it has regarded as the corruptions and worldliness of the existing churches. Sometimes, as in modern Africa, the motive for the founding of new religious movements has been the sense that the existing churches have derived too much from an alien culture. The process of integrating Christianity into a culture can in fact be just as divisive as the process of escaping from a culture.

At the other end of this spectrum there have been churches deeply involved in the social issues of their day. In present-day liberation movements, especially in Latin America, Christian faith is virtually equated with social or political action. The early Christian missionaries to Africa would not have seen their work in this light, nor thought of themselves as liberation theologians, but one of their main motives for going to Africa was to abolish the slave trade.

This is only a tiny glimpse of an enormously complex scene. Within it Anglicans have generally tried to keep a balance between involvement in the life of society and the recognition that the Church has a distinct life and integrity of its own. Different patterns have evolved in different parts of the Anglican Communion. A small church in a culture dominated by another faith can do very little in terms of helping to shape public policy; but it may witness to Christian love by the way it responds to individual needs. By contrast the witness of many denominations in South Africa, Anglicans included, has been a major factor in making apartheid morally unacceptable, and initiating political change.

Critical solidarity

In England, Church and society have been more closely connected than in any other part of the Anglican Communion, and this has to some extent shaped the general Anglican ethos. It is also true that in some parts of the world, notably in North America, Provinces were set up largely to escape the church/state relationship as it then existed in England. There remains, however, an identifiable ethos, usefully summed up in the phrase 'critical solidarity'. 'Solidarity' implies a willingness to be sympathetic towards the needs and aims of society, and the responsibilities of those in power. 'Critical' preserves the duality, the necessary distancing from power if the Church is to be true to itself. A snapshot or two from the history of the Church of England can show what this means in practice.

The English church existed before the English nation, and played a considerable role in forging and shaping it. From the earliest days bishops were chief advisers to the

Establishment

The Church of England is an established church, in the sense that it is officially recognised as the church of the nation. But it is not a state church like, for example, the Church of Norway. In Norway the government makes decisions on such matters as appointments of bishops and pastors, liturgy and clerical robes. Parliament is responsible for the church's budget.

In England the church receives no income from the state, and Parliament which has to give final approval to church legislation, may not amend it or initiate church legislation of its own. The main duty of Parliament in relation to the national church is to safeguard the rights of citizens insofar as these are affected by church policies. Diocesan bishops are appointed by the Queen, on the advice of the Prime Minister who has the right to choose one out of two names put to him by a Church Commission. Of the forty-four diocesan bishops, twenty-six become members of the House of Lords, in order of seniority, and for the duration of their episcopate.

As the official church of the nation the Church of England has to provide reasonable access to worship for everyone, and has a duty to baptise, marry or bury all who ask for these services. It also provides chaplains for hospitals, prisons and the armed services, for the most part financed by the Government, and in certain circumstances for schools, major industries and other bodies. Financially, apart from the above exceptions, it depends on endowments from the past, and on direct giving by its congregations.

king and, in a much reduced role, have remained so to this day as senior members of the Upper House of Parliament. The Church of England's established status, therefore, was not something imposed on it, but something which evolved in the process of nation-building. The relationship was not always an easy one, however, and in medieval times much controversy centred on how far the English church was national, and how far it owed a wider allegiance to the pope. An Archbishop of Canterbury, Thomas Becket, was martyred in AD 1170 on the orders of the king in a dispute on this issue.

At the Reformation in the sixteenth century the authority of the king replaced that of the pope as the main source of jurisdiction in the church. Church and state were thus tightly linked, and some of the links still remain, though in a much modified form. One result has been that the church has always seen itself as having responsibilities towards the whole nation. It has tried to maintain a comprehensive system of pastoral care, and before the days of welfare provision by the state most of what we now know as 'social services' were in the hands of the clergy. The church also pioneered universal education, and until the growth of secularisation and pluralism in the last 150 years, Christian values were universally regarded as undergirding public life.

These roles have not been performed without criticism and controversies. A strong tradition of religious dissent has meant that since the sixteenth century the Church of England has never had a monopoly, and this has been a valuable feature in setting limits to its power. The church has also itself been critical of Government and of the social order, and particularly since the early nineteenth century has been active in social reform. William Wilberforce pursued his campaign to abolish the slave trade as a Christian Member of Parliament, having been persuaded that this, rather than ordination, was his vocation. F. D. Maurice, a Church of England clergyman, founded a movement for Christian Socialism in 1848, and had much influence on the formation of trade unions and education for manual workers. Lord Shaftesbury, a prominent Church of England layman, was responsible during the second half of the century for a long series of reforms which regulated conditions in factories and mines.

The tradition of working for social justice continued

Christian Socialism

This was the name of a movement founded by an Anglican clergyman and theologian, F. D. Maurice, in 1848 in reaction against the frightful social conditions then being created by the Industrial Revolution in Britain. 'Socialism' for Maurice and his colleagues simply meant 'co-operation', in contrast with the fierce competitive spirit then prevailing in industry. The movement was significant in that it marked a transition from a type of church response to poverty mainly in terms of benevolence and charity, to a much more radical criticism of the social order.

It was succeeded by various other Christian social movements, many of them inspired by Anglo-Catholic clergy who deliberately went to work in the poorest urban areas. Social thinking in this tradition continued until the Second World War, with Archbishop William Temple as its most outstanding leader during its final phase. But it was never very politically effective, and socialism as a political programme developed from other sources, notably the trade unions.

Supporters of Christian Socialism claimed at one stage that it was the only true expression of Christian political ideals. Experience has shown that politics are both more complex and more ambiguous than that. It is now generally recognised, in British politics at least, that Christianity may find legitimate expression through any of the main political parties.

William Temple (1881–1944) 'was accused of interfering in matters which were none of his business'.

into the twentieth century, especially through the work of Archbishop William Temple, whose writings and speeches helped to lay the foundations of the welfare state. They were not always welcomed; in fact he was accused of interfering in matters which were none of his business. He was usually careful, however, not to put forward detailed social policies, but to lay down Christian principles on which those policies should be based. He and his colleagues developed the useful concept of 'middle axioms', i.e. statements about the general direction policies should take, halfway between broad Christian principles and particular policy options. Details, he constantly said, should be left to the experts.

Expressing the mind of the church

In more recent years the Church of England Board for Social Responsibility has been the main forum for giving advice on public policy issues, responding to, and when necessary criticising, government initiatives, and producing reports on social and ethical issues. A long series of reports on such matters as abortion, euthanasia, environmental issues, poverty, the welfare state, industrial relations, housing, nuclear weapons, values in society, the family, and many more, has been variously received. Some have criticised them as reflecting too obviously the spirit of the age. Others have criticised them for being unrealistic. This is not surprising, as those who try to

Clients at the 'Crisis at Christmas' shelter in Bermondsey 1994.

work with middle axioms usually find themselves under fire from both sides. The most influential church report in recent years, 'Faith in the City' (1985), was prepared by a special commission appointed by Archbishop Robert Runcie, and presented detailed evidence about the effects of poverty and unemployment in inner-city areas.

Working parties and commissions usually bring together people with very different backgrounds and opinions, and many types of expertise. This ensures that matters are thoroughly discussed; it also means that they frequently find it difficult to reach clear conclusions on complex issues. As a result the church is accused of not knowing its own mind and of failing to give prophetic guidance. In practice prophets are usually individuals or like-minded groups. They perform a valuable role in highlighting particular issues, arousing consciences by denouncing obvious evils, and holding out a vision of a better world. They complement the role of interdisciplinary working parties, with their emphasis on careful and objective analysis, which are needed to help translate such visions into realistic policies.

An attitude of critical solidarity towards the everyday world of secular expertise is not, of course, unique to the Church of England. It is an expression of the Anglican

Janani Luwum (1922–77), Archbishop of Uganda, was murdered when Idi Amin was president.

ethos which has always tried to take reason and experience seriously, and which has always emphasised that faith has to be lived out, both personally and corporately, in the context of daily life. The aim is neither to withdraw from the world, nor simply to accept it, but to work for its transformation through the presence and power of Christ.

These principles could be illustrated from many parts of the Anglican Communion. The Church of Uganda, for instance, was founded on the blood of martyrs. The martyrdom of Archbishop Janani Luwum in 1977 for his resistance to a tyrannous regime continued a great tradition. Only fifteen years later one of his successors as Archbishop was using his position as leader of the most effective educational network in the country to spearhead the fight against AIDS. He confessed that it was the Lambeth Conference in 1988 which had opened his eyes to its importance.

The Episcopal Church of the United States belongs to a country where the separation between church and state is a fundamental article of faith. It would claim that its independence of any connection with government has helped it in its concern for social justice and civil rights. It remains true, nevertheless, that some of its influence derives from the fact that many people in positions of authority belong to it.

In South Africa Archbishop Tutu's role has been both prophetic and conciliatory. He has spoken from intimate knowledge of those who suffered most from the injustice of apartheid, but he has also understood the realities of power, and the compromises needed in exercising it.

In South America where the strong Roman Catholic majority has tended to become polarised along the lines of social divisions, the tiny Anglican churches have for the most part managed to avoid this polarisation, and have concentrated on evangelism and on rescue work among the very poor.

Successive Lambeth Conferences have given a substantial part of their time to social issues. The 1958 Conference received a highly significant report on 'The Family in Contemporary Society', and endorsed the theological rationale for giving limited approval to the use of artificial methods of contraception. It was forced to defend this decision in 1968, following the publication of Pope Paul VI's encyclical *Humanae Vitae* that same year. The 1968

Christianity and social order

William Temple's book *Christianity and Social Order*, published in 1944 just before his death, summarised in popular form a long tradition of Christian thinking which assumed that society could be changed by defining the Christian principles on which it should be based. Some quotations can give the flavour of it.

> It is of crucial importance that the Church acting corporately should not commit itself to any particular policy. A policy always depends on technical decisions concerning the actual relations of cause and effect in the political and economic world; about these a Christian as such has no more reliable judgement than an atheist, except so far as he should be more immune to the temptations of self-interest.

> ... the Church may tell the politician what ends the social order should promote; but it must leave to the politician the devising of the precise means to those ends.

> The art of government in fact is the art of so ordering life that self-interest prompts what justice demands.

The last quotation shows Temple beginning to move in the new direction in social ethics set by Reinhold Niebuhr. Niebuhr's emphasis on the hard realities of politics, and his acknowledgment of the inevitable compromises required of politicians in a sinful world, spoke powerfully to a generation confused by the struggles with Fascism and Communism.

Subsequent Anglican social thinking has lacked the coherence which Temple tried to impose on it. In a world where most societies are now multicultural it is much harder than it once was to define clear aims and values. The use of interdisciplinary working parties, which may succeed in doing no more than define a variety of options, is now the most widely accepted method of bringing Christian insights to bear on complex social realities.

Church and politics

'I am puzzled about which Bible people are reading when they suggest religion and politics don't mix.'

Desmond Tutu

Lambeth Conference Statements

1978: 'The Church exists for God – to worship him and be a sign and agent for his Kingdom. Faithfulness to God through Jesus Christ in the Spirit is the basis of its existence, the inspiration of all it does and strives to become. As God in Jesus commits himself to our humanity, the worship of God through Jesus directs us towards every human search for freedom, fulfilment, and joy; and brings us up against everything that distorts, imprisons, or ignores the lives, needs, and hopes of men, women, and children. Because we worship God in his glory we are called to seek the glory of man.'

1988: 'The right and duty of Christians to speak and act on problems of social order needs no defence. It follows directly from our belief that this is God's world, and that he has shown his care for it in creation, incarnation, and redemption, and in his promise that all things ultimately will be brought to fullness in himself. Many of the most serious national and international conflicts have an obvious and strong religious or ideological dimension. Many of the most serious issues of social policy raise questions about the nature of human life, and about ultimate aims and values. For Christians not to play a part in the attempts to confront such issues would imply that the religious dimension is irrelevant. That would be a surrender to secularism.'

Conference also endorsed work done at the World Council of Churches' Conference on Church and Society in 1966. This had begun to develop ideas about the responsible society, economic justice, racism, and many other themes which have continued to dominate the ecumenical agenda as well as our own Anglican agenda.

Homosexuality made a first appearance in the 1978 report, which also expressed increasing concern about the degree to which modern life tends to be shaped by technological advance. This report began to face the problem of making ethical judgments in cultures where it is no longer possible to rely on a universally agreed set of values.

By 1988 issues of poverty and powerlessness and the abuse of human rights had come to the fore. A series of worldwide studies on the family had revealed how complex the whole area of sexuality and family life has now become. An important new topic was AIDS, and the Conference stressed the need to take it seriously as a threat, to reinforce traditional ideas of chastity, and to treat those living with AIDS with compassionate understanding.

All four Conferences made statements on war and peace, and expressed their concern about nuclear weapons. A significant addition in 1988 was a discussion of terrorism, but this only illustrated the difficulty in saying things which would not be misinterpreted in one or other part of the world. It is not true that one person's terrorist is another person's freedom fighter, but words may sometimes be twisted to give that impression.

Interesting cultural differences also emerged in 1988 on the subject of polygamy. The Conference accepted that a worldwide standard in this matter was not possible, without doing severe injustice to wives who might lose their homes and families if rules were applied too rigidly in certain countries.

This brief summary of what four recent Lambeth Conferences have said on social issues illustrates topics which are felt to be significant to the Anglican Communion as a whole. It would be wrong to leave the matter there, however.

Christ in the local church

The life of the church is not primarily expressed in meetings of bishops, valuable though these may be. Christ is present wherever two or three people meet together in his name, in the worship and work of the local church, and in the individual lives of those who love him and try to serve their fellow human beings. Issues of church and society are frequently most real, therefore, when they are most local. They need to be identified and grasped at the local level by those who care about the kind of society in which they live, who are both committed to it and critical of it, and who are faithful to our Lord's prayer 'Thy kingdom come'.

Questions

1. Do you think the Church should be involved in politics? What are the arguments for and against?
2. What evidence would you want to offer in order to refute someone who complained that Christians are too heavenly minded to be any earthly use?
3. How well does the church where you live keep the balance between involving itself in the life of society and sustaining its own distinct life and integrity?
4. What are some of the issues of public concern which we face today? What do you think is the best way for the Church to form a viewpoint and speak out?

3

Anglican belief

Bruce Kaye

Ernest Chau, from Hong Kong, ministers to a Chinese-speaking congregation in Sydney.

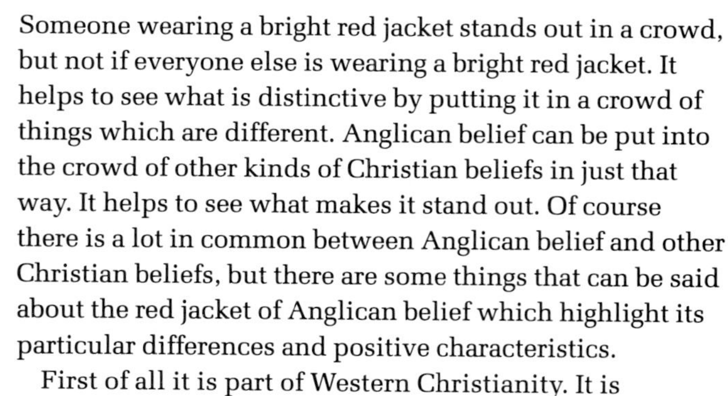

Someone wearing a bright red jacket stands out in a crowd, but not if everyone else is wearing a bright red jacket. It helps to see what is distinctive by putting it in a crowd of things which are different. Anglican belief can be put into the crowd of other kinds of Christian beliefs in just that way. It helps to see what makes it stand out. Of course there is a lot in common between Anglican belief and other Christian beliefs, but there are some things that can be said about the red jacket of Anglican belief which highlight its particular differences and positive characteristics.

First of all it is part of Western Christianity. It is different from all of the Eastern Orthodox traditions. It is obvious that its style and presentation is different. It is also different in its use of liturgy and symbols. Although it does not see itself as one of the family of Eastern Orthodox churches, there has often been a recognition of common perspectives, for example in the way the church finds its identity in worship.

In the Western Christian tradition, the Anglican way is clearly different from the Roman Catholic way. Anglicans do not share an allegiance to the Bishop of Rome as pope. Although Anglicans have come to see that they agree with a great deal in Roman Catholicism, they do not agree about the nature of authority in Christian faith. Roman Catholics focus much more precisely on the pope, in terms of how we may know what is truly Christian. Anglicans believe that authority is much more dispersed amongst the people of God. Anglicans are not part of the Roman Catholic institutional family.

Nor do they belong particularly to the continental Protestant church traditions. They do not share an allegiance to the theology of Martin Luther, as do the Lutheran churches. They do not share an allegiance to the theology of John Calvin and the Reformed tradition, as the Presbyterian and Reformed churches do. Anglicans do not believe that Scripture alone is the single source for our knowledge of God. So Anglicans, in their belief, are part of Western Christianity and are not Roman Catholic, nor Lutheran, nor Reformed nor Presbyterian. Anglicans belong to a Christian tradition, which was shaped from the very earliest times of British Christianity.

In the very early centuries of the Christian mission in Britain, the accidents of history meant that the Christian Church began and continued its mission in close interaction with the structure of British society. In the seventh century St Aidan and King Oswald, King of Northumbria, travelled together in missionary enterprises. From the very earliest times, the church leaders were absorbed into the social structures of early British society.

British Christianity has always been strongly enmeshed in society and its social structures; this tells us something about the belief of Anglicans. The Anglican way is open to that kind of inter-connection. Thus Anglican belief has a strong sense of openness to society and belief in the providential presence of God in human affairs. That sense of the presence of God in society is an important distinctive characteristic of Anglican belief. From the very earliest times the acceptance of Christian church leaders in the social authority structure was very distinctive.

It can be seen in the way in which Bede writes his history of the English people. The life of the church is an aspect of the life story of the people. Constantly God is seen to be present. We can see it in the Reformation. Unlike the continental Reformers, the English Reformers did not change much of the existing state church structure. We retained the order of bishops, priests and deacons. When the great defender of the Elizabethan church settlement, Richard Hooker (c. 1554–1600) gave a theological explanation of this Reformation settlement, he did so on the basis of the providence of God within human affairs. His was a very Anglican belief about the way in which God had providentially been present in the past in the life of the church and society.

State and church

'The beginning of the English was unlike that of some other national churches, and the difference in the manner of its origin marked itself in bold characters upon the Constitution and history of the English Church . . . in the several kingdoms the origin of the Church of Christ was sunned by royal favour. The sovereigns led the way themselves, or by their sovereign act opened the way for others to lead, with their express sanction . . . it was the Church element that entered upon a share in all business . . . the contrast between this state of things and that which obtained in the Church of Rome is very great, and it is of much importance that it should be kept in mind. That Church was fully organised, on its own lines, before its recognition by the State, and entered into combination with the State as a complete unity, accustomed to deal with all ecclesiastical and spiritual questions by and for itself alone.'

Canterbury Convocation Report on the position of the Laity in 1902

Providence and incarnation

One can see this doctrine of providence in the convictions which Anglicans carried outside the territory of England, even though the particular relationship of the church to the new societies was different from what existed in England. For example, in a sermon preached in Sydney on 12th November 1829, in acknowledgment of God's mercy in putting an end to the severe drought, Bishop W. G. Broughton said 'The foundation of all Religion must be laid in the belief of an over-ruling Providence.'

This emphasis on the providential presence of God in human affairs is connected with another distinctive character of Anglican Christianity, namely the central focus on the incarnation of God in the person of Jesus Christ for redemption in the world. Anglicans regularly talk about the incarnation. Historically they have most commonly talked about it in terms of bringing into focus in Jesus Christ the providential presence of God in the world. So the incarnation as a focus for our belief in a saving God is set against the background of a God who is providentially present for good in human affairs.

Anglicans have therefore shown a great openness to society and to social engagement. Anglicans have wanted to reserve strong conviction for central issues, but not to be absolutely committed to many other things: other things change and Anglican belief is open to that change. This Anglican belief has the appearance and the style of comprehension, or openness. That openness relates to what is accepted in the life of the church as much as to its engagement with society.

Anglicans are committed to trying to understand the human condition. So there is a strong tradition of Anglican scholarship. Anglican worship is about focusing upon the saving God who is present in Christ in the world. Anglican belief has led to a conviction about service in society and/or vocation in society. Anglican belief has a strong central core and a lot of flexibility around it.

Title page of the 1662 *Book of Common Prayer*. Anglicans define their core belief by reference to this book and the Thirty-nine Articles.

> There was nothing particularly 'middle' about most of the English Reformers' theological positions – even if one could decide between what course the middle way was supposed to lie. Their moderation consisted rather in a determined policy of separating the essentials of faith and order from Adiaphoria (things not vital) . . . Anglican moderation is the policy of reserving strong statement and conviction for the few things that really deserve them.
>
> *O. M. T. O'Donnovan on The Thirty-nine Articles*

The core of belief

In the modern world, Anglicans everywhere look back to the Reformation as being the crystallising, at a particular point in time, of the beliefs that hold them together. That is not the only source of those beliefs. Anglicans have always looked back to the early Church, and particularly the first four centuries and the teaching of the church fathers in that period, as being especially authoritative.

The Formularies of the Anglican Church are usually taken to include the Thirty-nine Articles, the *Book of Common Prayer* of 1662, and the Ordinal of 1662. Around the world Anglican Provinces regularly define their core belief by reference to the *Book of Common Prayer* and the Thirty-nine Articles. The commitment is expressed differently in different places. In the Church of England it is expressed in the Declaration of Assent, which is taken by an ordained person when they are licensed by the bishop to a particular ministry. They have to identify with the tradition of belief, which is expressed in the Thirty-nine Articles. In the Episcopal Church of the United States of America, their prayer book commits them to the teaching of the Thirty-nine Articles.

The Anglican Church of Australia, which has a formal Constitution, is committed to the doctrine and principles of the *Book of Common Prayer* and the Thirty-nine Articles.

It helps to understand the priorities in Anglican belief if we notice the order of the Articles of Religion. The first five Articles are about God, the next three are about the sources of our knowledge of God: Scripture, the Creeds. Then follow particular points of doctrine which were issues of debate at the time of the Reformation. These Articles also deal with the nature of our salvation, how we are saved and what that means. We are saved only by the Name of Christ, says Article 18. Only at this point do the Articles begin to talk about the Church and its authority and of the ministry in the Church and of the sacraments of baptism and the Lord's Supper. These things are not means of salvation, but the means of sustaining salvation. The last three Articles have to do with civil relationships and obviously bear the mark of the Reformation time.

What is important first and foremost in Anglican belief is *the nature of the God* whom we serve and worship:

An Anglican Constitution

'This Church being derived from the Church of England retains and approves the doctrine and principles of the Church of England embodied in the Book of Common Prayer, together with the form and manner of making, ordaining and consecrating of bishops, priests and deacons and in the Articles of Religion.'

Constitution of the Anglican Church of Australia, Chapter 2.4

The Declaration of Assent

Preface

'The Church of England is part of the One, Holy, Catholic and Apostolic Church worshipping the one true God, Father, Son and Holy Spirit. It professes the faith uniquely revealed in the Holy Scriptures and set forth in the catholic creeds, which faith the Church is called upon to proclaim afresh in each generation. Led by the Holy Spirit, it has borne witness to Christian truth in its historic formularies, the Thirty-nine Articles of Religion, the Book of Common Prayer and the Ordering of Bishops, Priests and Deacons. In the declaration you are about to make will you affirm your loyalty to this inheritance of faith as your inspiration and guidance under God in bringing the grace and truth of Christ to this generation and making Him known to those in your care?'

Declaration of Assent

'I, A B, do so affirm, and accordingly declare my belief in the faith which is revealed in the Holy Scriptures and set forth in the catholic creeds and to which the historic formularies of the Church of England bear witness; and in public prayer and administration of the sacraments, I will use only the forms of service which are authorised or allowed by Canon.'

Canon C15. Canons of the Church of England

> There is but one living and true God, everlasting, without body, parts, or passions; of infinite power, wisdom and goodness; the maker and preserver of all things both visible and invisible. And in unity of this Godhead there be three persons, of one substance, power, and eternity; the Father, the Son, and the Holy Ghost.
>
> *Article One*

The first Article, using some of the language of an earlier period, emphasises that there is but one true and living God. Then the Article reflects the Anglican belief tradition, by saying that this God is the Maker and Preserver of all things. This God is providentially present in the world, which God has created. Then the Article says that this one God has three persons, we might today say three dimensions, three ways of existing: Father, Son and Holy Spirit. Not persons in the modern sense of a personality, but persons in the sense of an agent of action.

The language is drawn from the disputes of the early Church, but the doctrine speaks of the reality of God. God the Father speaks of God as Creator by whom we are made, and Lord and Judge, to whom we are accountable. God the Son speaks of God as revealed in the incarnation of the Son of God in the person of Jesus Christ. He is Redeemer, Saviour, and deliverer from sin and separation from God. This gives a focus in the historical events of the life, death and resurrection of Jesus Christ. God the Holy Spirit speaks of God as continually present in the lives of individuals, the life of the Christian community, and in the life of humanity.

Past, present, historical and contemporary, Judge and Saviour, supreme and elevated, yet present and intimate. This idea of God is not singular, like a mathematical unit; it is more like the oneness we are as human persons. For example, we have one brain which operates in one way, and sustains the activity of one body and nervous system. Yet the brain is full of interacting stimuli. Its parts do different things and relate to other parts in the brain. It is singular and it is one brain, yet that oneness is full of life and diversity within its one coherent existence. So with God there is a social character to the unity.

The next emphasis in the Articles is on the *incarnation*. This means that God as Son was made truly human. Here the Articles of Anglican belief draw upon the debates of the early Church in order to maintain the reality of the salvation which has come in Jesus of Nazareth. This salvation which comes in Jesus is truly the work of God. This work of God is truly available to all human people. The utter humanity of this action of God is underlined by the belief in Jesus' descent into hell and resurrection to life.

Then the Articles draw attention to the work of the *Holy Spirit* as a divine activity in the lives of people.

This first and most important part of the Articles is the belief of Christianity in general, but it is expressed in ways which point to particular characteristics of Anglican belief: the openness of God's activity, the providential presence of God in the creation. Nothing compares in importance for Anglicans with this central core of belief. Nothing has equal status or standing in Anglican belief as this central belief about God. This is the core of Anglican belief.

The basis of belief

The Thirty-nine Articles go on to talk about the sources of our knowledge of God. First and foremost they mention Scripture. Scripture is not the only source for our knowledge of God, though it is the most important and the ultimate source. Scripture is important, because it is the Church's agreed testimony to God's activity in the experience of Israel and most importantly in the life, death and resurrection of Jesus. Anglicans do not believe in Scripture alone, but they believe in Scripture as the ultimate source of our knowledge of God. That it is said to be the ultimate source, means that there are others. Scripture provides the elements of the faith. That is why Anglicans believe that Scripture contains all things necessary to salvation. Anglicans believe, however, that the Church has authority in disputes, even disputes about the central nature of the faith.

Because Anglicans believe in a God who is providentially present and acting in the lives of people, they believe in a God who comes to us in all sorts of ways. As the community of Christian people, the Church is clearly a very important way, and so is the experience of people from previous generations. Our own experience and thinking and feeling are all important avenues for knowing God.

Anglicans often speak about the threefold cord of

Christ – the heart of the Gospel

'. . . men will often tacitly assume, and even openly avow, that its kernel is contained in the Sermon on the Mount. This conception may perhaps seem more healthy in its impulse and more directly practical in its aim; but in fact it is not less dangerous even to morality than the other: for, when the sources of life are cut off, the stream will cease to flow. Certainly this is not St Paul's idea of the gospel as it appears in the epistle to the Philippians. If we would learn what he held to be its essence, we must ask ourselves what is the significance of such phrases as "I desire you in the heart of Jesus Christ", "to me to live is Christ", "that I may know the power of Christ's resurrection", "I have all strength in Christ that giveth me power". Though the gospel is capable of doctrinal exposition, though it is eminently fertile in moral results, yet its substance is neither a dogmatic system nor an ethical code, but a person and a life.'

Bishop J. B. Lightfoot (1903) St Paul's epistle to the Philippians, p. ix

Scripture, reason and tradition. Scripture contains the elements which it is necessary to believe to be a Christian. Reason comprehends our experience as human beings who think and feel and act. Tradition is the reach of the past into the present; the way in which we inherit from the past the experience and knowledge of others who have shared our belief. This inheritance enables us better to understand and respond to the continuing presence of God in the world, the whole created order.

However, Anglican belief is always focused on the person of Jesus. It is about personal commitment and discipleship. The Articles talk about good works: today we would say, behaving Christianly and living a Christian life. These, the Articles say, 'spring out necessarily' of a true and lively faith (Article 12).

Sustaining belief

Anglicans believe that Christian faith is sustained by means of the Church and its community life. That community life, of course, involves different kinds of activities including private reading, prayer, reflection, discussion with others. But Anglicans believe that their Christian faith is sustained by a community whose life is open and public. It is a community of people in which God is able to speak through his Word and the two sacraments of Christ, baptism and the Eucharist.

Ministry and sacraments

In order to sustain this twofold ministry of Word and sacrament, Anglicans have maintained a ministry of bishops, priests and deacons. The distinction between lay and clergy is not absolute in the Anglican Church, but serves the purpose of sustaining the faith of Christian people through Word and sacrament. Throughout history, Anglicans have often changed their explanation as to why they want to maintain this threefold order. Some parts of the Anglican Communion declare that they will maintain this threefold order of bishops, priests and deacons, without any further explanation. In large measure this pattern is maintained on the basis that it has existed in the church from the earliest times. At the time of the Reformation the Anglican Church kept this ministry because it was seen to be the providential provision of God in the experience of the church and that, when appropriately reformed of the excesses of the medieval period, it did not have any fundamental disadvantages: it worked. It was unnecessary to change the threefold order.

By Word and sacrament, Christ is present among his people and in the hearts of believers. The sacrament of baptism is traced by Anglicans back to our origins in the incarnation of Christ. Baptism is that sacrament which symbolises our belonging to Christ and thus also to the Church. Anglicans believe that it is appropriate to baptise children, particularly children of Christian people, where those children are going to be brought up in a Christian environment. Traditionally, those baptised as infants have accepted the commitments made for them in baptism at their confirmation.

The value of received tradition

'Surely odious it must have been for one Christian Church to abolish that which all had received and held for the space of many ages, and that without detriment unto religion so manifest and so great, as might in the eyes of unpartial men appear sufficient to clear them from all blame of rash and inconsiderate proceeding, if in fervour of zeal they had removed such things.'

Richard Hooker, Laws of ecclesiastical polity. 4.14.6

Laity

The Church's community life is an arena in which the clergy exercise their ministry. That community life, through its worship and its interactions, serves to sustain the faith and vocation of lay people in the world. As well as their primary vocation in the world Anglican lay people have an important role in ordering the church's community life. Authority is dispersed within the Anglican way, not only to a variety of points, but to places

The General Synod of the Church of England comprises three 'houses' – Bishops, Clergy and Laity.

which are accessible to every member of the church. In that sense authority belongs to the whole church.

In England for many years most clergy appointments were controlled by lay people. Throughout the Anglican Communion lay people have a decisive voice in most appointments of clergy. Governance in Anglican churches is in most cases by Synod, in which lay people have an equal if not a majority voice in relation to the clergy. So the Anglican church community life is in very large measure under the influence of lay people and serves to sustain the faith of those lay people in their vocations in society.

Liturgy

The Anglican way is a liturgical way. The liturgy gives shape to our public worship, it guides and directs the content of that worship. It involves the participation of the various members of the church. The Anglican liturgy has always been imbued with Scripture and requires the preaching of God's Word and the celebration of Christ's sacraments. The way in which the liturgy is expressed varies greatly amongst Anglicans, according to cultural and physical circumstances, but the core liturgical character protects the orthodoxy of the faith, the involvement of the people as a whole, and the orderliness of the worship.

Anglican theology does not look back to a leading advocate, such as Thomas Aquinas in Roman Catholicism, or Martin Luther in Lutheranism, or John Calvin in Presbyterianism. Rather it attaches its primary theological formulations (the Thirty-nine Articles) to its book of worship (the *Book of Common Prayer*).

Worship and theology

'It is very significant that the formularies of the Church of England, included not only the articles, but the Ordinal and the Book of Common Prayer as well. The Church's theology is thus closely related to the Church's worship, prayer, and spiritual life and with the work of the pastoral priesthood.'

Michael Ramsey, 'Looking into the Future. Theology in Anglicanism', edited AA Vogel. Moorehouse, Barlow, Wilton. 1984, p. 160

Expressing belief

Because the Anglican Church has always been a form of Christianity enmeshed in society, so it is primarily expressed in the personal social life of Christian people. Their vocation is in the institutions of society: work, family, political, leisure. Every aspect of a person's life is an occasion for the expression of Christian belief. That is why Anglicans have always been engaged with society. This engagement takes different forms around the world, according to social and political circumstances, but the theme is continuous in Anglican belief. We are not a

Form-filling in the Vietnamese congregation in Sydney, Australia.

separated church, but an engaged church. It is for that reason that Anglicans around the world in different ways, have always had a history of social commitment, welfare, aid, care, social comment, participation in public education, politics and government. That engagement is reflected in Anglican theology. The Anglican theologian is someone who is intensely concerned to relate the faith which the church has inherited to the demands, the tragedies and the joys of the life which members of the church now live in society.

> To be a theologian is to be exposed to the vision of heaven and to the tragedies of mankind.
>
> *Michael Ramsey, 'Looking into the Future', p. 162*

Openness

Because of the very character of Anglican faith, its dispersed authority, its open community life, its commitment to social engagement, the church itself has always been an open and comprehensive community. Sometimes Anglicans have been abused for that comprehensiveness. But Anglicans need to be patient. Their faith makes them vividly aware that often there are not absolute answers to the meaning of Christian belief in the changing circumstances of modern life. As with the English Reformers, so throughout seventeen hundred years of Anglican belief, Anglicans have held strongly to the core beliefs, and left many other things open. This openness of the community life of Anglican belief is actually an aspect of openness to God in the world and openness to the future as belonging in God's providence.

At the time of the English Reformation when some people were arguing for very radical change in the way the church conducted its affairs, Richard Hooker defended the Anglican order on the grounds that it had been created by the providential will of God, and that in its newly reformed state, 'it did not work to the ill'. His opponents believed that there was one source of authority for all things, namely Scripture, and that Scripture taught Presbyterianism. Hooker believed, and in this he was truly Anglican, that there was no singular authority like that, no *sola scriptura*. He also believed that God guided his people through history for their good, through the central beliefs of the faith about the character of God and of salvation. These were the continuing things.

On another occasion, Richard Hooker argued that change was always possible, if not inevitable, because God providentially led his people in different circumstances to better understandings of the continuing central truth of his own character. Hence, the church is always open to change and reform according to this way of believing. The sixteenth-century puritan way of believing was more narrow and more particular than the Anglican way of believing, which was and is more open textured.

Failure and confession

Because Anglicans believe in this kind of way, they are vividly aware that they make mistakes: not only moral mistakes, but mistakes of understanding and of practice. That is why the General Confession stands prominently in the Anglican liturgies. We approach God as sinners, seeking the forgiveness of a loving God. Anglicans are confident to approach God in this way, because of what we have learned and been given in Christ.

Questions

1. How do Anglicans believe God speaks today?
2. What underpins the faith of Anglican Christians?
3. What do we mean when we say Anglicans are open?

4

A worldwide communion

Michael Nazir-Ali

It is one of the glories of the Christian Gospel that it is 'translatable' into the language, idiom and world-view of every culture. Throughout Christian history, this has brought about the emergence of churches firmly rooted in a local culture. There is, however, a negative side to the matter: churches, and even the Gospel, can become so identified with a people or a culture that this creates a barrier for cross-cultural mission and evangelism. In such situations, people of certain cultures may feel that the Gospel is alien precisely because it is 'owned' by people of other cultures. Even Christians may come to see the Gospel and their culture as so intertwined, that cross-cultural mission begins to be seen as a practical impossibility.

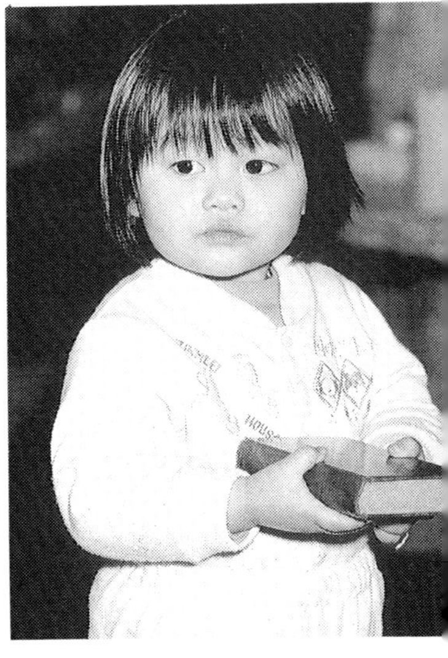

A young member of St John's, Campsie, Sydney.

The Reformation in England, as in so many other situations, emphasised the need for the Church of England to be truly a church for the people of England. The reading of the Scriptures in the vernacular, or common language of the people, the rendering of the Liturgy into English and the involvement of the laity (through Crown and Parliament), were all meant to ensure the 'Englishness' of the Church of England. At a time when national consciousness was emerging all over Europe, it is not surprising that 'locality' should have been understood as the nation–state and the Church as the national church. Not only the Church of England, but many other churches involved in the Reformation, came to see themselves in this way.

The Reformation and mission

It is well known that the Reformation, and the churches of the Reformation, did not produce, at first, a great sense of world mission. Many different reasons: geographical, political and theological, are given for this state of affairs. It is said, for instance, that these churches could not send people to other parts of the world because the sea routes, at that time, were controlled by Roman Catholic powers. The close relationship that these churches had with the states which protected them is often held to have made crossing political and cultural barriers harder for them. It was difficult for them to look beyond a particular people and a particular political order. They were often confined to one political system and even, perhaps, to one ethnic group.

It has been pointed out, however, that these churches did not merely lack the *means* for cross-cultural mission: they lacked even the *desire* for it. Many of the theologians of the period defended a peculiar kind of dispensationalism which held that worldwide mission came to an end with the passing away of the apostles. Those people who accepted the Gospel constituted the 'Christian nations' of the time. If God wanted the others to be converted, *he* would provide the means!

In striking contrast to the situation in the churches of the Reformation, the *Counter*-Reformation in the Roman Catholic Church was very missionary-minded. Taking advantage of the dominance the Roman Catholic powers enjoyed at the time on the high seas, both 'secular' and 'religious' missionaries reached widely-scattered areas of the globe. Not that their mission was purely opportunistic: it was undergirded by a properly universal view of the Church, accompanied by a well-developed understanding of its missionary task.

Although the Church of England, *Ecclesia Anglicana*, claimed continuity not only with the medieval church but with the ancient Celtic church which pre-dated the arrival of the 'Roman Mission' of Augustine, it is also, clearly, a church of the Reformation. How, then, did such a church spread beyond the British Isles?

The Anglican Church

Anglican comes from the Latin word which means 'English'. The Anglican Communion comprises those churches which recognise the leadership of the see of Canterbury and hence are in fellowship with the Archbishop. Today most Anglican churches would not be happy to be thought English. However, they share common roots in the prayer book, doctrine, and spirituality of English Christianity. They follow the Anglican way of worshipping, believing and living. There are about seventy million Anglicans in 31 self-governing churches in 164 countries worldwide.

How the Anglican Communion came to be

There are several different ways in which the Anglican Communion, as we know it, came to be. The first may be called the coincidental spread of the Anglican Church. Gradually, the predominantly Roman Catholic countries lost their hegemony over the sea routes, and other nations, including Britain, were able to take to the high seas to discover new lands, to trade with them and, sometimes, to settle some of their people in these parts of the world. Naturally, these people took their church with them and generally took great care to see that it resembled the church at home as much as possible!

The Anglican Church spread, in this way, into the Americas, Australasia, East Africa, India and other parts of the world. The first Anglican missionary societies: the Society for the Propagation of the Gospel (now USPG) and the Society for Promoting Christian Knowledge (SPCK), were founded, in 1701 and 1698 respectively, to assist in this kind of church expansion. Their main task, in the early years, was to provide Christian nurture and pastoral care for English settlers overseas. In time, however, they discovered that there was often missionary, or evangelistic, work to be done among the indigenous inhabitants of the colonies. The chaplains, attached to the trading companies, sometimes realised that they had a responsibility for the 'natives' as well as for the settlers. It is interesting to note in this connection that the 1662 *Book of Common Prayer* provides a form for the 'Baptism of Such as are of Riper Years', not only because of the growth of 'Anabaptism' (Anabaptists did not believe in the baptism of infants) but also because of 'natives in our plantations' and others converted to the Faith. In spite of this provision, Bishop Stephen Neill, in his *History of Christian Missions*, records that in the seventeenth century, only one Indian was baptised according to the rites of the Anglican Church even though there was a considerable Anglican presence in India at that time.

Even during this period of general disinterest in cross-cultural mission, there were some advocates of it in the Anglican tradition. One such was Adrianus Saravia (1531–1613). Saravia was a Dutchman who had been attracted to the Anglican way because he believed it had retained a primitive form of church order. Eventually he became a dignitary in the Church of England and one of the translators of the Authorised Version of the Bible. Saravia's work on the church's ministry expressly upheld the vocation of an ordered church to preach the Gospel to all nations. Such voices, however, were few and far between until the latter half of the eighteenth century.

The Anglican Communion

'The Anglican Communion is a fellowship, within the one Holy Catholic and Apostolic Church, of those duly constituted dioceses, provinces or regional Churches in communion with the See of Canterbury, which have the following characteristics in common:
(a) They uphold and propagate the catholic and apostolic faith and order as they are generally set forth in the *Book of Common Prayer* as authorised in their several Churches;
(b) They are particular or national Churches, and, as such, promote within each of their territories a national expression of Christian faith, life and worship;
(c) They are bound together not by a central legislative and executive authority, but by mutual loyalty sustained through the common council of the bishops in conference.'

Resolution of the 1930 Lambeth Conference

The evangelical revival and world mission

The churches of the Reformation were churches where the Bible was available in the vernacular and was avidly read. In time, people came to see that the God of the Bible has universal purposes and that he often uses human beings as the means to bring about the fulfilment of these purposes. David Bebbington, a church historian, points out that *means* was the key word signifying the whole apparatus of human agency in the fulfilment of God's mission. In the second half of the eighteenth century, people became more and more conscious of the need for world mission. In evangelical circles such consciousness was often related to the emergence of the *voluntary principle*.

In the eighteenth century, the Church of England was powerfully renewed by the evangelical revival. This renewal had to do, first of all, with a personal experience of divine grace and the forgiveness and empowerment which result from it. It had also to do with a renewed appreciation of the Church as community and of the sacraments as means of grace. The movement's moral concern extended well beyond the 'traditional' areas of individual and family behaviour. It led the way in the struggle to abolish slavery, but it was also active in improving the conditions of life for the poor in this country and in the task of proclaiming and living the Gospel in other parts of the world.

Those who felt they had a particular vocation in any of these areas organised themselves into voluntary societies or associations for the better pursuit of their aims, while remaining loyal to their church. The emergence of the Church Missionary Society (now the Church Mission Society) in 1799 was an aspect of the renewal of the church in this way. This was the first time that Anglicans had intentionally come together to take the Gospel across cultures. It began in a small way and was, at first, closely related to the need to resettle emancipated slaves in 'colonies' and to provide educational facilities for the ancient churches of the Middle East and India. In time, however, the effort extended itself to mission and ministry among those who were not Christians. Soon other Anglican societies were joining in this effort and new ones were coming into being. But this period of Anglican expansion we may well call *evangelical*.

Not that its greatest minds, such as Henry Venn

(1725–97) or even Roland Allen (1868–1949) wanted the churches being planted as a result of this effort to be Anglican. To them, this would have been almost a contradiction in terms. They worked for and prayed for churches that were truly indigenous, planted in the soil and culture of their country and people: churches that were 'self-governing, self-supporting and self-propagating'. (The three-self movement in the church in China goes back a long way!) Certainly, these churches would have 'special' relations with the Church of England. In the context of the Universal or Catholic Church of Christ, they would be in communion with the Church of England but with full autonomy in the ordering of their life. The relations that the Church of England now has with the united churches of South Asia, where Anglicans have joined Christians of other traditions, or with churches of non-Anglican origin, such as the Old Catholics, the Mar Thoma, the Philippines Independent Catholic Church and some of the Scandinavian and Baltic churches, are more like the relations envisaged by the architects of mission in the nineteenth century.

A thurifer (the person who carries the thurible in which incense is burnt at the Eucharist) and boatboy (his assistant) in Papua New Guinea, 1990.

The Tractarians and world mission

The Tractarian Movement in the Church of England, which took its name from a series of tracts published in the early years of the Oxford Movement (1833–45) was concerned to emphasise the divine character of the church. Whatever its relationships with the state, the church owed primary loyalty and obedience to God. Such a view tended to free the Tractarians from any commitment to simply maintaining the status quo. It is not surprising, therefore, that we find them addressing urgent social and political questions of their day. Nor is it an accident that many of the famous Anglican Catholic churches (as they came to be called) were located in the most needy areas of nineteenth-century England.

When David Livingstone made his famous plea in Cambridge in 1857 to replace the slave trade by 'commerce and Christianity', the Tractarians responded enthusiastically to this, and the Universities' Mission to Central Africa, for example, came into being in the same year. This inaugurated a new aspect to the history of Anglican mission: the *Tractarian*. Eventually, this tradition was to be hugely significant in the development of the Anglican Communion

Anglican bishops in the twentieth century have often offended those with power and authority in the land. Archbishop Michael Ramsey was unpopular with many when he was prepared to support the use of force to establish justice in Africa.

and in the emergence of particular churches, such as the Church of the Province of Southern Africa. These churches were rooted in the belief that the Church was primarily the Church *of God* and that it may, from time to time, have to stand over and against the secular order.

The tradition of '*loyal dissent*' goes back in the Anglican Church at least to the Non-Jurors of the late-seventeenth and eighteenth centuries. They got their name because they refused to take the oath of loyalty to William and Mary as they had already taken the same oath to the exiled James II! Many of them were deprived of their livings and even their sees, but they left a rich heritage of spirituality, liturgy and ecumenism on which the Anglican tradition continues to draw.

In many parts of the world, Anglican Catholics have nurtured this tradition of struggling against a given social order or against particular policies of the government, for the sake of society as a whole. A dramatic instance of such involvement is certainly the role of the Church and its leadership in the struggle against apartheid in South Africa. Nor is such witness limited to churches and leaders in the Catholic tradition: it has spread well beyond that and has made a significant contribution to the Anglican way as a whole. Even in England, establishment has not meant that the Church should be silent on social or political issues. In fact, its special place in society provides it with numerous opportunities for effective witness in this area.

Missions of assistance

Another kind of engagement in mission which we need to note is that of *fraternal assistance.* Since the early years of the nineteenth century, the Church of England and other churches of the Anglican Communion have responded to requests for assistance by the ancient oriental churches. These have been in the areas of education, medicine, theological education and even liturgical development. Almost the first of these was the response of the Church Missionary Society (CMS) to an appeal by the Indian Syrian Church, which wanted assistance in theological education and the early missionaries devoted themselves to this work. They were discreet and godly people and earned the respect of the church's bishops. Later on, the missionaries were not so wise and patient, and this led to conflict with the church leadership. Eventually, the Mission had to be terminated. In time, however, the seeds planted during this period led to tremendous renewal within the church – although this, in turn, led to division and the emergence of the Mar Thoma Syrian Church (a church in full communion with the churches of the Anglican Communion).

There have been similar Anglican missions of assistance to the Assyrian Church of the East and the Syrian Orthodox Church. In addition, CMS has worked with the ancient churches of the Middle East and BCMS (the Bible Churchmen's Missionary Society – now Crosslinks, founded in 1922) with the Ethiopian Orthodox Church. Both societies are now developing relationships with churches in Eastern Europe. A remarkable feature of this kind of engagement has been the clear intention of not proselytising and of trying to avoid the emergence of new Anglican churches in these contexts. There has been a commitment to the enabling and renewal of the existing indigenous church. Such an attitude has not always been wholly successful but it has earned the respect of the ancient oriental and orthodox churches among whom this work has taken place.

Has the Anglican Church got an ecclesiology?

Given the different ways in which the Anglican Church has spread, does it have a coherent ecclesiology? William Reed Huntington (1838–1909) was an American Episcopalian theologian of the nineteenth century who had an Anglican as well as an ecumenical vision. He was the first to articulate what later came to be called the Chicago–Lambeth Quadrilateral (1888). In doing this,

The Lambeth Conference

The first Lambeth Conference met in 1867 in the chapel of Lambeth Palace, London, the official residence of the Archbishops of Canterbury. 76 bishops attended. Canadian bishops had asked for it to take place to discuss important issues for Anglicans, such as the dispute between Archbishop Robert Gray of Capetown and Bishop Colenso of Natal over the authority of the Bible. The meeting was only for consultation. Decisions were to have no authority.

Lambeth Conferences have continued at roughly ten-year intervals ever since apart from a hiccup during the early part of the twentieth century because of the world wars. The growing size of the Conferences led to changes of venue. In 1988, 525 bishops attended the twelfth Conference in Canterbury.

Although at first the Lambeth Conference was only allowed to meet if it had no juridical authority, inevitably its influence grew over the course of its meetings. For example, when they met in 1888, the bishops agreed the Chicago–Lambeth Quadrilateral. This outlined four identifiably Anglican convictions which it would be necessary to hold if the divided churches were to be reunited.

Anglicans still recognise its importance. Since then, successive Conferences have discussed a wide range of issues, moral and political as well as spiritual, which are of concern to Anglicans worldwide. In a shrinking world the Lambeth Conference has carried increasing weight. It is both a forum for Anglican leaders and an organ to express their viewpoint.

Huntington was moved by his desire to see all the Christian churches in the United States come together. The implications of the Quadrilateral, however, were much wider than that: the 1888 Lambeth Conference recognised that the Quadrilateral could become the basis for discussions on unity with other churches. This it became and has remained ever since. The terms, set out by the Quadrilateral, are a common adherence to the normativeness of Holy Scripture, the sacraments instituted by Christ himself, the catholic creeds and the apostolic ministry of bishops, priests (or presbyters) and deacons.

It is, perhaps, important to remember that wherever Anglicans have united with Christians of other traditions, they have done so on the basis of the Quadrilateral. This is so, for instance, of Anglican participation in the Church of South India and the Church of North India. Adherence to the terms of the Quadrilateral has made it possible for these churches to continue to be received in the Anglican family, as well as belonging to other ecclesial families. Concordats with churches of non-Anglican origin, such as the Old Catholics, the Mar Thoma and the Philippines Independent Catholic Church, are also based on the provisions of the Quadrilateral. Discussions with the Lutheran churches in different parts of the world too continue to be 'informed' by the Quadrilateral as, indeed, do any ecumenical encounters of which Anglicans are a part.

It is interesting to note that the Quadrilateral is increasingly used in ecumenical circles to delineate the shape of the coming World Church. The Quadrilateral, however, is not simply an Anglican instrument for ecumenical conversations, but is also a way of understanding the basis and the coherence of the Anglican Communion itself: what we regard as essential for Christian unity is what is basic to our own life as a communion of churches. At the 1988 Lambeth Conference there was much discussion on 'instruments of communion', i.e. the beliefs and the structures which keep us together as a Communion. The instruments were identified as the Office of the Archbishop of Canterbury, who gathers the Communion together in different ways, the Lambeth Conference of Bishops, the Anglican Consultative Council, which brings together the bishops, clergy and laity, and the biennial meetings of the Primates of Anglican Provinces. It was also proposed that there ought to be a common declaration, based on the

Quadrilateral, which Anglicans all over the world could make. The form proposed in the report of the Conference is sensitive to the cultural diversity of the Communion and about our ecumenical commitment, but it also provides a basis for internal coherence in the Communion. It is to be hoped that such a common declaration will be finalised at the next Lambeth Conference.

The two poles

Huntington's view of the Anglican way had two poles to it. There was, first of all, the pole of *locality*. Huntington felt that the Anglican Church, in its fundamental doctrine, called the local church to be and to become the catholic church in that place. Such teaching may also be found, for instance, in the Preface to the *Book of Common Prayer* and in the Thirty-nine Articles of Religion. In actual practice, however, Huntington discerned two, mutually contradictory, elements. He referred to them as 'the Anglican Principle' and 'the Anglican System'. By 'the System' he meant all the 'ephemeral aspects' of Anglicanism: forms of music, choirs, robes and vestments, archaic offices etc. These may be appropriate in a given place and at a given time but are not necessarily so in every place and at every time. The tragedy often is that it is the System which is exported worldwide rather than the Principle being commended.

If one pole of the Anglican Principle is locality, the other surely is *catholicity*. A local church can be truly catholic only if it is in communion or fellowship with other local churches throughout the world. Such a relationship, if it is to flourish or even to survive, needs to be refreshed and strengthened through regular consultation and common decision-making. We have seen how Anglican organs of consultation and decision-making are gradually being strengthened; this can only be for the good of the Communion. It needs to be pointed out, however, that Anglican reluctance to develop powerful worldwide structures is rooted in the recognition that, in a divided church, no one part of it should pretend that it is the whole and that denominational structures should not be inimical to Christian unity.

The provisionality of the Anglican Communion

Such a view of catholicity has led successive Lambeth

Conferences to recognise the provisionality of the Anglican way. The words used by the 1930 Lambeth Conference echo in many other Anglican documents:

> . . . in its present character we believe that the Anglican Communion is transitional, and we forecast the day when the racial and historical connections which at present characterise it will be transcended and the life of our communion will be merged in a larger fellowship in the Catholic Church.

This is not to deny that there *are* permanent values or beliefs or ways of doing things. Anglicans treasure their precious heritage and hold it in trust so that it may contribute to and enrich the whole of Christ's Church. At the same time, they are deeply conscious that there are gifts which *they* need to receive from other traditions. Through the full participation of the united churches in its councils, the concordats with other episcopal churches and the approaching unity with different Lutheran churches, the Anglican Communion is gradually changing its character in the way foreseen by the Fathers of the 1930 Lambeth Conference.

A missionary Church?

An Anglican ecclesiology also leads to a *missionary* understanding of the Church. Already in the nineteenth century, as we have seen, the great mission thinkers of the time were looking forward to a fellowship of churches which were 'self-governing, self-supporting and self-propagating'. The Anglican Principle requires that local churches should be firmly rooted in local cultures and that they should be responsive to the challenges and opportunities provided for them by their locality. It is true, of course, that even such local mission cannot be exercised in isolation from brothers and sisters in other parts of the world. Indeed, there must be a partnership of giving and receiving even in such situations. In the end, however, the local church's role cannot be usurped by anyone else. In this matter, Anglican ecclesiology is profoundly Cyprianic: St Cyprian of Carthage (d. 258) had profound respect for the *Cathedra Petri* (or Chair of St Peter) but also held that each bishop had a certain autonomy and that in certain matters an ecclesiastical province, such as his in North Africa, could act independently.

The aspect of *locality* in the Anglican Principle leads us to a consideration of the different ways in which the people of God can be 'church' in today's world. The base communities in Latin America and the 'house church' movement in Britain are both challenging us to examine our structures. The parochial system is seen as a basis for church life, at least in England, and the parish may continue as a base for mission. But in the culturally plural situations in which the Church so often finds itself, a variety of responses is needed. Groups of people who come together to fulfil a particular task may well want to worship together as well. House Groups will develop a style of fellowship which the wider church will want to affirm. At the diocesan and provincial levels, the voluntary principle will need to be increasingly recognised. Bodies and agencies within the church will need recognition as having an ecclesial dimension.

The other side of the coin, of course, is that such bodies will be open to participation in the wider life of the Church and will seek to order their priorities in the light of the whole Church's vision of its mission. They should be enabled to do so. In the past, the Anglican Church has sometimes been unable to discern movements of the Spirit within its life: this was the case, for example, with Methodism. The consequence of this has been that the Church has lost many committed Christians and has lost out on the enrichment such movements can bring to the life of the Church. In a truly missionary church, there will be both discernment and direction of the movement of the Spirit.

The aspect of *catholicity* leads us to the view that the Church is not yet fully catholic because its missionary task remains incomplete! This is true, of course, in the local church's immediate vicinity, but it is also true of the world as a whole. Local churches are called, therefore, in partnership with each other and with voluntary movements in the Church, to reach out to the world in terms of witness and service.

A diverse Communion

A properly Anglican ecclesiology also results in a recognition of the multi-cultural and multi-contextual nature of both the local and the universal Church. By culture, I mean the traditions, customs, beliefs and world-views

Archbishop Desmond Tutu presides at an open-air Eucharist.

which people inherit from the past. By context, I mean their more immediate social, economic and political circumstances. In both these senses, the Anglican Communion as a whole, and various churches within it, present a plurality which we cannot ignore.

It needs recognition, first of all, in the way it affects the *leadership* of the church. In each culture and context, Christian leadership is inevitably affected and shaped by the patterns of other kinds of leadership in that situation. We should not be surprised, therefore, that the episcopate in Africa is affected by patterns of tribal leadership or that bishops in Asia are influenced by feudal models of leadership in their societies. In the West, similarly, we see the effects of corporate culture on the patterns of leadership and organisation in the church. As I say, this should not surprise us, but we should also be prepared to criticise these patterns in the light of our calling as servants of the Servant-King. The difference between the world and the Church at this point may well lie in the fact that we have the tools of self-criticism to hand. The Bible and Christian tradition should help us to both affirm and judge patterns of church organisation and leadership which we derive from our respective cultures. We should, therefore, expect both a diversity in the ways in which different churches organise themselves and a common thread which runs through all we do because we submit our structures to the scrutiny of Scripture and tradition. Whatever the appropriate cultural expression, in each context Christian leadership will be seen as gathering, enabling and directing, not as controlling, authoritarian and monarchical.

The fundamental Anglican documents already provide for *liturgy* which is in the vernacular and is, in other ways, appropriate for a given culture. There is an urgent need for churches to take this seriously at provincial, diocesan and parochial levels. Inculturation is not something that can happen only at the level of a 'macro-culture'; it can happen in relation to the various 'sub-cultures' which may exist within a particular locality. So it is not only in terms of African or European culture that inculturation should take place, but also in terms of young people, minorities, special-interest groups and so on; in short, wherever the church's outreach requires such a response.

In a widely scattered and diverse communion, it is important that ways of *living and acting* together should be effective. It is essential that the Anglican Communion Secretariat should be such that it can assist in gathering the Communion together. Whatever the financial arrangements and the major sources of funding, secretariat personnel should be drawn from right across the Communion and not only from the major, donor countries. The secretariat, along with provinces and their agencies, should encourage and monitor the regular exchange of people throughout the Communion.

At this time, there is a particular need for 'South-South' exchanges, i.e. people from Asia, Africa or Latin America being received in some other church in these regions. Churches and agencies in the 'North' should set their priorities in such a way that these exchanges are encouraged. Ways of consultation and decision-making need to be found which do not rely on adversarial styles of debate but are more consensual in nature. People taking the chair at inter-Anglican meetings, need to be trained in such a way that they do not notice only the dominating and articulate, but allow others to make a valuable contribution. The dominance of English, as a medium of discourse, should not be taken for granted and other languages should be used in the conduct of business. Lambeth Conferences already take this aspect of life

The Anglican Consultative Council

At the Lambeth Conference in 1968 the bishops of the Anglican Communion agreed the formation of the Anglican Consultative Council. By 1969 all the Provinces had approved. Since then the Council has met every two or three years in different parts of the world. In Anglican fashion, the Council has no legislative powers. It acts as a co-ordinating body, for example, 'to serve as needed as an instrument of common action'. It enables consultation to take place, and sometimes represents the Anglican Communion. Each Province and member church chooses up to three members. 69 bishops, clergy and lay persons make up its membership.

Following Lambeth resolutions in 1958 and 1978, other inter-Anglican initiatives have included the appointment of an Anglican Executive Officer (now known as the Secretary General) and the meeting of Anglican primates, or chief bishops of a Province. The primates meet every two or three years.

Towards consensus

The itch of disputing is the scab of the church.

Be calm in arguing;
for fierceness makes
Error a fault and truth
discourtesy.

George Herbert

seriously, but it needs a higher profile in other inter-Anglican meetings.

Whenever Anglican congresses have been held on a worldwide scale, they have not only encouraged clergy and laity alike but have also provided an impetus for thought and action. It is important that such congresses should take place at regular intervals. This will give people a sense of belonging together.

It is no longer realistic to expect that there should be one central college for training Anglican leaders. The concept itself betrays its 'datedness'; the Communion is too diverse for such an institution to succeed. It is still desirable, however, that there should be some 'common formation' of future leaders in a number of centres throughout the Communion. The initiatives taken by the Conference of Anglican Provinces of Africa, the CMS and USPG colleges at Selly Oak in Birmingham, Virginia Theological Seminary in the USA and Canterbury Cathedral are, therefore, worthy of note. Let us hope that other centres will emerge as we approach the millennium.

The Anglican Communion is a fellowship of churches from many different parts of the world. Within its life it holds people from many different cultural backgrounds and with many theological views. If it is to hold together and to make its contribution to the World Church, it needs to find a certain coherence in its fundamental beliefs and a certain effectiveness in its structures of consultation and decision-making. This is now beginning to happen and we pray that it may not be too late.

Questions

1. Why do Anglicans see themselves as belonging to a 'mission' church?
2. What is the mission of the Anglican Communion today?
3. In a multi-cultural world what have Anglicans to contribute?

Part 2

Belonging in the Anglican Church

5

Anglican origins and ethos

Elizabeth Culling

Most accounts of the Anglican Church begin with the divorce of Henry VIII and the separation of the English church from Rome. But the roots of the Anglican Church go back far deeper in time, and reach to the beginnings in Christianity in the British Isles. The Anglican Church was not created out of nothing in the sixteenth century: the slate could not be wiped clean in order to start again, even if the Reformers had wished to do so. It is equally important to avoid seeing everything as leading up to the Reformation, however important that period was for the formation of the Anglican way. The word 'Anglican' as a term emerged only in the nineteenth century, but its distinctive forms and practices had been in the making for much longer.

The British church

Christianity was probably first brought to Britain by the Roman army. Much of what we know about the early history of the church in Britain comes from the pen of St Bede. He gives us the name of the first known Christian, St Alban, who was martyred for protecting a Christian priest early in the fourth century. Other evidence suggests that the British church was being organised by this time on a diocesan basis, but the end of the Roman occupation and the barbarian invasions almost wiped it out except in the most remote parts of the islands. In 597 the Roman church sent a mission under St Augustine, but the work of Celtic missionaries from Scotland and Ireland had ensured that the Christian faith had not only been kept alive, but had spread through much of the north and west of Britain.

The Celtic church developed separately from the Roman church in the rest of Europe and had a different ethos. It was orthodox in doctrine, but the tribal and rural

Celtic Christianity

The Celts were originally pagan tribes who migrated across Europe to Gaul and the British Isles. They were subdued by the Romans and first came into contact with the Christian faith through them. St Patrick was a Roman Briton who was taken to Ireland as a slave and later returned to evangelise the Irish.

The Celtic church developed separately from the rest of the Church in Europe and although it was doctrinally orthodox, it differed in organisation and emphasis. It is these emphases which many are seeking to recover for the church today. They include a wholeness which avoided the mistake of compartmentalising life. Celtic prayers illustrate this quality in the way they embrace all of life from rising to going to sleep. The Celts had a deep awareness of Creation and experienced God through the natural world. This inspired awe and wonder, giving a sense of God's transcendence, though they also had an acute awareness of the presence of God everywhere, inspiring a sense of his immanence. While they recognised the glory of creation, they also knew it was fallen and in need of redemption. Thus the cross was also at the heart of their faith, and the great high crosses of the Celtic lands bore witness to this. They had a vivid sense of the supernatural which included a deep consciousness of the communion of saints, the presence of angels and the reality of evil which must be conquered in the name of Christ.

The Celtic mission

The Celts disliked rigid structure and organisation. They were a tribal, rural people and their church reflected this. Based on monasteries, each Christian community was independent and under the authority of an abbot. They were outward-looking, and mission-orientated. The natural wanderlust of the Celts thus became turned to wandering for the sake of Christ. This demonstrates their desire to transform culture, redeeming it for Christ.

nature of British society led to a church based on independent monastic communities rather than the more structured hierarchical church which developed out of the Roman Empire. Although the Celtic model gave way to the authority of Rome at the Synod of Whitby in 663, the ethos of the Celtic tradition was not altogether lost. Something of the simplicity and holiness of the Celtic Christians remained influential in shaping the native church of Britain and Ireland.

After the decision to submit to the authority of Rome, the church continued to grow, and was consolidated through the work of people like Archbishop Theodore (c. 602–90) and St Wilfrid (634–709). The fortunes of the church were closely bound up with the rest of the history of Britain and Europe, particularly the effects of repeated invasions in the eighth, ninth and tenth centuries. Officially under the authority of the pope, the identity of the church in Britain was subject to the political attitudes and activities of her secular rulers. Geography alone made England feel somewhat distant from the rest of Europe and did not foster intimate relations with the papacy in Rome. In any case, a unified Christendom in the West was little more than a fiction by the end of the Middle Ages, although the ideal persisted. Growing nationalism heightened the tension between England and a foreign papacy. Long before Henry VIII questioned the right of the papacy to hold jurisdiction in his realm, there were efforts to establish a measure of independence.

Historians of the English Reformation debate vigorously the question of whether the impetus for religious change and renewal came from above, by authority, or from below. There were problems and deficiencies in English ecclesiastical life as in the rest of the Catholic church, though many of these problems were not new. It has always been possible to uncover weaknesses in the church: poorly educated clergy and subsequent failure to emphasise the key elements of the Christian faith, superstition among the laity concerning the intercession of the saints and ways out of purgatory, mechanical participation in the sacramental and liturgical life of the church, low moral standards among the religious orders. But there is also evidence of high commitment to the church shown in bequests and building projects. There was also widespread piety with devotional aids figuring as the most popular type of literature in demand from the recently invented printing presses.

Were the English people so dissatisfied with their church that they cheerfully supported its radical reconstruction via king and Parliament? Many historians today would answer 'No' to this question. The church exercised a great deal of power in medieval society, with those at the top of the ecclesiastical hierarchy being as closely involved in secular government as in looking after the church. Their interests were thus bound up with affairs of state and the status quo. One of the most important 'causes' cited for the ease with which relations with Rome were broken is anti-clericalism, that is, opposition to the elevated position accorded to the clergy in society.

There were important forerunners to the events of Henry VIII's reign. Politically, papal power had already been limited by English monarchs reluctant to concede too much to the church. Theologically, John Wyclif had questioned the pope's authority and the doctrine of transubstantiation – the belief that the substance of the bread and wine at the Mass became the body and blood of Christ. His followers, the Lollards, had read the Bible in English in defiance of the authorities.

On the title page of the first publicly authorised version of the English Bible, Henry VIII is shown handing out copies of the Scriptures to an obedient and grateful people. But the English Bible was already in circulation and eagerly sought after by numerous people before 1539. By 1525 William Tyndale had translated the New Testament from the Hebrew and Greek. He was forced to work in exile because of hostility from the authorities in England, but with the help of English merchants he smuggled the newly printed Bibles back into the country. Copies of Tyndale's Bible were publicly burned by the bishop of London and the archbishop attempted unsuccessfully to buy up all the surviving copies. Tyndale's translation had an immense influence and he has rightly been called the 'Father of the English Bible'. In some ways it may be claimed that every translation since has simply been a revision of Tyndale. Ninety per cent of his words passed into the King James version of 1611 and about seventy-five per cent into the Revised Standard Version. He also translated parts of the Old Testament, but was burned at the stake before he could complete his work.

William Tyndale (1494–1536) translated the New Testament and parts of the Old Testament into everyday English. His translations have deeply influenced succeeding English versions.

The English Bible

Like the rest of the Catholic Church, the Church in England relied on the Latin Vulgate version of the Bible. The Celtic Church was responsible for producing and preserving precious manuscripts during the tumultuous period of invasions. The Lindisfarne Gospels were written at Lindisfarne in honour of St Cuthbert at the end of the seventh or early eighth century. No complete Bible in English exists before the Reformation, though there were translated selections found in other literature, and interlinear glosses of the gospels and Psalms in existence. Wyclif encouraged the cry for the Bible in the vernacular, but it seems that he did not translate it himself.

The invention of printing made the circulation of the Bible much wider and this was taken advantage of by the Reformers who wanted everyone to be able to read God's Word for themselves.

William Tyndale was the most important translator of the English Bible and indeed has arguably had more influence on the English language and culture than William Shakespeare. His English New Testament appeared in 1526. Others built on his work and in 1535 Coverdale's Bible was published, the first complete English Bible. Henry VIII authorised the first official English Bible, the so-called Great Bible in 1540 and every church was ordered to purchase one. Other translations followed, and in 1604 King James I sponsored a new translation at the request of the Puritans in the Church of England. This, the King James Version, remained the standard translation of the English churches until the twentieth century.

The church and Henry VIII

Theologically Henry and his government did not consider that they were establishing a new church when they broke from Rome. The king himself was a thoroughly conservative Catholic. Although he was prepared to dally with ideas of reform so long as they suited his political intentions, he had no desire to change anything theologically. It may be said that he could not have proceeded without the support of those in authority in church and state who did desire theological change, but not even reformers like Thomas Cranmer considered that they were introducing a new church. The church was being reformed. In Henry's reign the old services continued as before, and the administration was left unchanged. In the following reign, that of Edward VI, the English Prayer Book was introduced and more radical reforms which rejected Catholic ceremonies were undertaken, but services did not become unrecognisable. The reformers looked back as well as forward, believing that they stood in the true tradition of the church Fathers.

Thomas Cranmer was responsible for shaping much of the Reformation church. He became Archbishop of Canterbury in 1532 following advice given to Henry concerning his divorce from Katherine of Aragon. Cranmer was well read in the church Fathers and was a gifted liturgist with an excellent command of the English language. His own theological development was gradual and he preferred reform to come through gentle persuasion rather than by force. Like Martin Luther, he also believed in the role of the 'godly prince' whose task was to uphold a just society and give free rein to the Gospel.

Cranmer is often accused of inconsistency, but he was extremely consistent in his loyalty to the belief that the monarch was appointed by God and commanded obedience. As Archbishop he was responsible for the Great Bible, along with its prefaces, which was ordered to be placed in all churches. He was also responsible for the English Litany of 1544, and the two Prayer Books of 1549 and 1552. He produced the *Reformation of Church Laws*, published later in Elizabeth's reign, and a defence of the doctrine of the sacrament in 1550. He was mainly responsible for the Articles of the Church of England, the Homilies appointed to be read in the churches, and *The Institution of a Christian Man*, published in 1536 under the king's name.

Cranmer enjoyed much greater freedom to introduce reforms into the church in Edward's reign, and progress was much faster. The archbishop enlisted the support of a number of continental reformers who came to England to take up posts at Oxford and Cambridge.

The religious reaction of Mary's reign led to the deaths of the reformers Cranmer, Ridley and Latimer along with 300 others. The Queen did not reign long enough to consolidate the return to Rome, and Elizabeth inherited a legacy of religious as well as political upheaval. She herself was an unknown quantity when she ascended the throne and her intentions regarding the church were not clear. It is likely that she intended to proceed piecemeal with the settlement which followed. There was no preconceived model which could be imposed upon the country as a whole, for much of the church's liturgy and doctrine were in a state of flux. The royal injunctions set forth at the beginning of the reign probably expressed her mind most accurately, though judging by the Chapel Royal which displayed a crucifix and two candles, we can be sure that she liked the external ceremonies of religion. Despite this, however, there was never any question that she would accommodate Roman Catholicism, besides which the Catholics were in disarray following Mary's death, and were not a force to be reckoned with.

The church under Elizabeth

The new Queen's first action was to ensure that Parliament restored the Royal Supremacy, repealed under Mary. This Act of Supremacy passed in 1559 repealed Mary's ecclesiastical legislation, revived Henry VIII's laws against Rome and restored to the Crown the ecclesiastical powers that the latter had enjoyed. All ecclesiastics had to swear an oath of allegiance to the royal supremacy, although Elizabeth was known as Supreme Governor, not Supreme Head. Elizabeth was acknowledged as 'the only supreme governor – as well in all spiritual or ecclesiastical things or causes as temporal'. The Act also stated that the powers of Henry over the church should be restored 'by the authority of this present parliament'. Thus, it was the Queen-in-Parliament who now ruled the church, and in a modified form that continues in England today.

It is sometimes said that Elizabeth was forced in a more

Thomas Cranmer

Thomas Cranmer was born in 1489 in Aslacton, Nottinghamshire. Educated at Cambridge, he may have remained a diligent but obscure scholar had it not been for Henry VIII's desire for a divorce. The advice he gave to the king on the issue led to his promotion to Archbishop of Canterbury in 1532. He remained in this post for the rest of Henry's reign and the whole of Edward VI's reign. Under Mary he was deposed and burned as a heretic in 1556.

Cranmer stands as the great architect of the Church of England. He was a key figure in the break from Rome under Henry, and along with Thomas Cromwell the king's vice-regent, worked for the reform of the church. His achievements were limited until 1547 because of Henry's caution.

Besides his reforms at the national level, Cranmer worked hard to reform his own diocese of Canterbury. He also kept in close touch with the continental reformers and sought to find places for them in England where they could exert their influence. His burning desire was for people to know God and realise that they could approach him themselves through the Scriptures, through their own prayers and through participation in the life of the church. Criticised for being weak and fickle, Cranmer in fact exercised great bravery in standing up to King Henry (and surviving!), and in faithfully pursuing the cause of reform amid the political intrigues of the mid-Tudor court. He was consistent in his obedience to the monarch whom he believed held sovereignty by God's grace, until Mary tried to force him to deny his conscience before God.

Queen Elizabeth I (1533–1603). 'In Elizabethan England, to be English was to belong to the Church of England, and vice versa.'

Protestant direction than she would personally have liked, by enthusiastic reformers returning from the continent. There they had witnessed a more advanced form of reformation than anything hitherto established in England, and the exiles came home intending to set up the 'True Religion' among the English people who were seen as the 'Elect Nation'. It is of course difficult to know exactly what ordinary parishioners thought about the upheavals of recent years. It may well be that apathy and indifference were stronger than religious fervour of any sort, and peace and security were higher on the agenda in 1559. A number of the bishops accepted Elizabeth's position and her policies because they believed that this was the only way to secure the cause of reform in England. The Crown, for its part, saw the bishops as a bulwark against radical change in the social and religious framework.

Elizabeth used the church courts to enforce uniformity. The bishops were required to enforce the rules concerning church attendance and to see that churches were properly equipped for Protestant worship. Although there were some who wished to separate entirely from the established church, the majority who desired further reform were content to await its occurrence from within. Few were prepared to risk charges of sedition and the death penalty in order to bring about more radical change. In Elizabethan England, to be English was to belong to the Church of England, and vice versa. There were no alternatives, no deviations. The concept of toleration was unknown at this time. No one in the sixteenth century could have imagined anything other than one national church to which everyone belonged. It was 1689 before any Act of Toleration was passed allowing some freedom to dissent from the established religion.

Scotland, Ireland and Wales

In Scotland the Reformation was largely the work of John Knox who had strong connections with England and Geneva. With the help of other Scottish nobles he constructed a thorough-going Genevan settlement in Scotland, drawing up a *Confession of Faith* in 1560 and a *Book of Discipline* in 1561. He also produced a new liturgy, the *Book of Common Order* in 1564 and translated Calvin's *Institutes*. King James VI of Scotland who became James I of England grew up in this Calvinist atmosphere and embraced the Reformation in spite of his Catholic mother, Mary Queen of Scots. When he came to England, however, he was unwilling to concede ground to the Puritans who looked on him as their hope of further reform in the Church of England. Instead the Church of England became increasingly dominated by the High Church party under Archbishop William Laud.

Meanwhile in Scotland bishops were appointed, and there was subsequent pressure from England for liturgical conformity also. When a Prayer Book, similar to the English one of 1549, was introduced in 1637 there was so much opposition that it had to be abandoned. The Scottish bishops remained loyal to the Stuart dynasty during the upheavals of the monarchy in England, and in 1690 all the Scottish bishops became Non-Jurors, that is they refused to swear the oath of allegiance to William and Mary. The running of the church fell to their Presbyterian opponents and it has remained Presbyterian since that time.

Episcopalians found themselves a persecuted minority, especially after the rebellion of 1745 when severe penal laws were instituted. By the time of the death of Charles Edward Stuart, the diocesan and parochial system had collapsed. In 1811 the National Synod of the Church of Scotland was convened which passed a number of canons, including the acceptance of the Thirty-nine Articles. This marked the recovery of the Scottish Episcopal Church. It was organised into dioceses, but maintained some notable differences from other churches in the Anglican Communion. Thus the head of the church is the Primus, who holds office for life, while the bishops take an oath of obedience not to him but to the synod of bishops. From 1743 this church has had its own liturgical tradition which took Cranmer's First Prayer Book of 1549 as its starting point. This more Catholic tradition was taken up by Anglicans in the United States of America.

In Ireland the Reformation was imposed from above and was inseparably linked with foreign rule. Only a small minority belonged to the Anglican Church and it was very unpopular with the rest of Ireland. In the seventeenth century the plantation of English and Scots provided a stronghold of militant Protestantism in Ulster. In 1615 the Irish Articles, 104 articles of faith, were adopted by the Church of Ireland; these were more Calvinistic than the Thirty-nine Articles. The latter were accepted in Ireland in 1635. The Church of Ireland suffered general decline from the eighteenth century. In 1869 the English Prime Minister William Gladstone steered a bill through Parliament for the disestablishment of the Irish church. The bill passed amidst much opposition and the Irish church was disestablished and disendowed, although it remained in full communion with the Church of England.

In Wales the church followed England into the Reformation and remained part of the Anglican Church until disestablishment came about in 1920. Under Elizabeth I Welsh translations of the Bible and Prayer Book and the appointment of Welsh-speaking bishops gave the Welsh church its own identity. The influence of the Anglican Church in Wales declined in the second half of the eighteenth century. An increasing divide between nonconformists who represented the Welsh-speaking farmers, miners and industrial workers, and the Anglicans who were mainly English-speaking landowners and ironmasters, plus failure to adapt to population growth, led to disestablishment. At first traumatic, this enabled the church to put its own house in order and so build relations with the other churches.

Royal supremacy

Following the period of the Reformation, the institution of the church looked very similar to the medieval church. The ecclesiastical hierarchy was retained and the organisation of the church into Provinces, dioceses, archdeaconries and rural deaneries continued. The system of ecclesiastical courts , with a few additions, also continued as before. Holy Scripture, the creeds, sacraments of baptism, confirmation, the Eucharist, the threefold ministry of bishops, priests and deacons, were all as before. Elizabeth was careful to ensure that bishops were consecrated by others who were bishops already, which meant that the succession was maintained, and no one could accuse the church of discontinuity. As Elizabeth wrote to the Emperor Ferdinand, the Church of England followed 'no novel and strange religions, but that very religion which is ordained by Christ, sanctioned by the primitive and Catholic Church and approved by the consentient mind and voice of the most early Fathers'.

The Act of Supremacy, first passed in Henry VIII's reign, put relations between church and state on a new footing at a single stroke. By this declaration, the Crown claimed not only the headship of that English state in which the church existed, but also headship of the church which existed within and of that state. The Crown therefore claimed rights which exceeded mere loyalty: it claimed active rights of government, direction and initiation. Not everyone was easily reconciled to the Royal Supremacy, even though by the end of Elizabeth's reign its justification was well developed. Some Protestants had hoped that the Crown would eventually set in motion a thoroughgoing reformation of the church and then withdraw from further interference in ecclesiastical affairs. When it did not under Elizabeth they, like the Catholics, regarded the claim to supremacy as sacrilegious, especially when the monarch was female. Furthermore there was always the danger, as under Mary, that a change of monarch could mean a reversal of reform. Under Mary some went into exile rather than face the conflict of loyalties, while others, notably Thomas Cranmer, remained so loyal to the monarch that they came close to denying personal beliefs.

The medieval patronage system also remained as before. The dissolution of the monasteries greatly increased the proportion of lay patrons as parish livings passed from them to the Crown. Clergy were appointed by the Crown itself, by nobles, bishops, collegial bodies and local gentry with varying degrees of appropriateness. The Crown also continued to name the candidates whom cathedral chapters were expected to elect as bishops.

Doctrine and worship

Anglicans point not only to the Thirty-nine Articles as indicators of what the Church of England stands for, but also to the Prayer Book. 'If you want to understand us, come and pray and worship with us.' Thus doctrine and worship are closely connected in the Anglican tradition. The Reformation period was extremely formative for both. The medieval emphasis on sacrament over Word shifted in the Reformation, and the 'Word' took precedence. Although reformers of a more puritan persuasion like Elizabeth's first Archbishop, William Grindal, identified 'Word' with sermons, Hooker included scriptural readings, catechetical exercises and the homilies. He balanced Word and sacrament more evenly, and that balance remained fundamental. The combination of appealing to Scripture and antiquity, and the circumstances of controversy and upheaval surrounding the beginnings of the reformed Anglican Church, provided a creative framework for doing theology, and this has been an Anglican principle for doing theology ever since.

Hooker's writings demonstrate the close link between doctrine and worship. He displays a belief in authority but a mistrust of infallibility, of either the Roman Catholic or the Protestant variety. There is a sense of the mystery of divine truth, such that Hooker would be reluctant to define it too closely. Revelation, Reason and Tradition are the three foundations for doing theology, and are seen as complementary. Hooker sought the middle way at a time when many churches in the West were becoming more narrow in belief and practice. In fact the subsequent history of the Church of England has never been to maintain the middle of the road, but to swing back and forth, yet managing to contain the majority of its adherents under the Anglican umbrella. Hooker suggested that churches 'on all sides' should enter 'such consultation as may tend to the best re-establishment of the whole Church of Jesus Christ', sure that the 'calm and moderate' policy of the English church was the best way forward. The idea of holding to the 'middle way' has been regarded as a hallmark of the Anglican way ever since, despite the realities of history. By critics it is interpreted as weakness, a church which blows neither hot nor cold, but the ideal has enormous strengths and has enabled the Anglican Church to adapt and develop, and contain a variety of theological shades within her boundaries.

The Anglican Communion

From the eighteenth century the Anglican way underwent considerable transformation as the national churches of England and Ireland, along with the disestablished remnant of the Episcopal Church in Scotland, became part of a much wider Anglican Communion. These are in communion with the see of Canterbury, but self-governing, held together by common loyalties, and since 1867 by the participation of its bishops in the Lambeth Conference which meets every ten years. It is true to say that the expansion of the Anglican Church has been closely linked with British expansion overseas during the eighteenth and nineteenth centuries. Over ninety per cent of Anglicans live in countries where English is the official language. By the beginning of the twentieth century the Anglican way was rooted in all continents. The Anglican Communion, a term which first appeared in 1851, was becoming a genuinely worldwide fellowship. Anglican churches which had a missionary origin have become more indigenous and more autonomous during the last century.

As English explorers, traders and colonists travelled from the sixteenth century onwards, they took the Anglican way with them. By the early eighteenth century there were Anglican congregations in the Caribbean islands, along the north Atlantic Coast from Newfoundland to Georgia and were formed in territories of the East India Company on the Indian subcontinent. The Bishop of London had jurisdiction over all these, though with little practical effect. The founding of the Societies for 'the Promotion of Christian Knowledge' and 'the Propagation of the Gospel' around the turn of the eighteenth century meant the beginnings of some support and oversight. The charters of both of these mentioned evangelisation, but most of the efforts were directed towards settling 'the state of religion . . . among our own people abroad'. Beginnings were made, however, among native North Americans and African slaves, and support was given to the Royal Danish Lutheran missions in southern India. Out of the growth of the worldwide Anglican Communion has come the Lambeth Conference. It was not a Council to make decisions, but a Conference for the bishops to confer. It has become the meeting place of the leaders of autonomous Anglican churches which have shared roots and responded to similar influences.

Movements in the Anglican Church

It may be justly claimed that a distinctive Anglican theology began with the Elizabethan Settlement and has continued to take shape ever since. Thus to do justice to the ethos of the Anglican way we should look not only at Cranmer and Hooker and the Elizabethan clergy, but the influences which occurred in each of the following centuries.

Anglicans and the Ecumenical Movement today

1. Doctrinal conversations with different churches have established considerable common ground in matters of faith. Examples have been joint statements issued by Anglicans and Roman Catholics (ARCIC), Anglicans and the Orthodox, Anglicans and Lutherans, Anglicans and the Reformed churches.

2. Anglican Provinces have welcomed the 1982 Lima Document, *Baptism, Eucharist and Ministry*, produced by the World Council of Churches, which seeks to chart 'theological convergence' over matters that have divided Christians.

3. Anglican churches have played a significant part, with various Protestant churches, in the formation of united episcopal churches of the Church of South India (1947), the Church of North India (1970), the Church of Pakistan (1970) and the Church of Bangladesh (1971). Similar conversations with other denominations in England have not so far been successful.

4. An important development in Britain has been Local Ecumenical Partnerships (this used to be Projects). This term covers a variety of local arrangements in which Christians of different churches share an element of common life from sharing buildings through to forming a united congregation. Such co-operation is now made possible under Canon B44. There are now more than 800 LEPs that officially involve the Church of England.

5. The Church of England has now established working relationships with a number of regional or national churches in Northern Europe. In 1991 the Church of England and the Evangelical (Protestant) Churches in Germany recognised each other through adopting the 'Meissen Declaration' and committed themselves to a range of common action that includes mutual reception of the ➤

In the seventeenth century the Caroline divines (mainly church leaders during the reigns of Charles I and Charles II) expounded their understanding of the Anglican way through their scholarship, poetry and personal sanctity. They emphasised the episcopacy, loyalty to the Prayer Book, order and beauty in worship, and the central place of the sacraments. The church was also profoundly affected by the growth of scientific knowledge and the thought of the Enlightenment, otherwise known as the Age of Reason. The exaltation of Reason as the measure of all things led to the rise of Deism which abandoned all that was mysterious and supernatural in Christianity in favour of what was natural and reasonable.

The evangelical revival of the eighteenth century was in part a reaction to a cerebral religion and sought to restore the experience of the Christian faith to the church. The evangelical movement continued in strength into the nineteenth century and gave an important stimulus to the Reformation tradition within the Church of England.

Also in the nineteenth century, the Oxford Movement emphasised the Catholic tradition within the Anglican Church by pointing to the historic continuity of the church signified by the apostolic succession and its sacramental doctrine. Its influence was felt in the sphere of worship and ceremonial, in pastoral work in the slum areas of Britain, and in the restoration of Anglican religious orders.

Since the nineteenth century biblical criticism and theological liberalism have affected issues regarding the nature of belief and the traditional understanding of authority in the church. There has also been liturgical change including, in this century, revision of the Prayer Book. In the last twenty years there has been a proliferation of liturgical texts, a process which has involved experiment and ecumenical cross-fertilisation.

Many Anglicans have had a concern for Christian unity, and in recent history participation in ecumenical activity has been an important part of Anglican church life. The work of Archbishop William Temple in the twentieth century has been especially important in this area.

The tradition of distinguishing primary and secondary matters in theology, experience in handling Christian diversity, and the vision of Christians united in mission to a place have often shaped and encouraged a commit-

Eucharist although not yet a full exchange of authorised ministers. In 1995 the Church of England General Synod adopted the Porvoo Declaration with the aim of establishing working fellowship and full intercommunion with the Lutheran episcopal churches in Denmark, Estonia, Finland, Iceland, Latvia, Lithuania, Norway and Sweden. (In each case this depends on these churches also adopting the Declaration).

One of the first women to be ordained priest in England presides at the Eucharist (1994).

ment to ecumenism. At the same time the importance given to patterns of church life, such as episcopacy, which derive from the ancient church, has sometimes created barriers to institutional ecumenism. Anglicans are committed to closer relations with other Christians at many levels of church life.

As in every century, social change has affected the church and there have been a number of significant changes in the institution of the church. Archbishop Fisher began work on reforming church law, and eventually in 1969 a new set of Canons was produced. In the same year a new system of church government was introduced in the form of Diocesan and General Synods. The Anglican Church has experienced numerous changes over the centuries, the most recent being the ordination of women to the priesthood in the Church of England. The fact that in other parts of the Anglican Communion this was already happening demonstrates the diversity within the unity of the church. The Anglican Church is no longer the single dominant edifice it was at the end of the sixteenth century, but it remains the established Church of England, and has now become the Anglican Communion worldwide.

Questions

1. What main historical factors in the story of your church have shaped
   a) its worship,
   b) its physical appearance?
2. It is said that in every age the Church needs a reformation. Do you agree?
3. How important is it to hold on to the traditions of the past in the life of the Church?

6

The Anglican way of worship

Michael Vasey

At first sight Anglicans worship in very different ways. Here are some examples. In an ancient cathedral on an autumn evening a scattered congregation is listening to the appointed Psalms for the day, sung to Anglican chant. In a modern suburb a large and enthusiastic congregation is singing with hands outstretched after a lively illustrated address on Joshua crossing the Jordan river. In an African village a priest dressed in full vestments follows the traditional actions and gestures of the Western medieval Mass while choir and congregation participate with the drums and rhythms of traditional African music. In an Oxford church a congregation of young people uses an audiovisual presentation, prepared from secular music they like, to fill out the framework of a Rite A Eucharist.

Joyful young worshippers in Yambio Cathedral, Sudan (1993).

Fundamental principles

Although the appearance and musical style of these four events are very different, they have much in common and each is recognisably Anglican. In each case worship is a structured corporate act involving the interplay between customary forms and popular religion or devotion. People from one congregation might at first find it difficult to recognise the others as part of the Anglican tradition but in time they could come to see in the others the Anglican family likeness. Behind the diversity lie a common understanding and approach:

1. Worship is a corporate activity

In the cultures of the New Testament, as in many parts of the developing world, the response to an unusual event was the immediate gathering of a crowd (cf. Mark 1:33, 45; 2:2 etc.). By contrast, people in Britain respond to important news by going home to watch the TV or read a paper. Most English people are only used to relating to a small number of people at a time, for example in a home or maybe the corner of a pub, and find the gathering of a larger number of people for worship somewhat alien. Where people do come together in larger groups it is often to watch professional entertainment.

Worship involves a large group of people who are participants and not simply spectators. In this respect it is more like a dance – whether formal, disco or 'knees-up' – and, like any dance or social gathering, worship has conventions and skills which can at first seem fairly bewildering. One of the main tasks in introducing new people to worship is helping them feel comfortable enough to begin to learn how to participate.

A corporate event depends on a number of elements to make it work: appropriate space; well-thought out choreography; leaders with the knowledge and skill to enable the event to happen; a common understanding of the activity that is often focused on particular memories, symbols and focal actions; a clear and well-conceived programme; participants with sufficient confidence and information to participate. With worship, as with other corporate celebrations, music, movement and art are an essential part of the event. Worship is not just about words, although words are very important. The analogy of a dance perhaps exaggerates the physical demands of worship; listening – an active process – is an important part of worship.

2. Worship is a place of encounter with God

The Anglican Church has always recognised the central place of worship in a Christian's experience of God. In doing so it looks back to a major theme of the New Testament (Matthew 18:20; Acts 2:41–7; Hebrews 10:19–25; Colossians 3:16; Ephesians 5:18–20). Article 19 identifies worship as *the* mark of the church; it is a community in which worship takes place: 'in which the pure Word of God is preached, and the Sacraments be duly ministered according to Christ's ordinance in all those things that of necessity are requisite to the same'. Christian worship is not simply about meeting, teaching or singing although all of these are important; it is about encounter with God. By God's appointment and promise, and through the mysterious activity of the Holy Spirit, God is active in worship and human beings are transformed. Worship is about the presence of God, about transaction and re-creation.

Like the New Testament, the Anglican Church locates this activity of God primarily in the activity of Christ through the Holy Spirit (cf. Ephesians 2:18). Cranmer expressed this beautifully by the Collect, probably dating from the eighth century, that he put at the start of his Communion service.

Collect for Purity

Almighty God, to whom all hearts are open, all desires known, and from whom no secrets are hidden: cleanse the thoughts of our hearts by the inspiration of your Holy Spirit, that we may perfectly love you, and worthily magnify your holy name; through Jesus Christ our Lord. Amen

The fundamental structures of Anglican worship reflect the way in which God's presence is mediated to us. This can be summarised around four words: prayer, Scripture, sacrament, church.

Prayer

This includes praise and devotion as well as intercession. Prayer is not addressed to a remote and absent being. It depends on the activity of the Holy Spirit and involves access into the saving activity and presence of God the Holy Trinity made available for us in Jesus Christ. The provision of ordered public prayer makes a powerful statement about the reality and accessibility of God. Human life is not meaningless. Human beings are not simply autonomous, unaccountable and abandoned in the universe. God is concerned, active and accessible within the particular human communities in which our lives take form. Prayer is not a form of escape from the world; it is an acknowledgment that God is present to his world and has purposes for it.

Scripture

The Thirty-nine Articles refer to the books of the Old and New Testaments as 'God's Word Written'. This expresses the relationship between God's continuing activity in history focused in Jesus and the prophetic witness found in the 'sacred writings' of the Scriptures. The twenty-seven books of the New Testament are themselves evidence of the respect the first Christians gave to these writings which are both means of revelation and authoritative witnesses to the Apostolic faith. Both Jesus and the New Testament writers treated the Hebrew Scriptures of the Old Testament as more than historical documents (e.g. Luke 24:25–32; 1 Corinthians 10:11; Romans 15:4; 1 Peter 1:10–12). In the good purpose of God they have a continuing significance for the church today. This gives the Scriptures a central place in Christian worship; the Christian assembly is the primary place in which Christians are to meet Scripture. This occurs both through hearing Scripture read aloud (1 Timothy 4:13, Colossians 4:16), and also through celebrating its content in music, liturgy and teaching (Colossians 3:16).

Sacrament

The term 'sacrament' has had a number of different meanings in Christian history. The Thirty-nine Articles attempted to reserve the term for the gospel signs of baptism and Communion which they describe as 'effectual signs of grace, and God's good will towards us, by which he doth work invisibly in us, and does not only quicken [i.e. 'make alive'] but also strengthen and confirm our Faith in him' (Article 25). The New Testament treats baptism (Galatians 3:26–8; 1 Corinthians 12:13) and eucharist (1 Corinthians 10:16–17; 11:26, 29–34) as acts in which both the individual and the Christian community genuinely encounter God. They are ritual actions which make visible the Gospel of Christ and the kingdom of God; they communicate identity, vision and grace. Anglican worship attempts to take these two ritual signs seriously. It approaches them expectantly, celebrates them in ways which respect their ritual form, and expects them to shape the life of the individual and the community.

The doctrine of the Church of England

1. Canon A5, of the doctrine of the Church of England states: 'The doctrine of the Church of England is grounded in the Holy Scriptures, and in such teachings of the ancient Fathers and Councils of the Church as are agreeable to the said Scriptures. In particular such doctrine is to be found in the Thirty-nine Articles of Religion, the Book of Common Prayer, and the Ordinal.'
This canon is entrenched in the Worship and Doctrine Measure 1974 (5(1)). It is under this Measure that alternative forms of service to the *Book of Common Prayer* and new forms of declaration of assent for church office holders have been authorised.
2. The Worship and Doctrine Measure 1974 requires that 'every form of service . . . approved by the General Synod . . . shall be such as in the opinion of the General Synod is neither contrary to, nor indicative of any departure from, the doctrine of the Church of England in any essential matter' (S4(1)). S4(2) states: 'The final approval of General Synod of any such Canon or regulation or form of service or amendment thereof shall conclusively determine opinion as aforesaid with respect to the matter so approved.
3. In considering whether any rite is contrary to, or indicative of any departure from, the doctrine of the Church of England in any essential matter, reference should be made to (i) the Holy Scriptures; (ii) such teachings of the Fathers and the Councils of the Church as are agreeable to the said Scriptures; (iii) the Thirty-nine Articles of Religion, the *Book of Common Prayer* and the Ordinal of 1662; (iv) such forms of service, canons and regulations as have received the final approval of General Synod.
Attention will need to be paid to (iv) in weighing matters that have recently been in dis- ➤

Church

Anglicans are not alone amongst Christians in finding the church (whom they can see) harder to cope with than God (whom they cannot see)! – cf. 1 John 4:20. Some Anglicans are impatient with the institutional aspects of the church, often resent the rules the church lays down to govern worship, and are afraid that the church can become a substitute for God in the faith of some people. However the Scriptures treat the church with great seriousness as the place where the grace of Christ is made visible (Ephesians 3:8–11; 1 Peter 2:9–10), and where the barriers that divide humanity are broken down (Ephesians 2:13–22; 4:1–6; Romans 14:1–15; 7). Church is an important aspect of worship – not because the church mediates the presence of God, but because we come into God's presence with, and as part of, the church. This profound truth is made clear even in the opening phrase of the Lord's Prayer: 'Our Father'. The Anglican concern for the right ordering of worship is not simply fussiness; it arises because worship draws us into relationship with the rest of the church and with the church's struggle to embrace the Gospel. Belonging to Christ does not only mean enjoying an inner unity with Christians who think like us; it involves allowing ourselves to be formed into a community that includes people different from ourselves and reaching out to receive what God wants to give.

This also explains the great significance that the Anglican Church gives to the doctrinal content of forms of worship. Forms of worship are not simply a pastoral or teaching aid for the intellectually weak. Worship is the church's primary act of faith; it is the place where our understanding of God is both proclaimed and formed. This is one reason why General Synod gives such attention to the authorising of forms of worship. Anglicans treat the forms of the liturgy as the church's main doctrinal statements. Thus, while individual ministers have considerable freedom in leading worship, they are under obligation to ensure that services do not depart from 'the doctrine of the Church of England in any essential matter'.

The Creeds provide an interesting example of the way in which doctrine is articulated through worship. In the New Testament baptism is portrayed as 'calling on the name of the Lord' (Acts 2:21, 38–41; Romans 10:9–13); it involves acknowledging Jesus as Lord and entering into the life of the Trinity (Matthew 28:19). One result of this was that Christians used short acclamations or doxologies as a form of worship (Romans 10:9; 1 Corinthians 12:3; 1 Corinthians 8:6; 1 Timothy 1:17) as well as teaching new believers a summary of the faith (cf. 1 Corinthians 15:3–5; 1 Timothy 1:13). The characteristic form of baptism in the early Western Church took the following form: after a night spent with the church in prayer and listening to Scripture, the candidate went down into the water three times, being asked in turn:

'Do you believe in God the Father?'

'*I believe.*'

'Do you believe in Christ Jesus, the Son of God, who was born from the Holy Spirit from the Virgin Mary, and was crucified under Pontius Pilate, and died, and rose again on the third day alive from the dead, and ascended into heaven, and sits at the right hand of the Father, and will come to judge the living and the dead?'

'*I believe.*'

'Do you believe in the Holy Spirit and the holy Church and the resurrection of the flesh?'

'*I believe.*'

In time these three questions were turned into a short form which new Christians learned by heart and afterwards used as part of their personal prayer and rule of life. It is out of this simple practice that both the Apostles' and Nicene Creeds developed. Later Martin Luther was to urge Christians to recite the Apostles' Creed as part of their daily personal prayer; the same tradition is reflected in the *Book of Common Prayer*'s use of this Creed at Morning and Evening Prayer. It was in worship that the creeds gained their shape; from there they became part of the prayer armoury of individual Christians, and so, in time, made their way back into the regular liturgical life of the church.

pute in the Church of England. Where, in controversial matters, General Synod has taken care not to depart from the teachings or usage found in (iii), this should be respected.

from 'Patterns for Worship'.

3. Worship celebrates our humanity

Ancient prayers often speak of Christians 'being counted worthy to stand' in God's presence. The classic posture for prayer was to stand with hands outstretched (1 Kings 18:15; 1 Timothy 2:8). This expressed both openness to God and the dignity that God confers on us as human beings. Worship is a place where our humanity is acknowledged and transfigured (cf. 2 Corinithians

3:17–18). During their years of slavery it was in their worship that black Americans regained a vision of their dignity and held on to the promise of freedom. The link between worship and humanity is a major feature of Anglican worship.

Much Christian worship gives the impression of human beings frozen at a particular moment in their personal lives – with people permanently reliving their adolescence, or the first exuberance of their conversion, or the social and church culture of their childhood. Anglican worship at its best takes humanity, and its capacity for change and development, seriously. It respects the bodily and cultural aspects of what it is to be human as well as the rhythms and cycles of natural and spiritual life.

We come to worship not simply as souls or sinners but as human beings who express their identity, hopes and sins within a particular social and cultural context. Culture, like clothing, is an important part of what it is to be human. It is through the customs and art of a particular society that we are ourselves. Anglican worship honours this with its concern for art, movement and music. The deep Anglican interest in the art of liturgical celebration strikes many people as trivial, even repellent. While it runs counter to the functional materialism of much mass commercial culture, and often risks lapsing into sentimental nostalgia, its root lies in a deeply Christian respect for what it is to be human.

Human culture is neither static nor uniform. Article 34 asserts,

> It is not necessary that Traditions and Ceremonies be in all places one, or utterly like; for at all times they have been divers, and may be changed according to the diversities of countries, times, and men's manners [i.e. social customs], so that [= as long as] nothing be ordained against God's Word . . . every particular or national Church hath authority to ordain, change or abolish, ceremonies or rites of the Church ordained only by man's authority, so that all things be done to edifying.

This important statement from the Reformation expresses two principles that have guided Anglican worship: a willingness to adapt to changing social practice, and a realisation that such practice has an important role in sustaining social cohesion and unity in both church and society. These two principles often pull in two directions. In the sixteenth century Archbishop Cranmer carefully framed forms of worship that were suited to sixteenth-century society; at the same time he was opposed to local variations – and placed great emphasis on national unity.

Since the 1970s the Anglican Church has increasingly recognised the importance of cultural adaptation, not only internationally but at a parish level. This can be seen in the provision that the *ASB 1980* makes for local choice and creativity, and more recently in the official resource book *Patterns for Worship*. There is a danger that diversity will lead to fragmentation and disintegration; a collection of essays by the Liturgical Commission published in 1993, *The Renewal of Common Prayer*, sets out a strategy for balancing local creativity and wider unity. The demands of mission have to be balanced by a discipline that enables most Anglicans to make certain forms and prayers their own.

The conditions of modern life, both national and international, make the Anglican struggle to balance diversity and unity both difficult and important. Forms of worship celebrate the diversity and richness of human culture. Their richness and historical roots acknowledge the complex and layered nature of human identity. At the same time they attempt to resist the fragmentation of the human community and to press towards the unity, beauty and richness of the heavenly city (Revelation 21:22–22:5; Hebrews 12:22–4).

Another aspect of what it is to be human is seen in the various rhythms and cycles which are part of human life. In every part of life rhythm and change are important and need to be taken up into prayer. Much of the power of Anglican liturgical forms arises from their attempt to express and harness these moods and processes of human life. Some of these cycles reflect the dynamic of life as it takes shape in the struggle between sin and grace; life moves, for example, between lament and liberation, penitence and celebration, memory and hope. Part of Anglican affection for the psalms arises from the range of human moods and experience to be found in the psalter.

The Church year also brings one of the rhythms of the creation into relationship with the gospel story. Its origins lie partly in the festivals of the Jewish Calendar (cf. Leviti-

This tabernacle, to hold the reserved sacrament, in Gaba Chapel (Roman Catholic), Eldoret, Kenya, celebrates the richness of African culture.

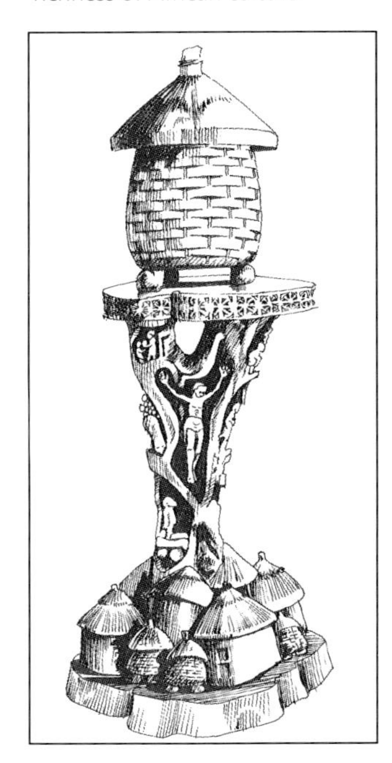

cus 23) and in the festivals of Passover and Pentecost that were taken over by the first Christians (cf. 1 Corinthians 5:7,8; 16:8; Acts 20:6,16). To this first cycle of the calendar later centuries added another cycle focused on the birth and baptism of Jesus. The emergence of a more developed and universal Christian calendar not only rooted the basic story of the Gospel more deeply in the culture and rhythm of church life; it also relates this great narrative – at least in the northern hemisphere – to the changing pattern of the seasons. Spring becomes an image of the resurrection; the mellowness of autumn becomes associated with themes of death, grief (All Saints/All Souls); the beginning of winter with anticipation and judgment (Advent); at Christmas Christ is symbolised as light shining in the darkness of human sin and suffering.

Another way in which Anglican worship acknowledges the movement of human life is in the rites and prayers that have gathered around birth, adolescence, marriage and death. The *Book of Common Prayer* sets out in order rites of Baptism, Confirmation, Marriage, Visitation of the Sick, and Burial. The vision that underlies this is of a human life as a journey lived out within the Christian community with each stage marked by appropriate prayer, ritual and Scripture. These pastoral rites – or 'occasional offices', as they used to be called – witness to the importance of relating the major moments and processes of human life to God.

Although the underlying vision remains valid and powerful, much of the detailed provision is currently being re-thought. In many particulars the scheme of the *Book of Common Prayer* reflects long-disappeared aspects of Tudor society; it was a world, for example, in which servants and apprentices shared the home, in which schoolmasters were licensed by the bishop, and where English society was perceived as one godly household under the Crown. Changes in society mean that these rites have somewhat lost contact with the human realities they were trying to express.

For example the funeral service, already abbreviated by Cranmer in order to remove medieval abuses over prayer for the Christian dead, has lost much of its contact with the processes of dying and bereavement: people often die in hospital away from the church, the journey to the funeral is no longer a walk with the community (cf. Luke

7:11,12) but a ride in the isolation of an undertaker's car, cremation is preceded by a brief ceremony to fit in with the timetables and budgets of undertakers and local authorities. Anglican churches outside Britain have often been more effective at resisting the shrinking and detachment of these rites. Thus, *A New Zealand Prayer Book* (1989) includes a form borrowed from Maori culture for prayer in the bereaved home following a funeral. Many denominations, including the Church of England, are now giving careful attention to revising pastoral rites so as to recover a living connection with the human experiences to which they relate.

Social change has had more drastic implications for the rites of baptism and confirmation. In Tudor society it was possible to treat baptism as also a birth rite and to make confirmation a public rite of admission into adulthood. Today in a secular culture, with many people coming to faith in Christ in adult life, and with a widespread desire to return to the ancient practice of giving children Communion from a very young age, the Tudor pattern is no longer seen as satisfactory. Modern rites of baptism and confirmation focus primarily on commitment to Christ, and the search is on to find other Christian ways of acknowledging birth and the entry into adulthood.

Historical developments

The principles that govern Anglican worship have their roots in Scripture but they have emerged and re-emerged through the long history of the Church in England.

'Thomas Cranmer (1489–1556) remains the most formative influence on Anglican worship.'

Thomas Cranmer (1489–1556) remains the most formative influence on Anglican worship. A gentle man of learning, he was the chief architect of the new liturgical forms adopted in the sixteenth century. He was responding not only to the new learning of the Renaissance and the recovery of the Bible which sparked off the Reformation but also to powerful social forces which saw the establishment of strong and independent nation states. His liturgical reforms began with the placing of an English Bible in every parish in 1539 and the publication of an English language litany in 1544. They blossomed in the brief reign of Edward VI with the publication of two English language Prayer Books in 1549 and 1552. In 1662 the second of these was taken as the basis of the Church of England's *Book of Common Prayer*. The earlier and more conservative version of 1549 became the basis of the Prayer Books of many other Anglican Provinces, particularly Scotland (1637, 1764) and the USA (1789).

Cranmer's Prayer Books have exercised an enormous influence on Anglican worship. This arose not only from the beauty of his language, but also reflects the maturity and creativity of his judgment at many points. His aim was to produce a liturgy that would unite both church and nation in a worship that was scriptural and edifying. His concern to make the Bible available to all emerges at many points. He devised a lectionary to ensure that the Scriptures were read. He devised new forms of daily prayer, based on the ancient monastic offices, which had at their heart readings from the Old and New Testament. He revised the ordination services in order to place Scripture at the heart of the life and ministry of the clergy. His reforms of the Eucharist concentrated on removing the late medieval idea that the Mass was an act performed by the clergy to obtain God's forgiveness. Cranmer emphasised that the Communion focused on the one atoning sacrifice of Jesus Christ on the cross. The Communion was an act of the whole people of God in which all were to receive 'these thy creatures of bread and wine' and so 'be partakers of his most blessed Body and Blood'. Because Cranmer was unable to persuade people to receive Communion weekly, his daily services became the main forms of Sunday worship until the later evangelical and Anglo-Catholic revival of interest in the Eucharist.

Cranmer's legacy can be seen at many points. It includes familiar and well-loved prayers – both his own and those culled from the riches of the past. Equally his influence continues to be felt in the structure and ethos of many services. One example is the 'conversational' structure of Morning and Evening Prayer constructed round their complementary readings from Old and New Testaments; this structure helped many Anglicans to respect the Old Testament and see it in a positive relationship to the New. Equally important was Cranmer's decision to continue the use of the whole psalter that was one of the discoveries of the early monastic movement; they saw the 150 Psalms as a mirror of the moods of the soul, a microcosm of Scripture, a prophecy of Christ, and a summary of the prayers of the church. Of course, at many points, Cranmer's work has not stood the test of time but this does not take away from his achievment.

Apart from the actual orders of service that Cranmer produced, there are three particular ways in which his liturgical reform has shaped subsequent Anglican liturgy.

First, unlike many continental Reformers, Cranmer did not see his liturgical reform as a new beginning. Both his method of working and his writing show a profound respect for tradition for the practice and teaching of 'the ancient Fathers'. This emphasis on continuity has proved very important for Anglicans and has contributed to their ability to respond creatively to social change. Cranmer's respect for tradition allowed the church to retain the wisdom of older practices, symbols and ideas of the church's worshipping tradition which have proved a source of spiritual strength and creativity within the Church of England. One example is Cranmer's keeping of the ancient 'Sursum Corda' which later scholarship has shown to be based on the Jewish prayer of blessing with which Jesus gave thanks over the cup at the Last Supper. As the traditional beginning of the Great Prayer of Thanksgiving at the Eucharist, the Sursum Corda puts Anglican worshippers in touch with an understanding that antedates many later controversies.

Although Cranmer produced a liturgy carefully tailored to the particular social conditions of the Tudor age, his method of working kept Anglicans in contact with the patterns, prayers and symbols of the ancient and medieval church. This has helped English culture respond to symbols of Christian faith that entered our culture with our first missionaries. It has also given the Church of England alternative patterns of prayer to which to turn as the Tudor vision of a single Christian church/nation has crumbled. Christians have had to return to the older pattern of a community, gathered around Word and sacrament and committed to the place in which they live – a pattern which shaped the liturgical forms which Cranmer used as his sources.

A second way in which the liturgical reform of the sixteenth century influenced the Anglican Church was in its reliance on the new technology of printing. Before the invention of printing, books had been a valuable community possession that had a variety of social functions. Those involved in worship tended to have handwritten copies of their own 'parts' rather than a complete script.

Anglican traditions

'. . . surely where the old may well be used, there they cannot reasonably refuse the old only for their age without betraying their own folly. For in such a case they ought rather to have reverence unto them for their antiquity, if they will declare themselves to be more studious of unity and concord, than of innovations and newfangleness . . .'

'Of Ceremonies'
Book of Common Prayer

Sursum Corda

'Lift up your hearts
We lift them up unto the Lord.
Let us give thanks unto our
Lord God.
It is meet and right so to do.'
(BCP)

Cranmer's *Book of Common Prayer* combined the different functions of doctrinal witness, liturgical manual and personal prayer book. Cranmer's desire to produce a single simple book also meant that he had to abandon much of the seasonal material which previously enriched the Christian year. Another result of printing was a further move towards a fixed and uniform liturgical text.

A third way in which the English Reformation influenced Anglican worship was by its particular approach to church law. A curious result of the doctrine of 'the priesthood of all believers' was that Cranmer's Prayer Books were authorised by Parliament. Parliament saw itself as the lay voice in the government of the church. This was to give the text of the *BCP* a permanence that Cranmer himself is unlikely to have intended. It has also strengthened the sense in Anglicans of the doctrinal importance of liturgical texts.

The legal situation was not to change until the creation of Church Assembly in 1919 (which became General Synod in 1970). In 1966 legal changes finally allowed the church to authorise Alternative Services without going to Parliament. Since the 1974 Worship and Doctrine Measure the Church of England General Synod has been the recognised body to issue new forms of worship provided that it makes no attempt to ban the *Book of Common Prayer*. After many years of fixity it became possible for the church to amend its forms of prayer. A process begun hesitantly in the 1960s led in time to the *Alternative Service Book 1980*.

The fixing of the basic liturgy texts in the sixteenth century had a number of important results. One was that popular devotion and liturgical creativity in English Christianity found its expression through hymnody. Great hymns were written in turn by Puritans, evangelicals and Anglo-Catholics and were then slotted into the fixed form of the liturgy. While this has made metric hymns one of the most important elements of devotion and teaching in Anglican life, it also tended to create a separation between music and devotion and the core liturgical texts of the church.

The legal entrenching of the *Book of Common Prayer* also made it difficult for the Church of England to adapt its liturgical forms to changing social conditions. This rigidity contributed to increasing distance from the Free Churches. It also led to a rigidity of mind about worship such that Walter Frere, a liturgical scholar and Bishop of

Truro, predicted in 1911 that it would take 'a long period of liturgical experiment' before the Church of England would be in a position to make 'instructed judgments' on liturgical matters. Fifty years later the Church of England finally began to go down the path that he had charted!

The fixed forms of Holy Communion and Morning and Evening Prayer led to increased demands for flexibility. In 1872 the 'Shortened Services' Act officially allowed a 'third service' in which clergy could devise forms of service for situations for which the *Book of Common Prayer* did not make provision. The effect of this was to encourage a more flexible approach to worship which resulted in Anglo-Catholic Mission Services, and later led to the development of Family Services and All-Age Worship. These last, like the Sunday Schools that they replaced, should be seen in part as a response to the collapse of Bible teaching in schools. In 1993 this emerging flexibility was given official recognition with the authorisation of *A Service of the Word*. Official resources and guidance for this finally appeared with *Patterns for Worship* in 1995.

Current and future directions

The First World War was to bring home to the Church of England the extent of the secularisation that had taken place during the nineteenth century and the degree of alienation of ordinary English people from the life of the church. In the previous century both Anglo-Catholics and evangelicals had been exploring ways of making the beauty and passion of the Christian faith accessible to people under the conditions of modern life. After the First World War this concern began to find official support and to draw on a movement of biblical and liturgical scholarship that came to be known as the Liturgical Movement. Although this was predominantly a continental and Roman Catholic movement it also involved some major Anglican figures such as W. H. Frere and Dom Gregory Dix. Probably the major flowering of this movement was seen in the very dramatic changes introduced into the Roman Catholic Church after the beginning of the Second Vatican Council (1963).

Liturgical renewal and cultural adaptation have become a major feature of the Anglican way. Many of its products are now familiar features of English Anglican life. The years that followed the Vatican Council saw serious

A Kenyan Blessing

This form concludes the new Kenyan Eucharist. It had its origin in changes to a Turkana litany of cursing made when the people came to Christ:

The people accompany their first three responses with a sweep of the arm towards the cross behind the Holy Table, and their final response with a sweep towards heaven.

Minister:
All our problems
People:
We send to the cross of Christ.
Minister:
All our difficulties
People:
We send to the cross of Christ.
Minister:
All the devil's works
People:
We send to the cross of Christ.
Minister:
All our hopes
People:
We set on the risen Christ.
Minister:
Christ the Sun of Righteousness shine upon you and scatter the darkness from before your path: and the blessing of God almighty, Father, Son and Holy Spirit, be among you, and remain with you always.
People:
Amen.

'Many Anglican Provinces have issued new Prayer Books.'

attempts by the different churches to learn from each other in matters of worship. An important illustration of this was the adoption between 1970 and 1975 of agreed English translations of the main texts used in worship. (A revised version of these, *Praying Together*, was published in 1990). Many Anglican Provinces have issued new Prayer Books that have been widely welcomed: e.g. USA (1979), Ireland (1984), Canada (1985), New Zealand (1989), South Africa (1989), Australia (1995). Other Provinces are publishing individual services – often with a larger book in mind: Scotland (1982/89), Kenya (1989/91), Wales (1992/94). Liturgical contact between Anglican Provinces is now focused on International Anglican Liturgical Consultations that take place every two years. In 1993 Anglicans in Africa held an important consultation on 'African Culture and Anglican Liturgy'.

While many people in the Church of England viewed the authorisation of the *ASB 1980* as the end of a painful process of modernisation, it has come to be seen simply as an important step in forging appropriate forms of worship for the modern world. The publication of *Lent, Holy Week, Easter* (1985) and *The Promise of His Glory* (1991) finally made official provision for the seasonal material that had been developing alongside Cranmer's Prayer Book. The report *Making Women Visible* (1988) proposed a moderate approach to the new issues raised by inclusive language. In July 1994 General Synod committed the Church of England to authorising new forms of worship to replace the *ASB 1980* after the year 2000. The proposals accepted by Synod envisage a 'core' book somewhat smaller than the *ASB*, supplemented by a book of Daily Prayer and other resource books. Although the processes of authorisation still focus on printed texts, there are many signs that Anglican worship in the future will be less dependent simply on following an order of service in a book. New developments in publishing and in information technology, the impact of the charismatic movement, new approaches to music and visual presentation, the wider involvement of lay people in the leading of worship, will all have their effect.

The importance of worship for the Anglican Church will remain with its capacity to lead people to God, to feed the spiritual life of individuals, and to shape the mission and impact of the church.

Questions

1. What do you most enjoy about Anglican worship?
2. How important do you think it is to balance local accessibility and wider unity?
3. Are there ways in which current Anglican provision presents a false view of God, and how could the defect be remedied?
4. What stock of prayers and Scripture are you building up on which you can draw in times of stress or weakness?

7

Word and sacrament

Philip Seddon

'Word' and 'sacrament' are not two different things. They are the two hands of God, mutually interrelated, a double eloquence.

In God's world things are not only 'things in themselves'; they can also point to – 'signify' – something else. Bread is bread; it also symbolises nourishment and sharing. A word is a word; it can also communicate terror or love. The water of baptism is water; it also points to death by drowning, and rescue to life. Word and sacrament are twin aspects of God's communication with us. Each needs the other.

In the Church, the Word is the *audible* word of God. It is the life-giving, creative Reality which speaks to mind and heart. It speaks of welcome, salvation, judgment and restoration.

The sacrament is the *visible Word* (to quote Luther). It is the reality of Christ – 'flesh and blood' as Hebrew puts it, 'body' and 'blood' in St John's words – given to nourish us, 'body and soul', as we say.

The Holy Communion service in the *Alternative Service Book 1980* is divided, after the Preparation, into two sections: the Ministry of the Word, and the Ministry of the Sacrament. This could be misleading: it does not indicate two ministries – rather two fundamental aspects of God's presence in Christ.

The power of the Word

The grass withers, the flower fades; but the word of our God will stand for ever.

Isaiah 40:8

The word of God is living and active, sharper than any two-edged sword, piercing until it divides soul from spirit, joints from marrow.

Hebrews 4:12

The Word

We must not confuse the Word with words. God's Word is not limited to words, but God wants to communicate. Some people are so tired of 'talk' that they want to abandon speech for symbol. But we must not despise language simply because of the tyranny of wordiness. Anyone who has experienced the 'direct hit' of the Word of God on their lives knows its power of penetration.

The Word of God comes to us in different forms:

- The Word of God is at work in creation and history. The Word of God can be both a spoken word but also an *act.* One Hebrew word – *dabar* – means both. God's Word achieves its purpose as surely as rain does (Isaiah 55:10–11). This sense is very strong in the prophets. The Word of God which came to them creates and recreates, judges and redeems; it is given 'to pluck up and to pull down . . . to build and to plant' (Jeremiah 1:10).
- The Word of God is also *written.* In Jeremiah 36 King Jehoiakim sliced and burnt Jeremiah's prophecies written down by Baruch. But he could not destroy God's Word. 'The king could not doom the word: the word doomed the king' (W. L. Holladay). Everything was rewritten – and more! The 1988 Lambeth Conference affirmed 'the sovereign authority of the holy Scriptures as the medium through which God by the Spirit communicates His Word in the Church'.
- The Word of God comes to us supremely in *personal* form in the *incarnation.* Jesus is the Word made flesh: the embodiment of God's love and faithfulness. There has been a strong witness to this in the Anglican Church. It should not be set in opposition to an emphasis on the cross; it is its foundation. Just as Jesus' life on earth is destined for sacrifice, so Eucharist and proclamation of the Word must follow the same pattern, reflecting the costly love of God made human.
- The Word of God is also *spoken* and *preached.* The Gospel which is Good News requires public announcement. The human proclamation of the written Word concerning the incarnation of the Son, God's Creative Word, has always stood at the heart of Christian ministry. Anglican history bears witness to a fine tradition of preaching, often combined with great learning. The names of Hugh Latimer, John Donne, Lancelot Andrewes, Charles Simeon, (Cardinal) John Henry Newman, Austin Farrer, John Stott and Desmond Tutu are but a few.
- The Word of God comes to us in *healing.* This means that God is not just concerned with minds but with our whole being. The goal of everything is not simply *understanding* but the *restoration* of the whole creation.

- Finally, we experience the Word of God in *visible* form: in the specific focus of Communion, and more generally in all of life. The God who specifically offers salvation in the form of bread and wine also speaks to us through anything and everything in creation: people, events, meetings, silence, beauty, horror.

The ministry of the Word should be seen as the life-creating speech of Christ, ministered through human mouths. Its power should never be minimised.

The life-giving Word

Break thou the bread of life,
dear Lord, to me,
As thou didst break the loaves
beside the sea;
Beyond the sacred page, I seek
thee, Lord . . .
And in thy Book revealed, I see
thee, Lord.

The sacraments

The Latin word 'sacrament' originally meant an oath of allegiance. It was then used in the Vulgate (the Latin translation of the Bible) to translate the Greek word *mysterion* (mystery). Partly because of the cultural associations of these words the Eucharist came to be seen as an isolated and exclusive form of Communion with Christ, almost on its own guaranteeing salvation and eternal life. It became separated from its historical reference to Jesus, and gained special powers in its own right.

However, we must not separate the sacraments from the Word, any more than the Word from the sacraments. Both, intertwined, are Christ's Presence given to us. Although the Holy Communion has always been regarded as the heart of the church's sacramental life, it is a mistake to isolate 'the Eucharist' from other blessings such as healing, deliverance, intercession – and, not least, 'the grace and comfort of the Holy Spirit'.

Catholics have tended to emphasise 'the sacraments', and Protestants 'the Word'. Both need to be deeply integrated. As with marriage, 'What God has joined together let no one divide.'

What is a sacrament?

In classic Christian theology, only three factors are required to constitute a sacrament:
1. It must have been instituted by Christ.
2. There is an action accompanied by a word. There must be 'matter' (the elements: water; bread and wine) and 'form' (words) – i.e. there must be elements of creation accompanied by appropriate words of redemption.
3. There must be the right intention (i.e. to perform the sacraments in the name of Christ).

For Anglicans the *Book of Common Prayer* (in the Catechism) defines a sacrament as 'an outward and visible sign of an inward and spiritual grace given unto us, ordained by Christ himself, as a means whereby we receive the same, and a pledge to assure us thereof'.

Anglican tradition has included a wider variety of opinion than the Roman Catholic Church on the 'effectiveness' of baptism and Eucharist. (The word Eucharist means 'thanksgiving' and is now the word most commonly used for the Lord's Supper, the Holy Communion or the Mass.)

Some hold to a more Catholic view that the sacraments function *ex opere operato* (as a result of the act performed). Grace is given without any qualification, because of the promise of God.

The grace of the sacraments

Neither is the effect of Christ's ordinance taken away by their wickedness, nor the grace of God's gifts diminished from such as by faith and rightly do receive the Sacraments ministered unto them; which be effectual because of Christ's institution and promise, although they be ministered by evil men.

From Article 26: 'Of the Unworthiness of the Ministers which hinders not the effect of the Sacrament'

Other Anglicans would emphasise more strongly what Catholic doctrine itself also states, namely that a proper attitude is required of those who receive. Compare Article 28: 'The mean whereby the Body of Christ is received and eaten in the Supper is Faith.'

Anglican doctrine is definite that the effectiveness of the sacraments does not depend on the personal merit of the minister *or the recipient*, because it is *Christ* who is at work in the Church, and it is *grace* that is given to the imperfect believer.

Modern convergence

Over the last seventy years there has been a tremendous convergence in the way in which different churches think about Christian faith – and particularly about Word and sacrament. A new spirit of partnership and respect has moved the churches beyond restating the arguments of the sixteenth century without people abandoning fundamental convictions. This convergence covers four areas:

- *Scripture:* a common appreciation of the biblical origins of the Eucharist.
- *Theology:* agreement on the centrality of the Eucharist as the focus of the Christian community.
- *Christology:* a clear focus of both Word and sacrament on Christ.
- *Philosophy:* a more fluid understanding of how the sacraments *work*, replacing a rather static sense of what they *are*. Some authors speak of 'trans-significa-

tion' to describe the way in which the elements of creation take on new meaning in the context of the events recalled in the Eucharist.

This, of course, does not mean complete agreement. In every church today there is a wide range of opinion, especially when you bear in mind the worldwide nature of the Church.

How many sacraments?
Article 25 acknowledges only two sacraments, on the ground of their institution by Christ. This does not mean that the Anglican Church does not give sacramental value to the other five recognised by the Roman Catholic and Orthodox Churches – Confirmation, Penance (or Rite of Reconciliation), Extreme Unction, Orders, Marriage. However these were not ordained by Christ and do not reveal those essential aspects of redemption to which baptism and Communion point.

Modern Christian thought has tended to expand the notion of sacrament and even to speak of a hierarchy of sacraments. One could envisage a series of concentric circles with Christ at the centre:

- Jesus Christ has been called 'the primordial sacrament' in some theology today. This means that Christ is at the root and heart of God's work by which salvation is offered and received.
- Scripture is 'the First Sacrament' – according to Olivier Clément, a contemporary Orthodox theologian – the life-giving Word of God; 'Scripture embodies the Word . . . the whole of the Bible is one moment of the incarnation.'
- The Church is (or, more cautiously, is called to be) the sacrament of Christ, i.e. the place where union with God through Christ is announced and enacted in Word and sacrament. The Second Vatican Council said, 'the Church is a kind of sacrament or sign of intimate union with God, and of the unity of all mankind' (*Lumen Gentium 1*).
- Since Christian believers are the sacrament of the Church, baptism and Eucharist are then the points in the Church's life by which we are shaped and placed 'in Christ'.

Sacrament as ritual

All cultures have rites of passage and rites of communion.

Baptism is a rite of *passage*. It marks entrance to the new community. Through drama a symbolic rite effects membership of the new group. Paul speaks of being 'transferred to the kingdom of [God's] beloved Son' (Colossians 1:13).

The **Eucharist** is a rite of *participation* and fellowship. It symbolises belonging to the new divine reality. Similar rites elsewhere often involve the use of blood, symbolising the cost and death required to enter the new life.

Death and life

Baptism and Eucharist both have a pre-history in Israel's delivery from Egypt. The salvation and judgment of the 'Passover', symbolised by the sprinkling of blood on doorposts and lintel, prefigure both the cross and the Eucharist. The crossing of the Red (really, Reed) Sea and of the Jordan anticipate baptismal water as the gateway to life.

'Our fathers were all under the cloud, and all passed through the sea, and all were baptised into Moses in the cloud and in the sea, and all ate the same supernatural food, and all drank the same supernatural drink.'

1 Corinthians 10:1–5

Death is present in the blood of death (smeared around the doors) and in the 'waters of death'. Life is present in the escape from Egypt and in the Promised Land. Both baptism and Eucharist embrace victory over death and are inextricably linked to Christ's triumphant death. So both are rites of participation. Unlike other 'sacraments' these two rites signify being joined to Christ.

Jesus chose to identify with lepers and other marginalised people in a special way

- Many people today would want to add, as a fifth level or circle, humanity. As Christ died for all, it is humanity that is blessed by virtue of the incarnation – it is in our humanity that we know and share Christ.
- The desperate poverty in many parts of the world forces some Christians to go further and speak of the 'sacrament of the poor' (cf. Matthew 25:40). Some writers speak of the 'consanguinity' between God and the poor, holding that God in Christ has chosen to identify with them in a special way, rooted in the incarnation of the Word in poverty. Here, the outermost circle touches the centre.

Baptism

The word 'baptism' covers a whole complex of realities: new birth, the gift of the Holy Spirit, being incorporated into Christ. Many New Testament texts on baptism refer primarily to the Spirit. 'In Christ' is one of the commonest phrases in Paul to describe Christian experience: Christ is the 'place' where we live. Christian experience is baptism *by the Holy Spirit* (cf. Mark 1:8) in the context of water. The Spirit enables us to share in the whole reality of Christ.

Jesus' baptism marked the arrival of the saving reign of God, the revealing of the mystery of the Trinity, and the coming of the Spirit for his calling (Matthew 3:1,16–17; 4:1). For Jesus it meant identification with us, self-surrender to his vocation, and an anticipation of his own death seen as a redeeming and saving 'baptism of fire' (Luke 12:49). For us, as for him, the public event of baptism cannot be separated from the life of discipleship nor from a deepening experience of the Spirit. It points backwards to Christ's saving death as well as foreshadowing death to the old order of sin.

Whereas baptism in Christian countries can almost become routine, it can be a costly and powerful witness in the context of other religions. The public confession of Christ has great power, whether it is gang-leaders in Hong Kong being baptised in the Spirit, or Africans renouncing witchcraft, and it often leads others to faith. More problematically, when a Jew or Muslim comes to faith in Jesus Christ and wants to be baptised, this is seen as a deep betrayal; centuries of confrontation between Church and these ancient religious cultures raise critical problems.

A believer's baptism in Benaco Refugee Camp, Tanzania, 1994.

The 1662 *Book of Common Prayer* treated infant baptism as, in effect, the pastoral norm. The secularisation of Western culture has meant that the baptismal rites of the *ASB 1980* were drafted with an eye to the adult who comes to faith. More recently the Roman Catholic Church has pioneered a more phased approach to baptism, attempting in the rites to mirror the process of incorporation into Christ and the Christian community. Anglicans in the USA now have similar rites, and the idea was welcomed by the Fourth International Anglican Liturgical Consultation in Toronto 1991. A Church of England report to the House of Bishops *On The Way* (1995) points out the extent to which this approach is already anticipated in much evangelistic practice – with people exploring faith in small nurture groups and being encouraged to see coming to Christ as a journey. This approach is likely to be adopted more widely. One of its gains is an attempt to recover the spiritual role of godparents – increasingly referred to as 'sponsors'.

All the churches are currently involved in the rediscovery of baptism as one of the focal points of Christian identity and calling. An important landmark in this was a 1982 statement reached through the World Council of Churches in Lima, Peru, called *Baptism, Eucharist and Ministry*. As baptism represents the transformation of the world in Christ it is not surprising that facing up to the challenges of baptism can be traumatic for churches as well as for individuals. This rediscovery of baptism has opened the door to new ecumenical relationships as well as raising questions about how infant baptism operates in some cultures. One outcome has been a search

Baptism a shared belief

'Churches are increasingly recognising one another's baptism as the one baptism into Christ when Jesus Christ has been confessed as Lord by the candidate, or, in the case of infant baptism, when confession has been made by the church (parents, guardians, godparents and congregation) and affirmed later by personal faith and commitment. Mutual recognition of baptism is acknowledged as an important sign and means of expressing the baptismal unity given in Christ . . .'

from the 'Lima Document', 1982

Baptism and children

'At the time when the cock crows first let prayer be made over the water . . . Baptize the little ones first. All those who can speak for themselves shall do so. As for those who cannot speak for themselves, their parents or someone from their family shall speak for them.'
from Apostolic Tradition, c. AD 215

'Parents and godparents, the children whom you have brought for baptism depend chiefly on you for the help and encouragement they need.'
ASB 1980

for appropriate ways for reaffirming baptism.

Secularisation has sharpened concern over the vexed question of infant baptism. Amongst those who accept infant baptism, debate often polarises between those who wish to assert the priority of God's grace and those who wish to ensure real incorporation into the believing community. It may be that more phased rites might help. The *Book of Common Prayer* followed ancient practice in asking those who bring infants to speak for the child. *ASB 1980* and other modern rites attempt also to spell out continuing parental responsibility for the Christian nurture of their children.

In general, Anglican orders of baptism have a number of elements in common:

- *Scripture and prayer.* Listening to the story and promise of salvation is part of the rite of baptism. In modern times prayer has often been focused in the prayer of blessing over the water. Increasingly the place of more extended prayer before the baptism is being explored.
- *Renunciation.* From early times a dramatic turning away from all that stands in the way of Christ has been an important part of baptism.
- *Sign of the cross.* Cranmer incurred the wrath of the Puritans for keeping the ancient sign of the cross in his baptismal rite. Used in many contexts by Christians it signifies ownership by Christ, protection from evil, and personal dedication to the Christian way. In the *Book of Common Prayer* Cranmer placed the sign after the baptism which led many to confuse it with baptism. Modern rites tend to place it earlier in the rite as a sign of ownership or protection.
- *Reciting the Apostles' Creed.* In the 1888 Chicago–Lambeth Quadrilateral the Anglican Communion affirmed the Apostles' Creed as 'the Baptismal Symbol', the sign of the Christian allegiance and faith being affirmed in baptism.
- *Water.* Both the *Book of Common Prayer* and *ASB 1980* stipulate 'dipping' or 'pouring' as the mode of baptism. Increasing numbers of adult candidates raise questions about the fonts in use in many churches.

Renunciation

'Dost thou, in the name of this Child, renounce the devil and all his works, the vain pomp and glory of the world, with all covetous desires of the same, and the carnal desires of the flesh, so that thou wilt not follow, nor be led by them?
Answer: I renounce them all.'
1662 BCP

A popular addition to the service which the *ASB 1980* has revived from medieval times is the lighting of a candle. It recalls the baptismal hymn quoted in Ephesians 5:14: 'Awake, O sleeper, and arise from the dead, and Christ shall give you light.'

Another vexed issue that has arisen in recent decades is the question of the age of admission of children to Communion. The ancient Church, like the Eastern Orthodox today, admitted children to Communion from their baptism as infants. In the Western Church Communion became separated from baptism between the eleventh and thirteenth centuries as a result of moves to protect the eucharistic elements from accident or misuse. As a result Cranmer inherited a pattern in which admission to Communion followed a later rite of confirmation and made this the basis of a liturgical framework designed to ensure that children were properly instructed in the faith. A return to the earlier pattern is currently under discussion in many Provinces, having been called for by two International Anglican Liturgical Consultations (Boston 1985; Toronto 1991). For many people an important consideration is the insight from many quarters that the experience of belonging is the basis for nurture and growth in the Christian life.

Confirmation

One result of the modern rediscovery of baptism has been to raise questions about the modern Anglican practice of confirmation. One of the problems is that the term *confirmation* has been used in different ways over the centuries.

The practice of a bishop anointing a candidate or laying hands on them after baptism (not always *called* confirmation) has had a varied history in the West. It seems to have arisen as part of the rich celebration of early baptisms. Its first meaning was probably simply an episcopal welcome but it soon became associated with prayer for the Holy Spirit. With anxiety about children dying unbaptised, and with problems of travel, the rite gradually became detached from the actual baptism and came to be seen as a rite of its own with its own name. In the Middle Ages it was understood in different ways but was usually seen as a rite of strengthening. In 1281, when people were lax about being confirmed, John Peckham, Archbishop of Canterbury, introduced the rule that admission to Communion should normally follow confirmation.

It was this practice that Cranmer regarded as 'traditional'

Four meanings of the word 'confirm'

1. *To establish or secure.* The earliest and non-technical sense. Used of an action in which the Church accepts and acts on baptism. It was applied to first receiving of communion as well as to episcopal anointing and hand-laying.
2. *A post-baptismal episcopal rite.* This technical sense emerges in the West in the ninth century.
3. *To strengthen.* This sense becomes widespread in the thirteenth century, arising from an adult's need of strength to witness and to resist temptation, and then specifically applied to children as they approached adulthood.
4. *To ratify.* The meaning of individual or personal ratification of baptism emerges in the preface added to Cranmer's Confirmation Service in 1662.

A confirmation in Georgia, USA. Confirmation has been important for Anglicans, although they have understood the rite in different ways.

and made the basis of the liturgical and educational strategy to be found in the *Book of Common Prayer*. In the seventeenth century, in the aftermath of the Puritan Commonwealth, being confirmed by a bishop also came to be seen as a sign of accepting the Anglican understanding of the Church. Ironically Cranmer's pastoral strategy seems to have remained something of a dead letter until the nineteenth century, partly because of the difficulties bishops faced in travelling to and around their dioceses. Confirmation as a lynch pin of a pastoral approach to adolescence really came into its own under the influence of evangelical and Anglo-Catholic bishops in the nineteenth century. In this way it could be seen as one of the first steps in the rediscovery of a theology of baptism, although grand confirmations ran the risk of overshadowing baptism itself.

The nineteenth-century approach to confirmation has run into a number of difficulties in the face of modern secularisation. Often it was seen to mark a transition from childhood to the less religious world of public adult life. It has also been unclear how confirmation relates to unbaptised people converted to Christ in adult life. Anglicans are not alone in wrestling with how to adapt this complex tradition to the realities of modern life. The 1995 Report *On The Way* identifies five important aspects of Christian conversion or discipleship which have come to be focused in confirmation, and which possibly need to be found another focus or home in the life of the church:

- Acknowledging entry into adulthood with its dangers and responsibilities.
- Encouraging and celebrating an individual coming to faith in Christ.
- Providing a framework for the nurture of those baptised as infants.
- Focusing prayer – particularly prayer for the 'charisms' [gracious endowments] of the Holy Spirit – in the initiation of the Christian.
- Encouraging responsible commitment to the life and mission of a local church.

Eucharist

Each of the names used for this service emphasises an important aspect of its nature:

- *Eucharist* comes from the Greek *eucharisteo,* to give thanks, and picks up the references to Jesus 'giving thanks' at the heart of the action (cf. Mark 14:22 etc).
- *Holy Communion* reflects the Greek *koinonia,* sharing, and is derived from 1 Corinthians 10:16–17.
- *The Lord's Supper* is mentioned in 1 Corinthians 11:20 (cf. Luke 22:20). It points to the fact that the ritual is a symbolic meal. It stands in continuity with the meals that Jesus enjoyed with his disciples, expressing fellowship with the living Jesus, the welcome he gives to sinners, and is a sign of the new order of the kingdom of God.
- *Breaking of Bread.* This phrase is used at the climax of St Luke's gospel (Luke 24:35) and is used to refer to the Eucharist in Acts 2:42,46. It expresses the fact that Christian discipleship involves the material sharing of lives.
- *The Mass.* This term derives not from the New Testament but from the Latin liturgy, when the priest at the dismissal said: *'Ite, missa est'* ('Go; you have been sent'). It can be seen as a reminder of mission and as an echo of Jesus' commission at the end of St John: 'As the Father sent me, so I send you' (John 20:21).

***Koinonia* – sharing**

The cup of blessing that we bless,
is it not a sharing in the blood of Christ?
The bread which we break,
is it not a sharing in the body of Christ?
Because there is **one bread,**
we who are **many** are **one body,**
for we **all** partake of the **one bread.**

1 Corinthians 10:16–17

The form of the service

Modern eucharistic rites in all the churches are best understood in terms of their structure. One effect of the Liturgical Movement has been a return to an ancient three-part structure reflected, for example, in our first 'eye-witness' description by the Apologist Justin Martyr. This gives a basic shape of Word: Prayer: Eucharist. Taken up into the modern rites this has given rise to the following pattern:

- *Gathering.* The assembly gathers in the presence of God. Although often cluttered, the rites of preparation have the essential aim of drawing together the people of God and focusing their expectancy and attention on the activity of worship.
- *Proclaiming and hearing the Word.* The assembly gathers round and appropriates the word encountered in the Scriptures. The solemn reading and reception of the gospel symbolises that this is an encounter with the living Christ. Cranmer's two Sunday lectionaries (schemes

A three-part meeting

'And on the day called Sunday an assembly is held in one place of all who live in town or country, and the records of the apostles or the writings of the prophets are read for as long as time allows. Then when the reader has finished, the president in a discourse admonishes and exhorts [us] to imitate these good things.

Then we all stand up together and send up prayers; and . . . when we have finished praying, bread and wine and water are brought up, and the president likewise sends up prayers and thanksgivings to the best of his ability, and the people assent, saying the Amen; and the [elements over which] thanks have been given are distributed, and everyone partakes; and they are sent through the deacons to those who are not present.'

Justin Martyr, c. AD 150

Readings more important than sermons

'In our speech of most holy things, our most frail affections many times are betrayed. Where when we read or recite the Scripture, we then deliver to the people *properly* the word of God. As for our sermons, be they never so sound and perfect, his word they are not as the sermons of the prophets were; no, they are but ambiguously termed his word, because his word is commonly the subject whereof they treat, and must be the rule whereby they are framed.'

Richard Hooker c. 1554–1600

Themes at the heart of the Eucharist

Memorial. Jesus shared with the OT a strong sense of memory. The Eucharist is an action which brings us into contact with the saving events of the first Easter. So at the feast of Passover 'you shall tell your son, "It is because of what the Lord did for me when I came out of Egypt"' (Exodus 13:8).

Incarnation. Jesus totally and really embraces humanity and the created order, identifies with its need, and transforms it from within.

Creation. The Eucharist builds on the reality of creation. Through the ordinary elements of creation, the church, an ordinary body of human people, anticipates the final restoration of everything.

Death. Right at the heart is the awesome death by crucifixion of the Son of God who loved us and gave himself for us (Galatians 2:20). Broken-hearted, we are fed by God's Heart-Brokenness; hungry and thirsty, we are fed by God's thirst for us.

for reading Scripture) have been replaced by a single scheme designed for the main Christian gathering of the week. The *ASB 1980* follows an ecumenical scheme from 1967 that organises the readings around a theme. Many churches, including the Church of England, are now committed to changing to the *Revised Common Lectionary*, an ecumenical three-year lectionary that reads through books of the Bible semi-continuously. *The Promise of His Glory* provided officially for the first time for alternative undated lectionary units derived from particular books of Scripture.

- *The Prayer of the People.* The intercessions are the priestly work of the gathered people of God and embody their calling as a royal priesthood. They are an action of the assembly which arises from their access to God and their presence and calling in the world.
- *The Eucharist.* The people gather round the table of the Lord to offer the solemn thanksgiving and to partake in the body and blood of the Lord. The Eucharist is a memorial action celebrating the death and resurrection of Christ and anticipating the heavenly banquet.
- *Dismissal.* In modern style this is concise and directs the assembly outwards to embrace its part in God's mission in the world.

The same concept of 'shape' provides the key to the way in which the Eucharist itself is presented. In 1945 an Anglican Benedictine, Dom Gregory Dix, published *The Shape of the Liturgy*, which crystallised this position. He showed that the Eucharist is at its heart not words said by a minister but an action done by the people of God. He drew attention to the way the four actions recorded by Jesus are taken up in the structure of the Eucharist: 'he took bread, and blessed, and broke it, and gave it to them' (Mark 14:22).

This has led to an older and more biblical understanding of what action consecrates the bread and wine. The 1662 *Book of Common Prayer*, unlike Cranmer's Prayer Books, laid down that the minister should imitate Jesus' actions while recalling the institution of the Eucharist. Modern rites see the eucharistic prayer as a single action, imitating Jesus' giving of thanks. In this they follow the old Jewish (and biblical) understanding that it is thanksgiving (blessing God) that consecrates (cf. 1 Timothy 4:4–5).

The Body and the body

The Eucharist cannot be separated from the community that celebrates the feast of its redemption. The community adds its own meanings to the celebration by virtue of its experiences.

Many parts of the church celebrate their joy in Christ in the midst of awful suffering. They celebrate the victory of Christ over death in the midst of daily experiences of death and destruction. They celebrate the cross and resurrection in a world that has almost become a crucifix. Holy Communion calls us to solidarity with Christ in his body around the world. He stands with us and with them, and so we stand alongside those of whom the world is not worthy (Hebrews 11:32–8). There was a deep meaning in the fact that Oscar Romero, the Roman Catholic Archbishop of San Salvador, who opposed injustice in his country, was assassinated while celebrating Mass.

It is not surprising that the Eucharist has attracted to itself such a wealth of music, seen for example in the huge variety of eucharistic hymns. From Gregorian Chant to Palestrina, from Byrd to Bach, from Beethoven to the Misa Criolla, from Berlioz to the Misa Luba, from Mozart to Bruckner, the passion and praise, humiliation and joy of Christian communities throughout the world have drawn the highest and most varied expressions of human art that human creativity has been capable of.

Questions

1. What evidence do we have that God acts in Word and sacrament?
2. How could we gain a stronger sense of the identity and calling that God confers through baptism?
3. Is the Eucharist worth the fuss?
4. How do we make connections between liturgy and life?
5. What are the links between worship and mission?

8

Churchmanship

Jonathan Baker

Why is it that Anglican churches are so very different from each other? Anyone who has worshipped with more than one Anglican congregation will have discovered that even in next-door parishes there can be enormous differences in forms of service, vestments (the clothes worn by the clergy), music, ritual, and the involvement of lay people as well as in ways of understanding God. At times it can be hard to believe they are all part of the same church! To help us as we look at the variety of Anglican belief and practice (i.e. at different kinds of 'churchmanship'), let us begin with the help of three imaginary case studies.

Holy Saviour

Holy Saviour is a gothic-style Victorian church richly decorated with stained glass, painted statues, frescoes, mosaics, wrought iron and glazed tiles. The worship is dominated by the Eucharist, which is celebrated every Sunday, and also every morning during the week. The main Sunday service is dignified and formal. The priest is robed in colourful embroidered vestments and is accompanied by robed acolytes whose task it is to swing incense, ring bells at the altar, and assist the priest with the preparation of the bread and wine.

The worship at Holy Saviour's is full of awe and beauty, symbolism and mystery. Here, the praises of God's people on earth join with those of the saints in heaven. This is suggested by the music (which will often include ancient hymns from the early or medieval church), by the sight of clouds of incense, by the colour of the robes and vestments, and by the solemnity with which the priest leads the service.

Such worship engages all the senses, and is much more

than the hearing of words and the giving of intellectual assent; there is plenty to watch, to listen to, to smell, and at the moment of receiving Communion, to touch and taste as well. The words of the liturgy (many of which are sung) are like the words of a drama, in which the priest is the principal actor; the service is full of movement and action from the opening procession onwards, reaching its climax as the priest moves to the altar for the consecration of the bread and wine and the congregation files up to the sanctuary rail to receive Communion. Such worship is not casual or familiar, but quiet and reverent, and when members of the congregation finally go forward to receive the wafer and the wine, there is a sense of going up on to holy ground, of going to meet with the living God, of something momentous and a little frightening being about to happen.

The ministry of Holy Saviour is bound up closely with the ministry of the priest, who places great emphasis upon visiting his parishioners (especially the sick and housebound), regardless of whether they attend church. The role of the laity in any explicitly religious activity is limited, save insofar as it supports the work of the priest.

Anglo-Catholic worship 'is full of awe and beauty, symbolism and mystery.' (Mass at St Peter's, London Docks.)

Christ Church

Christ Church is the next-door parish to Holy Saviour. It is a modern brick building, plain and unpretentious, and inside the movable seats are set in a semi-circle so that worshippers are conscious of each other as they gather before God. Communion services alternate with Morning Prayer, a more word-based service centred on a substantial sermon. Children and young families are much in evidence, with the youngsters going out to Sunday School classes after the first part of the service. There is a small singing group and a band with electronic instruments who help to lead worship. The music is modern and lively, with the words of songs displayed by overhead projector.

The atmosphere at the Lord's Supper is informal and relaxed; there is a sense of closeness between members of the congregation who clearly enjoy being in church. Some of them lift their hands during the singing, and there is great stress laid on drawing near to God. There are no processions and little in the way of liturgical drama; perhaps the sharing of the Peace is the most significant piece of

At All Souls, Langham Place, London, an orchestra often leads the lively worship.

movement, when people greet each other enthusiastically with handshakes and hugs. The vicar does not always wear robes when he leads non-eucharistic services; in fact, his role is more that of worship leader than as the representative of God, except when he is preaching, when he applies the Bible directly to the lives of the people with great authority. God is expected to speak through the Bible and sermon, and people's sense of God's presence is enhanced by the high degree of expectancy with which they listen to the preacher.

Members of the congregation play a very active part in the worship. They read from the Bible and lead prayers (which often include time for open prayer in which anyone may pray aloud or share words of prophecy). They make up the music and drama groups and help to distribute the bread and wine at Communion. Sometimes there is an opportunity for healing ministry after the Communion, during which individuals may go forward for prayer and the laying-on of hands from members of the lay leadership team. After the service, coffee is served and worshippers are encouraged to stay and chat. A high degree of commitment is expected of church members, who often attend the church not only for worship on Sundays, but for a variety of other meetings and activities during the week. There is a great stress on evangelism in the parish and missionary work overseas, based on an awareness of the distinction between Christians and non-Christians.

St James'

St James' is the ancient parish church in the centre of the same town as Holy Saviour and Christ Church. St James' has a first-rate choir and there is a full-time organist. Choral music undergirds the worship and connoisseurs travel some distance in order to enjoy Choral Evensong.

The parish priest is a woman who, after some initial hesitation, has been warmly welcomed by the congregation. The services are a mixture of old and new. Sunday Evensong and Morning and Evening Prayer during the week all come from the old *Book of Common Prayer*; services of Holy Communion come from one of the approved modern liturgies; whilst Family Services and liturgies for special occasions (such as 'Homelessness Sunday') are put together by the priest herself. Much of the worship is formal, in keeping with the building and the music. Prayers, for example, are normally read from a book and address themes which are timeless and universal rather than topical and local. Sermons, on the other hand, whilst lasting only a few minutes, usually reflect upon a current news item or local issue, and often urge the congregation to greater social involvement.

Few people live in the parish itself, which is filled chiefly by shops, offices and small businesses. There are problems locally with the number of unemployed and homeless, although the church does run a support group for the one and a soup run for the other. At the other end of the social spectrum the church also welcomes the mayor and local dignitaries at the annual Civic Service and on Remembrance Sunday; in this respect it tries to serve the whole parish and not just its own members, and as a result tends to expect a relatively low level of commitment from its congregation (with the exception, of course, of the choir). The congregation of St James' is a mixture of the cultured middle class who appreciate the music and those from more varied backgrounds who value the church's stance on various local issues. Money is always tight at St James', chiefly because of the huge cost of maintaining the ancient building. On the whole those who give generously do so out of a strong sense of civic pride rather than out of awareness of principles of discipleship.

The Anglican spectrum

Christ Church, Holy Saviour, and St James' are imaginary, but realistic, examples of different strands of churchmanship within the Anglican way. Historically, there are three 'corners' to the Anglican 'triangle'; these are the Anglo-Catholic tradition (represented here by Holy Saviour), the evangelical tradition (such as Christ Church), and a moderate, or liberal tradition of churchmanship (such as St James'), which rejects the extremes of the other two and which for many outsiders embodies the typically reasonable and temperate face of the Anglican Church.

What is more, within each of these three main ways of being Anglican we can make out a number of sub-species; there is, for example, the charismatic movement, with its emphasis on the Holy Spirit and his gifts, the ministry of every member of the church, and lively worship. This has its roots in the evangelical tradition, although charismatic Anglo-Catholic churches are not uncommon. The Anglo-Catholic tradition has produced the Liberal Catholic way, which combines catholic ritual and worship in a traditional form with critical awareness and a dislike of dogma; whilst from the central, or broad-church tradition has emerged a more radical strand of liberal thought which is not afraid to submit orthodox belief to rigorous questioning in the light of modern knowledge, and to reach controversial conclusions.

Scripture, tradition and reason

The reason for such a variety of belief and practice in Anglican churches is to be found chiefly in the absence of a central source of authority; unlike Roman Catholicism, there is no central office or institution in the Anglican Church which can impose uniformity. Instead, Anglicans have always based their faith on a combination of three sources: Scripture, tradition, and reason. Sometimes Ecclesiastes 4:12 has been quoted: 'A threefold cord is not quickly broken'!

There is a clear connection between each of these sources and the three main streams of churchmanship; evangelicals stress the authority of Scripture, Anglo-Catholics stress the authority of tradition (especially that of the first four centuries of the Church), and liberals stress that faith must be reasonable.

This does not of course mean that each type of Anglican recognises only one kind of authority; differences in churchmanship have more to do with how the balance between Scripture, tradition and reason is understood. For example, all Anglicans acknowledge the supreme authority of Scripture in theory; but in practice they understand this belief differently.

For evangelical Anglicans, Scripture is the Word of God which continues to speak directly to believers today; the only interpreter it needs is the Holy Spirit, illuminating the text and applying it to the heart. Scripture is therefore treated on an altogether more exalted level than any other authority.

For Anglo-Catholics, Scripture is authoritative as it is brought to us and interpreted for us in the traditions and teachings of the church. Since Scripture is itself the product of the early Church, its primacy is not quite so clear cut for the Anglo-Catholic as for the evangelical.

For liberals, Scripture is authoritative as an historical source; there is no way to approach the human figure of Jesus except through the pages of the New Testament. As an historical source, Scripture must therefore be examined with all the tools of historical criticism in order to understand as much as possible about its origins, its authorship, its first readers and so on. Scripture is perhaps not so much a revelation to be proclaimed as a riddle to be solved under the guidance of the Holy Spirit. It is more a source of questions than of answers.

Depending upon one's churchmanship the balance between Scripture, tradition and reason can shift. The result of this dynamic relationship is a tremendous variety of ways of talking about God and expressing our faith in him. Let us now turn to consider some of these in more detail.

The Anglo-Catholics

Anglo-Catholics trace their descent from the more conservative wing of the English church at the time of the Reformation, which wanted to preserve continuity with the medieval Roman Catholic Church as much as possible. However the distinctive influence of the Anglo-Catholic tradition today owes much to the nineteenth-century Oxford Movement (known also as the Tractarians because of the tracts they issued to promote their views).

As a result of government interference in the affairs of the church in the 1830s, the Tractarians were first known as staunch defenders of the church's independence from the state. They developed an exalted doctrine of the church which was based upon the role of bishops as the successors and representatives of Christ's apostles (the doctrine of 'apostolic succession'). This developed alongside a renewed interest in the history, theology and worship of the early Church in the first few centuries after Christ.

For Anglo-Catholics today the doctrine of the incarnation is fundamental; that is to say, the conviction that in Jesus Christ the eternal Son of God took human flesh and became a human being as we are, yet without surrendering his divinity. Anglo-Catholics draw much inspiration from this; in particular the incarnation can help us to see God as present within the created world itself, and poten-

God's grandeur

The world is charged
with the grandeur of God.
It will flame out,
like shining from shook foil . . .

Gerard Manley Hopkins (1844–89)
(from a High Anglican family; later he became a Roman Catholic priest)

tially in every human being. Because of the incarnation, Anglo-Catholics are able to affirm the basic goodness of God's creatures and creation, and can see the physical world as the thinnest of veils through which the reality of heaven may at any moment burst.

This has also proved to be a powerful motive for the work of mission. Anglo-Catholics have a noble history of making the love of God incarnate in slums and run-down urban areas, perhaps most famously in the East End of London. There clergy and religious communities such as the Society of St John the Evangelist have put flesh on the Gospel by identifying with the local people in their poverty and serving them in practical ways. It is however a criticism of such work that it has tended to be almost exclusively clerical; perhaps the other side of an emphasis on bishops and clergy as representatives of the visible church is the risk of undervaluing the work of the laity.

The importance of the church for Anglo-Catholics is also clear in their emphasis on the sacraments. Here the incarnation is again stressed, as God is believed to be present in, and working through, the water of baptism and the bread and wine of the Eucharist. Baptism is therefore a decisive moment in which the candidate (whether adult or infant) receives forgiveness and is joined to Christ. In the Eucharist Christ's sacrifice on the cross is not just a past event remembered in the bread and wine but a present sacrifice in which each communicant identifies with Christ's broken body and poured out blood, in order that he or she may also share in his resurrection.

If the incarnation has helped Anglo-Catholics to develop a special concern for this world, they also have an appreciation of other-worldly spirituality, of withdrawing from the world the better to intercede for it and serve it; both male and female religious communities were revived during the Oxford Movement, and retreats, individual spiritual direction and contemplative prayer are Catholic characteristics which are now appreciated by much of the wider Anglican Church.

The Anglo-Catholics have had an influence in the Anglican Church over the last 150 years far outweighing their numbers. Many features of the Anglican way which are taken for granted today owe their origin to the Anglo-Catholics; clergy dress and vestments (including the so-called 'dog-collar'), candles on the altar, retreats, religious communities, weekly Communion services, English translations of ancient hymns, and the arrangement of the furnishings inside a typical Anglican church, are all due to Anglo-Catholic influence.

On the other hand, there are weaknesses in the Anglo-Catholic way, chiefly stemming from its view of authority; Anglican bishops are not in a position to interpret and apply the tradition with the kind of authority which a doctrine of apostolic succession really requires (such as is found in the Roman Catholic or Eastern Orthodox Churches). As a result Anglo-Catholics tend to look back with fondness on the pre-Reformation church when bishops did have such authority; in doing this they can appear backward looking and unable to adjust to new circumstances. It is the wing of the church which has found it hardest to come to terms with the ordination of women as priests; its high doctrine of apostolic succession and priesthood has also created difficulties for dialogue with other denominations.

John Keble (1792–1866)

Country parson, poet and hymn writer, Oxford don and man of God, John Keble embodied many of the qualities associated with the Oxford Movement. Although a distinguished scholar (he got a double first and was Professor of Poetry at Oxford), he valued holiness of life above academic excellence, and he was revered for his deep spirituality and moral influence. He had a profound sense of the beauty and mystery of God, and in his poetry he expresses deep awareness of the presence of God whilst preserving a sense of the mystery. For Keble, all creation was a sacrament, and all theology was prayer, insights which he explored in his book of devotional poems, *The Christian Year*. This was hugely successful, running through 92 editions within Keble's lifetime, and was widely appreciated across all shades of churchmanship.

The evangelicals

Evangelicals have tended to be uncomfortable bedfellows with other Anglicans. This is partly a matter of temperament, for they see themselves as the heirs of the Protestant Reformation, for whom protest against ecclesiastical authority runs in the blood. It is partly a matter of experience, for on more than one occasion those representing the evangelical heritage have been expelled from the Church of England (one thinks of the Puritans evicted under Charles II, and the Methodist followers of John Wesley). It is also partly a matter of nostalgia, for the doctrine of the Church of England set out in the *Book of Common Prayer* and the Thirty-nine Articles is profoundly evangelical; but the Articles have never won the universal assent in the church which their official position suggests should have been the case. Evangelical Anglicans have frequently felt that their loyalty to the Anglican Church was being tested, either because other Anglicans have not taken them seriously enough, or because of invitations from the Free Churches to join them.

Having said that, the evangelical movement is enjoying an upsurge of popularity at the end of the twentieth century, and with growing numbers and influence there has come a broadening of outlook. This has led to a deeper commitment to the Anglican Church on the part of evangelical Anglicans whose loyalty in the past has been ambivalent. Alongside this there has been something of an identity crisis, as evangelicals have struggled to answer the question, 'What is an evangelical?' Precise definitions risk excluding many of those clearly influenced by evangelicalism, or else embrace those who would not think of applying the label to themselves!

What we can say is that at the heart of evangelical Anglican faith there is the Bible. Doctrine and practice are submitted to the Bible's teaching. The devotional life of individuals is nourished by Bible reading and prayer. A feature of evangelical church life in all denominations is the appearance of small groups formed for the purpose of studying the Bible; and in congregational worship there is a stress on expounding and applying the Bible from the pulpit. The supremacy of Scripture leads to a corresponding downgrading of other sources of authority, not least because each individual Christian is able to read the Bible for him- or herself; the ministry of every church member is emphasised and clergy are valued as preachers and teachers of the Bible rather than as priestly mediators representing God to the people.

At the heart of the Bible is the message of Jesus Christ, and so the evangelical way is marked by a strong devotion to the person of Christ, and an emphasis on his death and resurrection. If Anglo-Catholics tend to stress the doctrines of creation and incarnation, evangelicals are inclined to stress the doctrines of the fall and redemption. Whilst this can lead to a gloomy 'sin-soaked' piety among some evangelicals, it more commonly leads to a warm personal devotion to Christ, a joyful quality of worship, and a desire to share the experience of Christ's love with others. The evangelical appeals to inner attitude rather than to outward display, and can present the Gospel as a simple message requiring a simple response; for such reasons it can be especially attractive to young people. Evangelicals are Gospel people, for whom the gift of Jesus Christ is radical and life-transforming, literally 'Good News'.

Evangelicals expect the Gospel to make a difference in the world; they tend to be natural activists, and in terms of their spirituality they are much more at home with intercessory rather than contemplative forms of prayer.

By the same token they have a concern for evangelism and missionary work. It is no accident that the majority of Anglican missionary societies have an evangelical origin. Evangelical churches are much involved in supporting missionaries and in evangelistic work in their own parishes. Care is taken to ensure that parents wanting children baptised and couples wanting to be married in church are prepared beforehand and are made aware of the claims of Jesus Christ and the Gospel promise of forgiveness of sins in his name.

The weaknesses of the evangelical way largely reflect its strengths. The stress on personal faith in Christ can lead towards excessive individualism. The message of redemption from sin can be unduly spiritualised so that it leads to greater withdrawal from the world instead of greater involvement; evangelical churches can appear sectarian, drawing a distinct boundary between the church community and the outside world. At the same time the emphasis on the Bible can lead to laziness in relating the Gospel effectively to contemporary society, as if appealing to biblical texts was enough by itself to persuade everyone; confidence in the Bible as the Word of God can also lead at times to a sense of certainty bordering on arrogance. Nevertheless, such weaknesses are less prevalent today than they were, and the signs are that evangelical Anglicans are poised to play a more influential role in the life of the church in the future.

Evangelical spirituality

Although he was not an Anglican, the hymns of Isaac Watts (1674–1748) have long been favourites with Anglican evangelicals, and none more so than this, which expresses the heart of evangelical spirituality:

When I survey the wondrous cross
on which the Prince of glory died,
my richest gain I count but loss,
and pour contempt on all my pride.

Forbid it, Lord, that I should boast
save in the death of Christ my God;
all the vain things that charm me most,
I sacrifice them to his blood.

See from his head, his hands, his feet,
sorrow and love flow mingled down;
did e'er such love and sorrow meet,
or thorns compose so rich a crown?

Were the whole realm of nature mine,
that were an offering far too small:
love so amazing, so divine
demands my soul, my life, my all.

The charismatic movement

Since the early 1960s many Anglican churches have been deeply influenced by charismatic renewal. Broadly speaking, charismatic spirituality celebrates the work of the Holy Spirit in the life of the church and the individual. It was initially a reaction to the overly formal and intellectual expressions of Christianity which for centuries characterised the Western churches.

Renewal manifests itself as an intense experience of God's love in which the Holy Spirit touches the emotions at the deepest level. The result can be like the uncorking of a champagne bottle, expressed sometimes (but not always) in uncontrollable laughter or weeping, shaking or falling to the floor. It is often accompanied by 'speaking in tongues', which is best thought of as a private prayer language emanating from the heart rather than the intellect.

In charismatic congregations 'the Holy Spirit touches the emotions at the deepest level'.

Such emotional intensity is not continuous; but it leads to a heightened expectancy that God can be directly experienced, and it creates an awareness that worship is not something we do for God, but is a gift of God's Spirit.

The worship in charismatic Anglican churches at their best is marked by a strong sense of freshness and spontaneity. Music tends to consist of modern worship songs led by an instrumental group rather than hymns led by choir and organ. There is a strong awareness of the Church as the body of Christ and of the ministry of every member. There is often a strong supernatural content, with the exercise of spiritual gifts of healing or prophecy, or singing in tongues. In some churches there has been a renewed emphasis on delivering people from the powers of evil, and the language of spiritual warfare is much used.

Charismatic spirituality

The simple directness of charismatic spirituality is expressed in many songs and choruses. Although written long before the modern charismatic movement, this chorus catches the dominant theme:

Spirit of the living God,
fall afresh on me
Spirit of the living God,
fall afresh on me
Break me, melt me,
mould me, fill me
Spirit of the living God,
fall afresh on me.

Charismatic worship can seem strange and even threatening to those who are familiar only with traditional styles of worship. However, it can also be exciting and more accessible for those with no church background at all. Anglican churches which are growing and attracting folk with no previous church involvement often turn out to have been influenced by the charismatic movement.

The liberals

Liberal Anglicans strive to maintain a faith which is guided by human reason rather than one which relies on external authorities such as revelation or dogma. Commonly, they affirm central Christian truths but draw back from trying to define details. A reasonable faith is not necessarily less than orthodox; it is simply a faith which has been submitted to the claims of truth and is not afraid of being questioned. It is likely to be undogmatic and modest in its claims. Such a faith can be attractive to those on the fringes of the Church who find traditional faith literally incredible, and yet who still see Christ as leading in some sense to God. As such its strength lies in its tolerance of doubt and questioning rather than in offering a distinctive package of positive beliefs and practices.

Liberal Anglicans value the search for better relations with other denominations, and indeed with other religions; unfortunately their discomfort with traditional doctrine can be a disadvantage when they are confronted by those outside the Anglican fold who are unsure of exactly what the Anglican Church stands for.

Liberals are very conscious of how easily the Church can cut itself off from the concerns of ordinary people in the outside world, and advocate an active involvement in society. Their key theological motif is that of the kingdom of God, which makes them aware of the activity of God in the world and not just in the Church. They think of Christ not so much as God incarnate or God the redeemer as God the servant, and they stress that the Church's mission is to be understood in terms of serving the wider community, rather than in terms of converting non-Christians. The Church is thus one, but by no means the only, means of bringing about the kingdom of God.

Liberal Anglicans are not afraid of getting involved in controversial political and social issues such as opposing racism or nuclear weapons. They are often advocates of change within the Church, for example in attitudes towards homosexuality or women priests. By stressing the importance of reason and the individual conscience, liberals value the integrity of truth and the integrity of the individual and are not afraid to question what others have accepted perhaps too uncritically.

On the other hand liberal Anglicans have been accused of being 'cuckoos in the nest' because of the tendency in unfettered liberalism to undermine traditional belief without putting anything positive in its place. Those Anglicans of the middle way who want to emphasise the essentials of the faith and so leave room for disagreement on secondary matters have not found it easy to draw a boundary around a 'core' body of belief immune from critical enquiry. There are some liberal Anglicans who as

The liberal approach

The poetry of Robert Browning (1812–89) reflects the honest integrity of the liberal approach, as in this extract from 'Bishop Blougram's Apology' in which the bishop affirms the ambiguity of his faith:

> Our interest's on the dangerous edge of things.
> The honest thief, the tender murderer,
> The superstitious atheist, demirep
> That loves and saves her soul in new French books.
> We watch while these in equilibrium keep
> The giddy line midway: one step aside,
> They're classed and done with. I, then, keep the line
> Before your sages

(demirep means 'a woman of suspect chastity')

a result of their questioning remain faithful to traditional forms of belief; there are others who by the same means have ended up abandoning belief in the God of the Bible altogether. Such radical liberals believe that the word 'God' is simply a way of describing all that is potentially best in human life, a term for fulfilled humanity. The ultimate danger for liberal Anglicans is that of losing any recognisably Christian Gospel, and of the Church simply accommodating itself to the changing social and cultural trends of society without offering anything in return.

The Anglican Communion

A number of problems are presented by the range of churchmanship within the Anglican Church. For example, the differences do not always owe their existence to conviction so much as to historical accident. This is particularly true in some of the Provinces of the Anglican Communion which share the same shade of churchmanship as their founding fathers in the missionary movement. Where the missionary societies were decidedly evangelical, the dioceses which sprang up in their wake tended to be evangelical too; some Anglican dioceses in South America and in much of East Africa are good examples.

The Anglo-Catholic churchmanship of those dioceses first established by Tractarian bishops is even more pronounced, because they were established not only as a result of missionary work, but in order to demonstrate and express catholic principles of church order. In the end Anglo-Catholics have made a more lasting impact on the Anglican Communion than evangelicals because they were concerned not merely to convert the 'heathen', but to embody Anglo-Catholic beliefs about the Church. The results are with us today; the churchmanship of the Church of the Province of Southern Africa reflects that of its energetic first Bishop of Capetown, the Tractarian Robert Gray (1809–72); and the Anglican Church of New Zealand has similarly been shaped by its first Bishop, George Augustus Selwyn (1809–78), to give but two examples.

Because of the influence of the early missionaries, many dioceses in the wider Anglican family reflect a more homogeneous churchmanship than any diocese in the Church of England. The Anglican Church of Canada, for example, would find the extremes of churchmanship described in our three case studies untypical; whilst the Anglican Church of Australia would recognise an even more marked contrast between Anglo-Catholic and evangelical, but in neighbouring dioceses rather than in neighbouring parishes. When the lines of division fall along national or diocesan boundaries, competing forms of churchmanship can become entrenched because they can exist independently of each other. Where the differences are in neighbouring parishes, such isolation is more difficult to sustain and it is easier for folk of varying churchmanship to appreciate one another's traditions.

The common ground

The tolerance of such different shades of belief and practice within one church has led to a number of criticisms. It is charged, for example, that the Anglican Church is incoherent and is held together only by its institutional structures rather than by any internal unity. It is also charged that dialogue with other churches is impossible because Anglicans have not properly begun the task of internal dialogue, and internal prejudices are reinforced by partisan attitudes reflected in theological colleges, patronage trusts and church newspapers and journals.

There is some truth in these criticisms, but it must not be overstated. The varieties of churchmanship have not sprung up independently, but have to a large degree stimulated each other's development as each tradition has tried to correct and counteract the weaknesses and overemphases of the others. What is more, churchpeople of all shades agree upon a great deal. All are agreed that the Anglican Church is a scriptural Church, and that prominence should be given to the public reading of the Bible, and that its interpretation should be open and not manipulated or controlled by some official church authority. All are agreed that the Anglican Church seeks to maintain a balance between the local church and the universal catholic Church of which the national or local church congregation is a particular manifestation. There is a common adherence to the sacraments and to the apostolic orders of bishops, priests and deacons. There is agreement that Anglican clergy should be pastors working in partnership with the laity and not be a separate priestly caste.

Perhaps most important of all, there is agreement that the truth expressed by the Anglican Church is incomplete and provisional; the church is not perfect but is in constant need of reform; the meaning of the Scriptures is never exhausted, for 'the Lord has yet more light and truth to break forth from his word'; and the conclusions arrived at by human reason are always open to amendment.

To these truths the varieties of Anglican Churchmanship bear witness in a unique way. When the followers of particular forms of churchmanship see themselves as the sole guardians of the truth, the existence of such different traditions within one church can be uncomfortable, even destructive, and Anglican 'comprehensiveness' can appear rationally indefensible. But where the distinctive insights of each tradition are held with humility and modesty, they can inform and complement each other to produce an unrivalled richness in ways of understanding and expressing the grace of God.

Questions

1. How would you describe the churchmanship of your local church? What are its main characteristics?
2. How aware is your local church of the insights of different traditions? What could it learn from them?
3. Is the existence of a wide variety of churchmanship in the Anglican Communion a source of strength or weakness?

Part 3

Following the Anglican way

9

Praying our way through life

Graham Pigott

Anglicans are essentially practical about living the Christian faith. They seek to say their prayers, go to church and love their neighbours. Each is an activity, an element in a way of life; something Anglicans do, rather than something they are. Yet in the doing they are seeking to become more Christian in character and practice. They will say their prayers at home. They will worship in their local parish church, or another nearby if the way of worshipping (i.e. tradition of churchmanship) is of particular importance to them. They will often contribute to their local community through voluntary activities which provide social care, and support local and national charities. In addition they will give to Christian organisations which seek to share Christian faith, including Christian mission and aid overseas. Their daily work, if they are employed, will provide a further way of serving others and contributing to the common good of society. Together, these three strands of personal prayer, public worship and community service, give shape and content to Anglican spirituality. Spirituality means the way people live their religion.

Anglicans have a wonderful spiritual heritage to explore, though frequently many have only a limited appreciation of its richness. This is partly due to the effect of different traditions of churchmanship, and therefore ways of worshipping, which have been a feature of Anglican comprehensiveness. Yet this can also make us suspicious. Our diverse heritage includes thoughtful writings, poetry, hymns and choral music, often in the setting of beautiful cathedrals or historic buildings such as King's College Chapel in Cambridge. To some this has given the impression that Anglican spirituality is elitist, for the educated and the traditional rather than for ordinary people. Certainly some of these features of English culture have been taken to many parts of the world and are often evident, for example in church architecture overseas. Again, in most Christian missionary work there was a concern to provide education from basic reading and health care skills to university level, usually in the context of Christian teaching and worship. In this way the particular beliefs and practices of the Anglo-Catholic and evangelical traditions within the Church of England became formative for many Anglicans around the world. These are now being re-evaluated with greater respect for local context and culture, which in turn can provide valuable insights for Anglican churches in the developed world. They are having to change their focus from a pastoral role to mission in response to an increasingly secular world.

In recent years there have been new influences such as the charismatic movement with its emphasis on personal experience of the Holy Spirit. There has also been the renewal of the liturgy and new patterns of worship. In the search for a spirituality in a busy world, there is a rediscovery of Christian meditation, which is a prayerful thinking, often on a passage from the Bible, and contemplative prayer, which is a looking with desire towards God and the Lord Jesus. The practice of going on retreat for a few days to give time to prayer and reflection and talk with someone about one's faith journey is growing. There is also a new openness to other Christian traditions and new ventures in faith sharing and social concern amongst Anglicans worldwide.

These developments have led to even greater diversity. Tensions have arisen between traditional practices and new forms of worship as Anglicans seek to face the challenges that arise from major changes in society. So the three strands of personal prayer, public worship and Christian service now come together in different patterns. This is because of the way the Anglican Church has evolved over many centuries, taken root in many parts of the world, and is now adjusting to the current changes that it faces.

One way to appreciate this diversity is to consider Anglican spirituality under a series of key formative elements which each contribute to its richness.

1. Churches and cathedrals

Many churches and cathedrals, even in other parts of the Anglican Communion, are part of the heritage of historic public buildings which bear witness both to early British Christianity and the developments since. They are a reminder of the importance of places of public prayer and worship for local communities. For families, and individuals too, these are the places where they are baptised, married or attend the funerals of people with whom they have shared the gift of life. Sometimes these places have been the focus for national celebration, thanksgiving or grief at significant moments in history.

Often they are the places of memorials in stained glass, carved wood or stone. Many have been cared for and generously financed to keep them in good order and care. Within them are key symbols of the Christian faith: crosses and crucifixes, tapestries and embroideries, liturgical colours or plain white linen cloths covering the altar or communion table. All these are an immediate clue to the way the worship is conducted in a particular place. As a result, the minds, memories and the imaginations of the worshippers are formed for future years and the personal practice of their faith. There are organs and choir stalls, and frequently the evidence of adaptation and change. Pews have been removed or the communion table brought forward into the nave, or modern seating introduced, ceilings repainted and gilded, stonework repaired and cleaned.

What is familiar to, and valued by, Anglicans in their churches and their forms of prayer and worship can

This communion table in Zaire is made from an Apolo's tree.

distinguish them from other expressions of Christianity, and other religions worldwide. This is also true within the Anglican Communion overseas, for instance where a crucifix may be of a black Christ. New churches, communion vessels, embroidery and clergy dress will often express the designs and skills of local craftspeople, but still bear a distinctively Anglican form and style.

For these reasons Anglicans are often deeply attached, for better or worse, to their places of worship. They rally to keep them from being closed or made redundant. Church buildings are symbols of the history and presence of God, even in a modern age unsure of what to believe and disinclined to share in public worship. In Britain, they also bear witness to the old religious divide of church and chapel, which in turn frequently reflected difference in social class. As local churches work together, that distinction is now being healed.

One of the features of the twentieth century, and not only in Britain, has been the repair and care of parish churches and cathedrals and the huge increase in visitors through the growth of leisure time and tourism. So now cathedrals have toilets, cafes and shops for the modern pilgrims who come by car and coach. They buy prayer cards and picture postcards, icons, candles and guide books. These are tokens and reminders of their spiritual heritage, conveying a reminder of God's grandeur and grace, embodied in the history of a place. Perhaps they kneel at Cuthbert's tomb in Durham Cathedral and are reminded of the Celtic contribution to English Anglican Christianity. Or they wander through to the chapel that houses the tomb of the Venerable Bede, the Jarrow monk who wrote a history of the English church and people in AD 731. There they read his prayer and glimpse his faith, inscribed now in modern gold letters:

CHRIST IS THE MORNING STAR
WHO, WHEN THE NIGHT OF THIS WORLD IS PAST
BRINGS TO HIS SAINTS THE PROMISE OF THE LIGHT OF LIFE
AND OPENS EVERLASTING DAY.

Anglican spirituality worldwide has a strong sense of place that helps to witness to the presence of God alive in a changing world. Such places are reminders of the communion of saints and the generations who in their time honoured and served God. Many of its churches and cathedrals provide an opportunity for personal prayer and thanksgiving to be made silently and anonymously, or to listen to worship being faithfully offered, without ever having to be formally attached to a congregation. In this sense the Anglican way is open to all comers at the level they choose to participate. Its worship is public and its buildings bear witness to this. To these they come to worship, whether regularly, or a few times a year, or at key moments in their lives. And from these they go, to serve and work and live their daily lives. They take with them the memory of the place of prayer and the worship and many other associations which convey an experience of God.

2. Prayer books and Bibles

Anglican spirituality has been shaped by the words of two kinds of books: Bibles and prayer books. The Bible is of great importance. To show this it was often beautifully decorated and scribed. The Lindisfarne Gospels (c. AD 698), the work of the monks of Holy Island, off the Northumberland coast, are a fine example. They are now on display in the British Library. The Bible has been made available for everyone, which was precisely William Tyndale's intention when publishing his translation of the New Testament into English in 1525. He was motivated by his desire that even a ploughboy would be able to read it for himself.

The Lindisfarne Gospels. Initial P at the beginning of St Jerome's Preface to the four gospels.

This began the momentum of translation into English which led to the Great Bible in 1539, and eventually to the King James Bible in 1611. It became known as the Authorised Version because it was the official translation that was to be read in parish churches. As a result its phrases are quoted in English literature. Some are still present in common speech, such as 'an eye for an eye'. It is particularly familiar among the older generations, because it was used in schools as well as churches until the 1960s. In the twentieth century modern translations began to appear. These include the very popular paraphrases by James Moffatt and J. B. Phillips, the *New English Bible*, with its more literary style, and, later, the most accessible translation, *The Good News Bible*. Others have followed since. The result has been that the Bible can now be more easily read. However, there is a significant problem. It is less easily remembered, as people may both use and hear more than one version. For example, the English *Alternative Service Book 1980*, includes extracts from a variety of translations including the Roman Catholic *Jerusalem Bible*.

Hearing Scripture read was for Thomas Cranmer light for a man's darkness, food for his hunger, and fire when cold. He recognised that the Daily Office, the daily pattern of prayer in the early Church, was grounded in reading most of the Bible. So he made provision for the public reading of the Scriptures through introducing Morning and Evening Prayer in his original *Book of Common Prayer* in 1549. These two services are an adaptation of the eightfold Latin monastic office so as to provide a Daily Office of prayers, with psalms and Bible reading for clergy and lay people alike. It is a shared activity, not a private practice. This reflects the Benedictine monastic tradition with its emphasis on stability of place, common prayer and meditative *lectio divina*, or divine reading. Ever since, Anglican prayer has ideally been the morning and evening activity of Christians. Of course, prayer can be breathed and offered at any time of the day. John Hackett wrote in his Christian Consolations (1671): 'Prayer is the key to open the day, and the bolt to shut-in the night.'

The Anglican ideal of saying Morning and Evening Prayer, with the public reading of the Bible in the common language, was classically lived by the poet priest George Herbert (1593–1632). He tolled the bell to summon the people of his parish to come to hear God's Word and to pray with him and his family twice a day. Cranmer's collect for the second Sunday in the season of Advent in the *Book of Common Prayer* expresses this prayed partnership of the Bible and the Prayer Book:

> Blessed Lord,
> who hast caused all holy Scriptures to be written for
>   our learning;
> Grant that we may in such wise hear them,
> read, mark, learn, and inwardly digest them,
> that by patience, and comfort of thy holy Word,
> we may embrace and for ever hold fast the blessed hope
>   of everlasting life,
> which thou hast given us in our Saviour Jesus Christ.
> Amen.

In recent years, changes have taken place in some churches. The late-night monastic office of Compline has been adapted for personal and public use. Sometimes it is used as an alternative to Evening Prayer as a service at the end of the day. Another new resource is *Celebrating Common Prayer*, a comprehensive version of the Daily Office in a single volume prepared in conjunction with the Anglican order of the Society of St Francis. The Archbishop of Canterbury, in the foreword, drew attention to its emphasis on celebrating together, or, if alone, being in partnership with the church's common prayer, rather than 'saying the Office' as a private and clerical obligation. This renewed understanding of common prayer lies at the heart of an Anglican understanding of prayer. It has always included the saints in heaven, whose days are marked with special collects and readings. These highlight the union of the Church on earth with the communion of saints and its pilgrimage through history.

Cranmer's provision of common prayer was also intended to correct the habit in his time of people saying private prayers during the medieval Mass from personal prayer books; these were called manuals and primers. His desire was for people in every parish to pray together twice daily as well as receive Holy Communion weekly. He also wanted them to be able to understand what they were doing by using prayers and Bible readings in their own language. But this vision and ideal was never fully realised.

So for much of their history Anglicans have been people of two books: the Bible and the *Book of Common Prayer*. Of the two books, outside the evangelical tradition within the Anglican Church which has always emphasised the prior place of the Bible, the *Book of Common Prayer* 1662 has been the most formative influence spiritually. It has shaped the language of personal devotion, both through public and personal use. It has also entered deep into the memories of generations of people, and so has become a dearly loved book around which a society has been formed. However, in all parts of the world it is now being supplemented, if not replaced, by the new liturgies. Even so the Latin tag, *lex orandi, lex credendi*, which means the law of praying is the law of belief, still sums up the Anglican way. It lies at the heart of Anglican spirituality. Archbishop Michael Ramsey (1904–88) endorsed this when he suggested that Anglicans, when asked what they stand for, will offer the enquirer an invitation to come and pray and worship. Through participating they will then come to understand what Anglicans believe. This process is continued within the new services which are rich in Scripture and Christian beliefs that can be absorbed through common use.

In private prayer Anglicans have tended to lean in one of two contrasting directions. The distinctive emphasis of the evangelical tradition has been to encourage a daily quiet time beginning with a Bible reading, often using daily notes that provide a brief commentary. This is followed by personal prayer from the heart, in preference to any form of written prayers, with an emphasis on intercession: asking on behalf of others. It is home based and Christ centred.

In contrast, the Anglo-Catholic tradition has encouraged early morning Communion and the keeping of saints' days, together with the Daily Office of Morning and Evening Prayer, sometimes followed by a period of silent prayer. By necessity it is church based, and centres more in Christ through his Church. These two very different forms of Christian devotion, although variants, each continue elements of Cranmer's vision and can complement each other.

The majority of Anglicans have more varied ways of praying their way through life. Due to personal and practical necessity they cannot maintain the ideal. They will use books of prayers and meditations, some Bible reading or other Christian reading during the week, and share in the worship and community life of their local churches as often as they can. Most are affected by the constraints of their work and family life. For the retired, sick or disabled, regular radio and television services and programmes can provide a valuable way of sharing in Christian worship and learning.

3. Priests, poets, preachers and thinkers

For anyone who wishes to explore the way Anglicans have lived, prayed and thought, there is a gallery of godly people to meet through their writings, poems, prayers, sermons and hymns. They are all seeking to express something of the mystery of God who is present through his creation, becomes fully human in Jesus, and offers the gracious gift of his Spirit. Life in the present can be an anticipation of sharing fully in his glory. In this way Anglican spirituality is rooted in an appreciation of the incarnation and the indwelling of God, God present in human life, first in Jesus, then through his Spirit within us. So God can be known in everyday experience. Only a sample of these people can be included here. They can be an encouragement to explore further this immensely rich treasure trove.

Early on are the prayers and writings of Anselm, Archbishop of Canterbury (1033–1109). Then came the English mystics, people with a deeply intuitive awareness of God. Their writings have become very popular in the renewal of meditation and contemplation mentioned earlier. Among these were Mother Julian of Norwich (c.1342–1416), who wrote of her *Revelations of Divine Love*, and the unknown author of the spiritual classic, *The Cloud of Unknowing*. This mystical dimension has consistently emerged in the writings of Anglicans. It reflects the Christian belief that all human beings are creatures with deep longings, whose true end and fulfilment is God himself. The purpose of Christ's coming is to transform human nature by participation in the divine.

Cranmer's formative contribution through the *Book of Common Prayer* must never be underestimated. It has been accompanied in the centuries since by books of prayers and devotions, catechisms, and writings on practical direction for living a spiritual life. These were written by Anglican leaders of great literary skill and depth of Christian reflection. They include Lancelot Andrewes (1555–1626), Archbishop William Laud (1573–1645), Bishop John Cosin (1594–1672), Jeremy Taylor (1613–67), William Law (1686–1761) and Bishop Thomas Ken (1637–1711). Their writings reveal a strong sacramental and mystical sensitivity, an awareness and expectation of meeting God within creation, through meditation and Holy Communion, and in the daily duties of life. They shared a conviction that we feed on what we read, but digest only what we meditate on. Therefore what begins with understanding needs to end in affection, uniting the person with God and leading to a communion based on love. As Jeremy Taylor wrote:

> 'Take good, gracious God as he is, and lay him as a poultice on your sick self as you are. Or, if I may put it otherwise, begin with your disordered self and, just as you are, reach out in desire to touch good, gracious God as he is.'
> *The Cloud of Unknowing*

> Love is the greatest thing that God can give us; for Himself is love: and it is the greatest thing we can give to

Batter my heart, three personed God; for you
As yet but knock, breathe, shine, and seek to mend;
That I may rise, and stand, o'erthrow me, and bend
Your force, to break, blow, burn and make me new . . . for I
Except you enthral me, never shall be free,
Nor ever chaste except you ravish me.

John Donne

God; for it will also give ourselves, and carry with it all that is ours.

'Holy Living', Chapter IV, Section 111

This continuing emphasis on recollection and meditation as part of prayer and personal devotion has produced a harvest of poetry, including that of John Donne (1571–1631). Some poems were used later as hymns; these express a vision of prayer and praise and show how an awareness of the ordinary can be the place of encounter with God. Bishop Ken's words, later sung to Thomas Tallis' Canon, capture this quality of praise:

Glory to thee, my God, this night
for all the blessings of the light;
keep me, O keep me, King of kings,
beneath thy own almighty wings.

Praise God, from whom all blessings flow,
praise him, all creatures here below,
praise him above, ye heavenly host,
praise Father, Son, and Holy Ghost.

George Herbert (1593–1632) expressed this spiritual vision of God being present through consecrating the details of daily life:

Teach me, my God and King,
in all things thee to see,
and what I do in anything
to do it as for thee.

All may of thee partake;
nothing can be so mean
which, with this tincture, *For thy sake*,
will not grow bright and clean.

This aspect of the Anglican spiritual tradition has continued in the twentieth century through the work of T. S. Eliot (1885–1965), W. H. Auden (1907–74) and R. S. Thomas (b.1913).

The eighteenth and nineteenth centuries in England saw the growth of the contrasting spiritualities and churchmanship of the evangelicals and Anglo-Catholics, mentioned already. They co-exist within the Anglican Church today worldwide. Yet in response to change they are learning from each other, both in mission and spirituality.

Evangelicals at prayer

Evangelicals align themselves with the Reformation in Europe, but developed from the evangelical revival of 1738–42 in which the preaching and hymns of John Wesley (1703–91) and his brother Charles (1707–88), both Anglicans, were instrumental. The effects of the revival could not be contained within the Church of England due both to the enthusiasm and emotion, and the approach to mission through open-air preaching and the formation of midweek class meetings. Yet a significant number of clergy and others influenced by the spiritual renewal remained within the Anglican Church. They were dubbed 'evangelicals' because of their emphasis on Scripture, personal conversion and assurance.

John Newton (1725–1807), one-time slave trader, was deeply converted. As a vicar he wrote hymns for his midweek meetings, including 'Amazing Grace'. Henry Venn (1725–97), founded the Clapham Sect. This was a group of Christians who sought to make practical social changes that reflected Christian beliefs and values in response to the new industrial society which had created many injustices. They also believed that through Christian missions the world would eventually come to faith in Christ. This conviction led to the founding of the Church Missionary Society (1799), now the Church Mission Society, which has played a significant role in the development of the Anglican Church overseas.

Amongst the evangelicals, Charles Simeon (1759–1836) was influential as a preacher and leader. He was concerned to have them as clergy in the pulpits of English parishes. The prayer meeting and intercession (prayer for others) were considered hallmarks of spiritual vitality along with Bible study. The Keswick Convention (1875) in the English Lake District was developed to teach an evangelical Christian holiness and seek revival. The East African Revival, when it arrived in England in 1947, reflected a similar spirituality with an emphasis on personal repentance and holiness. Since then, the Anglican Church in East Africa has experienced great suffering with many martyrs among their bishops, clergy and laity, including the Archbishop of Uganda, Janani Luwum (1922–77).

Amazing grace (how sweet the sound)
that saved a wretch like me!
I once was lost, but now am found,
Was blind, but now I see.

'Twas grace that taught my heart to fear,
and grace my fears relieved.
How precious did that grace appear
The hour I first believed!

Through many dangers, toils and snares
I have already come:
'tis grace has brought me safe thus far,
and grace will lead me home.

The Lord has promised good to me,
his word my hope secures;
he will my shield and portion be
as long as life endures.

John Newton

Anglican evangelicals have also been prominent in the Christian Union movement in universities and higher education, particularly as a consequence of the preaching and writings of John Stott (b.1921). They welcomed the evangelistic missions of the American evangelist Dr Billy Graham. All this has contributed to their present ascendancy within the Church of England and vitality within the Anglican Communion. But they are no longer as united. The impact of critical scholarship on the study of the Bible has created tensions between more liberal and conservative ways of interpreting Scripture. The rise of the charismatic movement since the 1960s has affected the whole church, especially evangelicals. It has encouraged more informal and intuitive ways of worshipping in church services and small groups, seeking to use the gifts of the Holy Spirit listed in some of the New Testament letters (e.g. 1 Corinthians 12:4–11). The Anglican evangelist, David Watson (1933–84) was a leading charismatic evangelical. This worldwide movement has brought new spiritual life to many within the different traditions of churchmanship within the Anglican Communion.

Anglo-Catholic spirituality

Anglo-Catholics have a spirituality which contrasts with that of the evangelicals, who have stressed lay participation in witness and Christian mission. They developed through the Oxford Movement in the 1820s, led by John Keble (1792–1866) and John Henry Newman (1801–90), who later became a Roman Catholic. They developed the high church and sacramental elements already present within Anglican spirituality. The place of ritual and symbol within worship was revived. Priests began to wear vestments, embroidered in the colours of the Christian year. The sanctuaries in many parish churches were richly adorned. They encouraged the practice of going on retreat and pilgrimages to holy places, such as Walsingham in Norfolk. Sacramental confession to a priest was encouraged. He would then give absolution, the formal assurance of God's forgiveness for any personal wrongdoing that had been admitted.

The Anglo-Catholics also encouraged disciplined patterns of prayer, sometimes with fasting, going without food as a form of self-control and self-offering. These disciplines were related to the keeping of the church year, especially the season of Lent and Holy Week. They used the stations of the cross. This is a way of prayer, favoured by Roman Catholics, which uses images of Jesus' journey to the cross as the focus for meditation and personal response. Their emphasis on receiving Holy Communion regularly helped Anglicans towards the current practice of Parish Communion services. In these the Word and sacrament, that is preaching and Communion, are held together in a single service as the central act of worship each Sunday.

The Anglo-Catholics also revived the religious life and orders within the Anglican Church and these flourished. Examples are the Society of St John the Evangelist, founded by R. M. Benson (1824–1915), and the Community of the Resurrection within which Bishop Trevor Huddleston (b.1913) served. He lived for some years in their community house in Soweto, South Africa, campaigning against apartheid. His presence and commitment helped Archbishop Desmond Tutu discover the Christian faith and his vocation to the priesthood.

Trevor Huddleston (b. 1913) campaigned against apartheid in South Africa.

Anglican faith and searching

Between these contrasting ways of being Anglican there has always been the desire to find a middle way. Much Anglican thinking and living has been characterised by a prayerful vision which combines Scripture, tradition, human reason and personal experience. This is evident in Richard Hooker (c.1554–1600), who believed in the essential place of reason and conscience as God-given. Benjamin Whichcote (1609–83) believed that the spirit in man is the candle of the Lord. The same emphasis was present in F. D. Maurice's Christian Socialism and Archbishop William Temple's vision for a Christian society. Yet it was tested deeply in the experience of Studdert Kennedy (1883–1929) as an army chaplain among the trenches of the First World War. His faith and searching were graphically expressed through his poetry. He concluded that God somehow shares in the anguish and horror of human suffering, yet in a healing way:

> Father, if He, the Christ, were Thy Revealer,
> Truly the First Begotten of the Lord,
> Then must Thou be a Sufferer and a Healer
> Pierced to the heart by the sorrow of the sword.

> Then it must mean, not only that Thy sorrow
> Smote Thee that once upon the lonely tree,
> But that today, tonight, and on the morrow,
> Still it will come, O Gallant God, to Thee.
>
> *'The Unutterable Beauty', Oxford, 1983, pp. 12–13*

Later, Evelyn Underhill (1875–1941) brought an appreciation of mysticism to her thinking of prayer as a school of charity. Austin Farrer (1904–68) combined scholarship and experience in his preaching. C. S. Lewis (1898–1963) wrote popular Christian apologetics, including his *Screwtape Letters* – letters from a senior to a junior devil. The Narnia stories, which he wrote for children, are enjoyed by all ages. In them, Aslan the lion is like a Christ figure.

Archbishop Michael Ramsey (1904–88) 'combined great intellect with contemplative prayer'.

One of the outstanding Anglicans of the twentieth century was Archbishop Michael Ramsey (1904–88). He combined great intellect with contemplative prayer and an appreciation of the Eastern Orthodox Christian tradition, to convey a deep Christian humanism in response to the secularism and spiritual searching of the twentieth century. He recognised how Anglican belief and thought has developed under the sound of church bells, with worship, prayer, doctrine and practice interrelated and informing each other.

The development of Anglican spirituality clearly includes very diverse influences. Whilst the evangelical and Anglo-Catholic strands are very distinct, there are also a choral and a high-church tradition, a liberal tradition, and now a significant charismatic influence affecting each of these. There are clear signs of interaction and the weaving together of different ways of praying and worshipping. And now the Anglican Communion around the world is beginning to contribute its prayers, poetry, thinking and liturgies. These arise out of very different social and cultural contexts to challenge, inform and enrich Anglican ways of praying and living. Two prayers from Africa, one ancient and the other modern, illustrate this new and growing contribution:

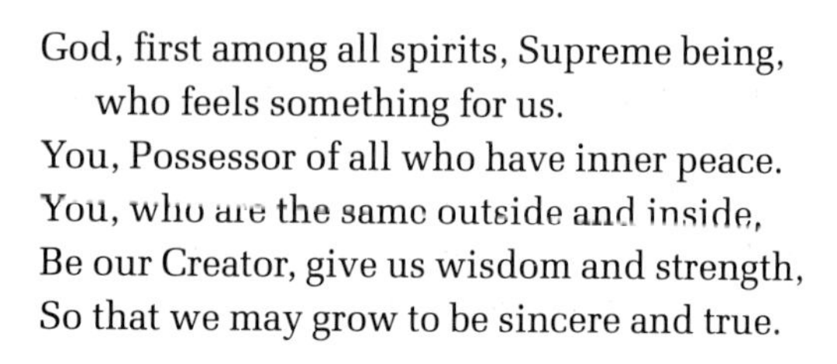

> God, first among all spirits, Supreme being,
> who feels something for us.
> You, Possessor of all who have inner peace.
> You, who are the same outside and inside,
> Be our Creator, give us wisdom and strength,
> So that we may grow to be sincere and true.

And, you, God, Master of everything
Grant us your help to live for others
So that we may live for you.
In Christ's Name. Amen

An Ancient African Prayer

Come, Lord, and cover me with the night.
Spread your grace over us as you assured us you
would do.
Your promises are more than all the stars in the sky:
Your mercy is deeper than the night.
Lord, it will be cold.
The night comes with its breath of death.
Night comes, the end comes,
but Jesus comes also.
Lord, we wait for him day and night.

A Prayer from West Africa

A pilgrim way

Clearly Anglican spirituality has been moulded by history and evolved in each century. We are now in a period of even greater social change, affected by mobility, mass media and a revolution in communications. So there is a movement towards even greater diversity. The new challenge can be seen in a simple fact. No single liturgy or service book now unites Anglicans worldwide, not even English Anglicans. Our day has seen the development of the *Alternative Service Book* and other liturgical resources throughout the Anglican Communion. A new generation of people has different expectations about Sunday and worship. Tapes, CDs, videos and computers are the basis of a growing culture which has less interest in book learning and more interest in leisure activities. Yet each has potential for providing Christian learning and spiritual resources for prayer and worship.

In this context Anglicans are now having to ask what are the essential characteristics and key elements in their long spiritual tradition which they wish to sustain and hand on. There has always been a strong sense of going on a pilgrimage through time, with the rhythms of daily prayer, morning and evening, weekly worship, and the Christian year. Ash Wednesday, Lent, Holy Week, Easter, Ascension Day and Christmas especially, together with the rites of passage that mark the stages of human life from birth to death, have been important milestones. Yet these patterns and frameworks are in danger of being lost in a secular world.

Anglican spirituality is bound up with special places, shared words, and hearing the Bible story. It is liturgical and sacramental, personal and communal, a pilgrim way where Word and sacrament belong together through an open Bible, common prayer and the sharing of bread and wine. It is also sacramental in the sense of being open to the presence of God through the wonder and mystery of creation, human creativity, the search for justice, suffering, care and kindness.

Greater freedom is a central desire in an age of many uncertainties and much spiritual searching. A disciplined way of life can be difficult to sustain in an age of major change and increasing fragmentation. An Anglican spirituality that is true to its roots will encourage a prayerful life, through reflection and meditation, using the Bible and spiritual reading, in the context of faithful worship centred in the receiving of Holy Communion. Each is a way of feeding on Christ, by faith, with thanksgiving. These sources of spiritual renewal will lead to practical Christian action, generous giving, and a compassionate respect and care for other people. Each Christian will need to accept responsibility for his or her own choices that can lead to the maturing of their personal faith in Jesus Christ. Encouraging a contemplative dimension amid the bustle and stress of modern life will give birth to the non-possessive love, compassion and generosity that can transform human living through being open to the presence of God in all of life.

The strengths of the Anglican way of praying and living are its moderation, comprehensiveness and diversity; its sense of place and commitment to a locality. It is non-sectarian. The Anglican Church is a church with blemishes, seeking to be open to God and open towards the diverse societies it seeks to serve. Christian holiness, humility, humanity and the willingness to live a hidden life of prayer and practical goodness go hand in hand in the Anglican way. This is rooted in coming together faithfully for the public worship of God and Jesus Christ through common prayer, an open Bible and Holy Communion. As Archbishop William Temple believed: prayer and worship are supremely important. Conduct tests them.

The Christian's duty

The Bishops of the Church of the Province of South Africa described the duty of all Anglican Christians of our church thus:

'The Father expects all his people to witness to the Lord Jesus Christ, and in the power of the Holy Spirit to bring others to a knowledge of him.

The Anglican Church in Southern Africa shares in this call, and every baptised and confirmed member must share in God's mission to the world.

To this end your lifestyle as a Christian should include these responses to God's love for you: to

- come to God in personal prayer every day
- read the Bible daily
- receive Holy Communion frequently and in expectant faith
- follow the example of Jesus openly, as the Lord whom you know
- work for justice and reconciliation
- uphold Christian standards in marriage
- bring up children to love and serve the Lord
- give money for God's work and to consider the claims of tithing
- give personal service to the church and your neighbour
- let your life be marked with self-denial and simplicity.'

The Catechism, An Anglican Prayer Book (1989), Church of the Province of South Africa

Questions

1. Can you give examples of the way Anglicans combine the three strands of their spirituality: personal prayer, public worship and practical service?
2. What are the essential characteristics of Anglican spirituality? What are their strengths and weaknesses in the present time of social change?
3. How can various practices within the different traditions of the Anglican Church contribute to growing Christian maturity?

10

Sharing our faith in the world

Amiel Osmaston & Alison White

What is our faith?

The Gospel is the good news that forms the heart of the Christian faith. The Gospel is not a set of doctrines, it is a person – Jesus Christ himself. As the Anglican Thirty-nine Articles phrased it long ago, 'For Holy Scripture doth set out unto us only the name of Jesus Christ, whereby men must be saved' (Article 18). This Gospel of salvation 'means entering into a relationship with the person of Christ. It means acknowledging our need for him: for his healing and forgiveness, experiencing and accepting that we depend totally on him' ('Mission in a Broken World', ACC8, 1990). This essence or core is shared by all the Christian denominations worldwide. The Anglican Church does not preach a different Gospel from everyone else! So for example, Anglicans can agree with the Roman Catholic encyclical *Redemptoris Missio*, which summarises the Gospel like this:

> The subject of proclamation is Christ who was crucified, died and is risen: through him is accomplished our full and authentic liberation from evil, sin and death; through him God bestows 'new life' that is divine and eternal. This is the Good News which changes humanity and their history, and which all peoples have a right to hear. *'Redemptoris Missio', para 44*

Jesus proclaimed the good news of a coming kingdom, which he defined in the Lord's Prayer as being a time when God's will shall be done on earth, as it is in heaven. The faith and actions of Christians are part of the way in which God is bringing his kingdom into being in the world – like the influence of yeast spreading through dough. So when Christians talk about the Gospel and faith, they are not just talking about having a personal spiritual experience, or about joining a church. They are talking about God ruling as King in every place, eternally.

How do we witness to the Gospel?

The bishops of the Anglican Communion, meeting in Cyprus in 1989 to prepare the ground for the Decade of Evangelism, commended this definition of witness and evangelism:

> Jesus commanded his disciples to 'go and make disciples of all nations . . . and be my witnesses . . . to the ends of the earth' (Matthew 28:19; Acts 1:8). To evangelise is to make known by word and deed the love of the crucified and risen Christ in the power of the Holy Spirit, so that people will repent, believe, and receive Christ as their Saviour and obediently serve him as their Lord in the fellowship of his Church (see also John 20:21; Luke 4:18f).
>
> *'Mission in a Broken World', pp. 119–120*

So God has given us a mission (from the Latin *missio*, meaning 'I send out'). Sharing our faith is not just a matter of words, it is a matter of reflecting Jesus in what we do, and in the whole way we live our lives. This mission is not unique to the Anglican Church. We join with the whole Universal Church in God's mission to his world.

The five marks of mission

Mission is characterised by five marks:

- To proclaim the Good News of the kingdom;
- To teach, baptise and nurture new believers;
- To respond to human need by loving service;
- To seek to transform unjust structures of society;
- To strive to safeguard the integrity of creation and sustain and renew the earth.

The Anglican Consultative Council

A model for Anglican witness

'The Acts of the Apostles describes the way in which the community of the church communicated the good news of Jesus Christ in their world. The activity of evangelism is seen primarily as God's task, and they allow themselves to be the vessel of communication. Communication took every form and shape then known to the world: word of mouth, witnessing to the power of God to change life, healing signs, miracles, martyrdom, worship, example, the life of the community, writing, preaching, nurture, caring, a willingness to stand up to government and to those in high places, a passion for right living at both the individual and the social level'.

(From Roger Herft, Bishop of Waikato, New Zealand, on 'The Gospel and Communication' at the Anglican Consultative Council 8 in 1990. 'Mission in a Broken World', p. 68)

What about cultural differences?

Obviously the way in which we witness to the Gospel will depend on who we are and where we are. How we speak and what we do has to fit with the culture and the context in which we are living. This means that every church is shaped by the culture in which it evolved. The Anglican Church is no exception: it has been shaped by British culture and history.

However, it has now spread across all five continents. The Anglican Church was caricatured as 'the British Empire at prayer'. Now the Empire has fallen, but Anglican churches remain, and have grown and become increasingly indigenous and independent. The Anglican Communion now has around seventy million members, nearly half of them in Third World countries. Some are in countries that were affected by very different colonial powers, e.g. Chile (ex-Spanish), Zaire (ex-Belgian), Korea (ex-Japanese).

With such a richness of different cultural contexts, it is not surprising that many answers have emerged to the question of how to maintain an Anglican identity while also finding creative and appropriate ways to witness to Christ in a particular culture. I remember joining with Kenyan Anglican friends in a market-place, as they asked passers-by 'Are you saved?' I found myself thinking 'You'd never get away with this in England!', yet in Kenya it seemed acceptable and it worked.

The liveliest growth in the Anglican Communion is in Africa south of the Sahara, in Asia and in Latin America. By contrast, the 'older' Anglican churches of the north can seem spiritually dry and apathetic or nervous about witnessing to the Gospel. However, there are still big differences between the 'northern' countries. Adult churchgoers form 40 per cent of the population in the USA; 27 per cent in Australia; and 10 per cent in Britain (i.e. 3.7 million people, of whom 31 per cent are Anglicans) (P. Brierley, 'Christian England', Marc Europe 1991, pp. 35 and 59).

What every country has in common, whether 'south' or 'north', is that the Gospel is being proclaimed in a pluralistic context, where Christianity is only one choice among many faiths and philosophies on the supermarket shelf. The Anglican way took shape in the comfortable womb of Christendom, but has had to learn methods of mission that can cope with the modern 'open market'. Of course some Anglican churches do not even have the luxury of an 'open market' – in countries such as Iran and Burma they struggle to find ways of witnessing even though explicit Christian evangelism is illegal. For some of them, as for the earliest Christians, their witness has even led to martyrdom.

What's special about the Anglican way of sharing faith?

If the Anglican churches worldwide exist in such different contexts, do they really have anything in common about the ways in which they share the Gospel faith? Are there any characteristics which are 'distinctively Anglican' compared with other denominations? The answer is 'Yes', although they will not all be true of every Anglican diocese. Most of these special characteristics have their roots in English culture and history, but have been adapt-

What is the parish system?

The parish system began to develop after Christianity became the official religion of the Roman Empire in AD 312. Parishes were based on the existing Roman civil and administrative divisions. As churches multiplied, dioceses and parishes sub-divided. In England, the wandering Celtic missionary bishops began to be replaced by the more static Roman system. Theodore of Tarsus (Archbishop of Canterbury 669–90), created a network of dioceses, each with a bishop under the authority of Canterbury. Parishes were created, often as the local lord of the manor gave land, and built and endowed the church. In the sixteenth century, Henry VIII nationalised the church and took over the appointing of bishops but the parish system remained much the same. In the nineteenth century the explosion of population and the rush from the countryside to the new industrial towns led to a revival of the ancient strategy of subdividing and creating new dioceses and parishes.

Since the First World War, there has been a decline in church attendance and in numbers of clergy. This, together with new ideas about the value of co-operation and teamwork, has led to a number of parishes being clustered together in group or team ministries. More recently, there has been significant growth in some areas, and many churches have planted new congregations – often in new housing estates or in marginalised or deprived areas of their parish. However, with all these changes and adaptations, the principle underlying the parish system remains the same: to create viable geographical units within which the church can witness to the Gospel by offering ministry to every member of the population.

ed and put into practice in new ways as the Anglican way has spread overseas. We will look at six of these special Anglican characteristics.

1. Being rooted in a place

Being human has much to do with the places to which we relate. From New Testament times place has also been important for the self-understanding of the Church (see 1 Corinthians 1:2; 1 Thessalonians 1:1 etc.). Respect for locality is a significant part of the Anglican vision. In England this has been expressed through the parish system. Each church has responsibility for mission within a defined geographical area, and every member of the population belongs to a parish. This means that most churches are deeply integrated into the life of the community, and have a strong sense of local identity and historical continuity. So when people see this kind of church, what does it say to them about the Gospel? It proclaims that our faith is incarnational – that in Jesus, God chose to become flesh, to become local, rooted in place and history. He is a God who acts in our situation, here and now. On the other hand, the huge scope and variety of the worldwide Church reminds us that he is also God of the whole universe and cannot be domesticated or 'made in our own image'.

2. Being open and accepting

Because the Anglican Church developed at a time when virtually everyone in Britain was assumed to be Christian, it meant that everyone automatically belonged in some sense to the church. Everyone had a right to the church's services – for example baptisms, weddings and funerals. You didn't have to do, say or believe anything in particular before being allowed to attend worship. The Anglican Church holds firmly to the principles of personal liberty and 'reasonable tolerance'. Peter Meiderlin's well-worn phrase sums it up well: 'Unity in things necessary, liberty in things unnecessary, and charity in all.' (Though of course this does not resolve the problem of how to decide what is 'necessary'!)

Christian churches and denominations vary enormously over how much it is necessary to do or believe in order to belong. It is worth looking at how these differences affect the ways in which they witness to the Gospel. How

WHO DO WE 'REACH OUT' TO IN MISSION?

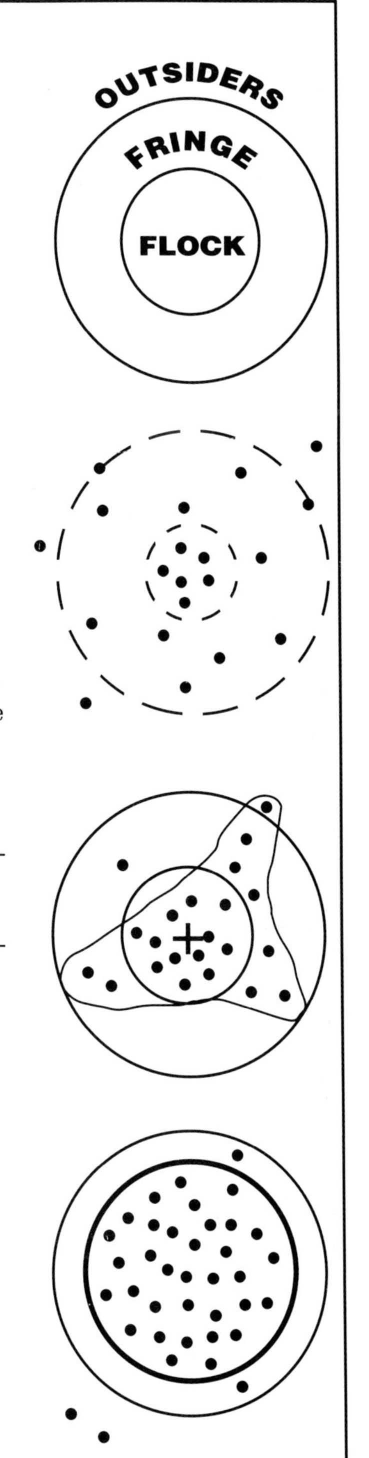

Look at the church in terms of its 'circles of belonging':

'The Flock' = those who are known to be Christians and/or attend church fairly regularly. They are clearly 'in' and belong.

'The Fringe' = those who attend only very occasionally, but feel they have links with the church and belong in some sense.

'Outsiders' = those having no contact with the church.

Churches vary as to where they put the boundaries between flock, fringe and outsiders:

A fuzzy church:

A church where membership is not really defined. It is not clear who to reach 'out' to, as nobody is really 'out'. Anyone can feel included. There is a huge fringe (e.g. some liberal churches and some community-based and village churches). For evangelism, church members have good links and friendships in the wider community . . . but may not be able to express the Gospel message clearly in words.

A centred church:

A church where membership is defined in terms of individual relationship to the centre (i.e. to Christ). Boundaries are fluid. What matters is which way people are moving. Even an 'outsider' can belong if he/she is beginning to move towards Christ. More emphasis on 'my personal faith journey' than on belonging. A danger of individualism.

A bounded church:

A church where membership is carefully defined by believing or doing certain things and not others.

Boundaries are firm, it is clear who is 'outside', and evangelism involves encouraging them to jump in over the boundary wall. There is only a small fringe. (e.g. some Plymouth Brethren/House churches).

A strong committed fellowship . . . but to outsiders it can look like a clique, odd and unfriendly.

For evangelism, they have a clear Gospel message, but probably few natural links and contacts in the wider community for sharing it.

does the church decide who is 'in' and who is 'out', and therefore who to reach 'out' to in mission? (See p. 147.)

Traditionally in Britain the Anglican Church has tended to be more like the 'central' or the 'fuzzy' models. However, the threat of an increasingly secular society has meant that some Anglican churches have become more like the 'bounded' model. This is particularly true of some of the Anglican churches in the Third World who have had to establish a clear identity and membership for themselves in order to exist at all.

However, compared with most other denominations, the Anglican Church worldwide is fairly 'open-edged'. It is possible to be drawn in gradually (for example through friendships) and to grow slowly into faith and membership. Research shows that more people become Christians through this kind of evangelism than through sudden challenges or big rallies (John Finney, *Finding Faith Today – how does it happen?* Swindon, Bible Society, 1992). The openness of the Anglican way proclaims the Gospel of a God whose arms are always open to receive us. He is infinitely patient and does not cut us off.

3. Witnessing through caring

We have already looked at the way in which the Anglican Church sees itself as rooted in a place or parish, and open

A Church Army evangelist in Newcastle offers a helping hand for the blind.

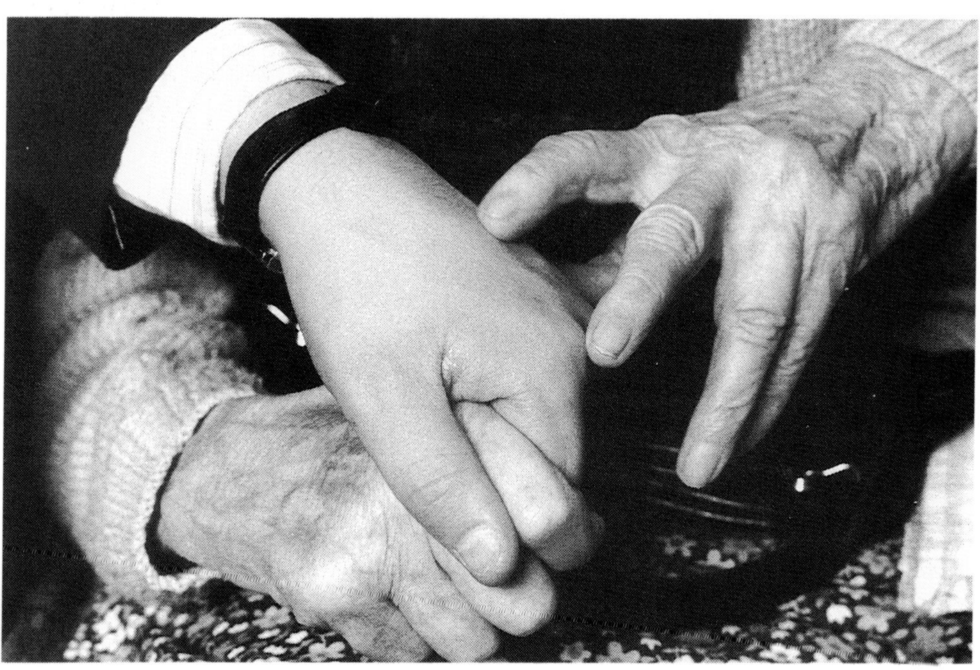

to the whole community so that nobody is cut off from belonging and care. Because of these characteristics, the church has witnessed chiefly through offering care and nurture, rather than through direct evangelism and verbal proclamation. It is a pastoral model, with the priest being seen as shepherd of the flock, and entrusted with the 'cure of souls'. Even the Anglican missionary societies followed this model, sending out missionaries to set up hospitals, schools, agricultural training centres etc. It is true that actions speak louder than words, but the church is becoming increasingly aware that it has often been too hesitant about putting the Gospel clearly into words as well. However, caring action has pointed people to a God who loves and gives himself sacrificially to us, who listens and cares about our smallest practical needs. The church tries to reflect Jesus, who did not just preach a message – he served and healed people, and he reached out to those who were excluded, despised, hurt or powerless.

The church's ministry of healing

William Temple, Archbishop of Canterbury (1942–44), wanted to see the church and the medical profession working together for the healing of the whole person. The church's ministry of healing was strongly affirmed by the Lambeth Conference in 1978.

'The Conference praises God for the renewal of healing within the Churches in recent times and reaffirms:

1. that the healing of the sick in his name is as much part of the proclamation of the Kingdom as the preaching of the good news of Jesus Christ;
2. that to neglect this aspect of ministry is to diminish our part in Christ's total redemptive activity;
3. that the ministry to the sick should be an essential element in any revision of the liturgy.'

(Resolution 8)

Today, about half of all parishes in England include some form of healing service weekly in their regular worship. This usually takes place in a eucharistic setting. It frequently involves clergy and laity, health workers among them, working together. The purpose of the church's healing ministry is not to offer a cure, counselling or crisis intervention so much as care in the context of the church's prayer.

4. Challenging and shaping society

Sometimes it is not adequate simply to care for those who have been damaged by life and by the society around them. Sometimes the social structures that are causing the damage need to be challenged and changed. We must deal with the causes of evil, not just the symptoms. This is a vital part of spreading the Gospel and proclaiming the kingdom.

As the state church in England, the Anglican Church has been intimately involved in the life of the nation from the start, and has had enormous influence in shaping the laws and structures of society – from the highest levels of government down to the grassroots level in parishes. Sometimes the church has become too closely identified with the ruling powers, and has helped to support and justify the 'status quo'. However the Anglican Church has also played a vital role in challenging injustices, and in trying to build a society based on Christian principles.

Some Christian denominations tend to encourage their members to withdraw from the dangers and deceptions of 'the world'. By contrast, the Anglican Church has never been afraid of getting its hands dirty, and encourages its members to be fully involved in the society around them. This has often meant speaking and acting on behalf of people who are oppressed or marginalised by society. It has also meant challenging laws, institutions, systems and patterns of behaviour which are seen as evil and incompatible with God's will.

When the Anglican Church spread to other countries where it was no longer the state church, it still kept its concern for challenging and shaping society in accordance with Gospel principles. Many bishops have been persecuted for voicing the church's challenge to the ruling powers – such as Janani Luwum, killed when Idi Amin was President in Uganda. Others have been a catalyst for radical changes in their society – such as Desmond Tutu, involved in the overthrow of apartheid in South Africa.

5. Holding opposites together

The Anglican Church tries to be balanced and to avoid theological extremes. There have always been arguments between Christians who say that mission is mainly about evangelism (telling people about our faith), and other Christians who say that mission is mainly about social action (getting involved in caring for people and in shaping society). These arguments have existed between different pressure groups in the Anglican Church too. However, on the whole the Anglican Church does try to hold together these different approaches, saying that they are all necessary. We aim to share the Gospel in a full and balanced way: through practical action and caring; through reasoned and biblical proclamation; and through involvement in worship. The comprehensiveness of the Anglican approach presents a Gospel that touches and transforms every aspect of people's lives – body, mind and spirit.

6. Expressing faith through worship

In the Anglican Church, the authorised liturgy used in church services plays a much more important role than it does in most other Protestant denominations. The *Book of Common Prayer* and the *Alternative Service Book* and its revisions, are very powerful ways for people to express their faith together. The liturgy is full of quotations from Scripture, prayers and creeds which celebrate the Christian faith at the same time as communicating it. We absorb the Gospel as we repeat the heart of it together each Sunday, and newcomers or seekers are drawn into this process. Worship is not individualistic. As we use the faith-inheritance of Scripture and liturgy in our worship, we are united with each other, united with all those who have worshipped down the centuries, and united with the worldwide Church. Of course there has to be diversity within that unity, as the liturgy is revised, translated and adapted to different cultures and to succeeding generations. Through it all, the forms of Anglican worship weave a rich tapestry that witnesses to the Gospel and draws people into faith. Worship is about being in relationship, with God and therefore with each other. It is in worshipping God the Father through Jesus Christ in the power of the Spirit that we meet God the Holy Trinity face to face, and the Good News comes alive to us.

Question
Are these six characteristics true of your local Anglican church (or the one that you attend)? What are the particular strengths and weaknesses about the way your church witnesses to the Gospel?

From the cradle to the grave

We have already seen that two of the special ways in which the Anglican Church witnesses to the Gospel, are through caring for people, and through helping people to meet God in worship. These two come together in the way the church reaches out to people at turning-points in their lives. We offer care through 'rites of passage' or special services such as baptism, confirmation, marriage, and funerals. We try to care and to point people towards God, literally from the cradle to the grave! Particularly for Anglican clergy in England, this work can take up a great deal of their time, since every person living in the parish has the right to a wedding or funeral service in the Anglican church.

Baptism and confirmation

For most Anglicans, the normal pattern has been to be baptised as an infant, and to be confirmed during their teenage years. Baptism in water in the name of the Trinity, is the mark of being a Christian. It is 'a sign of new birth whereby they that receive baptism rightly are grafted into the church, and the promises of the forgiveness of sin and of our adoption to be the sons of God by the Holy Spirit, are visibly signed and sealed' (Article 27). Baptism is a sign of God's grace, which enables us to respond to him in faith. Of course an infant cannot make a conscious response – the parents do this on the child's behalf. Traditionally, confirmation has provided an opportunity for the young person to affirm his or her own faith publicly, and to receive the bishop's laying-on-of-hands and prayer for the gift of the Holy Spirit. When someone who was not baptised as an infant becomes a Christian in adult life, then he/she is usually baptised and confirmed in the same service.

Some Christian denominations (such as the Baptists) will not baptise infants because they insist that the person must be able to understand and accept the Christian faith for themselves before being baptised. The Anglican Church has always continued the ancient Catholic practice of baptising infants, because they want to emphasise that God reaches out to us in grace even before we are able to understand or respond. Of course this can cause difficulties for the Anglican Church – often families who have little Christian faith and who never normally come to church, will ask to have their children baptised, perhaps as a sort of superstitious 'spiritual insurance policy'. This appears to devalue the significance of baptism, so many churches now ask parents to attend a short baptism preparation course. For many adults, this has helped them to understand what it really means to be a Christian, and they have come to faith in Christ for themselves.

The Anglican Church has had a very strong tradition of teaching the faith to children, through Sunday Schools, youth groups, church schools (many established by Anglican missionary societies), confirmation classes, and various uniformed organisations.

Marriage

According to the Anglican wedding service, marriage is a gift from God:

> Marriage is given, that husband and wife may comfort and help each other, living faithfully together in need and in plenty, in sorrow and in joy. It is given, that with delight and tenderness they may know each other in love, and, through the joy of their bodily union, may strengthen the union of their hearts and lives. It is given, that they may have children and be blessed in caring for them and bringing them up in accordance with God's will, to his praise and glory.
>
> *ASB 1980, p. 288*

According to church law, marriage is a serious public commitment. 'The Church of England affirms, according to our Lord's teaching, that marriage is in its nature a union permanent and lifelong, for better for worse, till death them do part, of one man with one woman, to the exclusion of all others on either side' (Canons of the Church of England, B30). This ideal of marriage is a picture of how much God loves us and is committed to us. He has chosen us, and longs for us to return his love. He holds out to us the offer of a covenant relationship which cannot even be broken by death – eternal life with him, now and for ever. So at its best, a Christian marriage witnesses powerfully to the good news of God's love.

The Anglican Church upholds that ideal. However, it is clear that many marriages actually fall short of the ideal, and increasing numbers end in divorce. To those who suffer the pain of a broken relationship, the church longs to show the Gospel of a gracious God who can forgive us, transform us, and give us a fresh start. The long-running discussions about whether, and in what circumstances, divorcees should be remarried in church, show how hard it is to get the right balance between upholding marriage as a lifelong commitment, and witnessing to a forgiving God.

'The Mothers' Union is a powerful arm of the church's ministry.'

The Christian understanding of the meaning and purpose of marriage will continue to be hotly debated, as people wrestle with questions about homosexual couples, common-law 'marriage', polygamy etc. Meanwhile, the Anglican Church tries to support couples and families, by offering marriage preparation, counselling, marriage enrichment and parenting courses. A great deal is done by the Mothers' Union to support family life – especially in many Third World countries where motherhood has high status, and the Mothers' Union is a powerful arm of the church's ministry.

Funerals

The funeral service in the 1662 *Book of Common Prayer* makes the charitable assumption that the deceased is a Christian. This is natural, given the context of Christendom, when to be English was by definition to be Christian! In countries where the Anglican Church is not the state church, the approach of the 1662 liturgy is largely acceptable because clergy normally only bury members of their own church. However in England, the vast majority of the population are still buried by Anglican clergy or

Anglican generosity

In the seventeenth century the bishops replied to the objection of the Puritans to the assured language of the Burial Service:

'We see not why these words may not be said of any person whom we dare not say is damned, and it were a breach of charity to say so even of those whose repentance we do not see: for whether they do not inwardly and heartily repent, even at the last act, who knows? And that God will not even then pardon them upon such repentance, who dares say? It is better to be charitable, and hope the best, than rashly to condemn.'

Readers, with a service at the church or crematorium. Therefore the *Alternative Service Book* and other modern Anglican liturgies try to express Christian confidence in the face of death, without presuming to judge whether the deceased is 'going to heaven' or not.

Many people come to funerals who do not normally attend church. Often the shock of a friend's or relative's death makes them ask questions about God, faith, life after death, purpose and meaning. The Anglican Church has a tremendous opportunity and responsibility to present the good news of the hope of resurrection in Christ. This needs to be done through the liturgy, the sermon, and in pastoral care for the bereaved before and after the funeral.

In most Western countries, the funeral is a fairly brief business – perhaps a bare twenty minutes at a crematorium. However, funerals in places as far apart as Peru, Uganda and Indonesia can last for several days. This gives much more opportunity for caring and for witnessing to the Christian Good News. At one Anglican funeral in Uganda that lasted three days, around two hundred people gathered. The Mothers' Union took over the catering – a mammoth task. A long queue filed slowly past the body of the much-respected Christian as he lay in state in an open coffin. People sat with the bereaved family day and night and comforted them. There was much singing and some special funeral dances. This was interspersed with people standing up to give obituaries and to share memories of the dead man. Several people preached semi-impromptu sermons, and others gave testimonies of the ways in which Christ had saved, healed, helped, forgiven and changed them. A number of people came to faith in Christ through attending that funeral. It seems a very appropriate witness to the truth of the cross and resurrection, that new life should come through death.

Question

Should the Anglican Church still continue to perform baptisms, weddings and funerals for virtually any inhabitant of the parish who asks? Does this help our witness to the Gospel, or not?

Witness in the wider community

We have seen that Anglican witness to the Gospel is characterised by the church being part of the local community or neighbourhood. Sometimes this is difficult in areas where there has been a great deal of change and people do not have a sense of belonging to a place or the people who live there. Many big towns and cities have created very different settings for churches. The word 'community' may mean little when people live in one place and work many miles away. Nonetheless, the Anglican Church continues to work out its commitment to those around it who may have little to do with its regular life and worship. This is an important part of an Anglican understanding of Christian revelation which is not for a chosen, privileged few, but for everyone.

Anglican churches have a mission to make available to everyone what God has made known about himself and to make it possible for people to respond in ways which they find appropriate. This will often mean personal ministry to individuals at key moments in their lives – on the occasions of baptisms, marriages and funerals. There is also an important role for the church in being involved in the corporate life and events of a neighbourhood, a town or a group with common interests. By playing this kind of part, there is an opportunity to express the fact that Christian faith is not simply personal and private. It also has insights about how we live as human societies and how we might try to make sense of life together and acknowledge that God has created us both for him and for one another.

The local Anglican church reaches out to everyone in the community.

There are many ways that a church can help the Gospel to be part of local life. We will look at five ways in which Anglican witness is carried out.

1. Presence

If, as we have seen, there is something important about being open and accepting and witnessing through our actions, then it is vital that there is easy access to experiencing this kind of Christian life. This is what lies behind the Anglican commitment to the parish system. It is not realistic to imagine that everyone will want to go to church and so it is important that Christian faith is not only to be found hidden away in church buildings. Anglicans want to affirm that God is to be found in the many different aspects of our life, that he is involved in the everyday, ordinary events of our lives and not just in special times and holy places.

There is in many places, for example, a role for the Anglican Church in the running of schools, which will provide not only education for those attending but also offer a chance for pupils and staff to work within a Christian ethos. There are sometimes opportunities in state and

Church planting

A renewed emphasis on mission has led many Anglican churches to adopt a strategy of church planting. Familiar as a mission tactic in the developing world, it has offered hope to Anglican churches which seem to be losing ground. A House of Bishops' report in the Church of England, *Breaking New Ground* (1994), commended church planting as both effective and lawful. Since 1990 there has been one church plant a fortnight in England. Bishops are encouraged to adopt church planting as a lawful supplement to the traditional Anglican parish strategy of mission. Church plants take various forms. To use horticultural images:

1. 'Runner' – a church establishes satellite congregations or out-stations.
2. 'Graft' – a sizeable planting team from one congregation joins another.
3. 'Transplant' – part of a congregation moves to another location to form a new church.
4. 'Seed' – a small team of church planters relocates to help another congregation grow.

independent schools to help in taking assemblies, visiting Religious Education classes and running Christian clubs during the lunch break or after school. Some youth organisations welcome an Anglican minister as a chaplain to the people who are involved, as for example in the Girls' Friendly Society, or the Scouting movement. Other organisations have been established through the Anglican Church, such as the Church Lads' Brigade.

The areas where we live change: villages and towns grow or dwindle; houses are built and new estates developed. Often this means that there are large geographical areas that do not have a church in them. The parish church may even be miles away and difficult to reach. The Anglican Church in many different parts of the world is responding to this situation by starting new churches. The Archbishop of Canterbury wrote about church planting, 'I am convinced that church planting is a mark of a vigorous and outgoing Christianity and is a sign of hope for the future' (G. Carey et al, *Planting New Churches*: Eagle 1991, p. 22). This is not a gimmick or a passing trend. In many ways it is reinterpreting the Anglican vision of witness and care for the whole population. There are many different ways in which new churches can be established. Not all of them will involve building a church building. Many churches find a home in a local school or community building. Often a new church will be a joint project between two or more denominations, which is also an important part of the witness to the Gospel, as we will see later.

2. Involvement in local life

A typical way in which Anglicans witness to the Gospel is by being involved in local community projects, providing voluntary services to those with particular needs in the area. This might include anything from visiting and care for elderly people or campaigning for public amenities. (See Chapter 11 for much more information about this aspect of Anglican life.) Sometimes it will be individuals from a local church who will be working in this kind of way and it is important that they are supported and prayed for by the congregation even though they are not going on behalf of the church. Sometimes the church as a whole will become involved in a scheme or may even start one of its own. These are important ways of witnessing to the fact that the Gospel is about the coming of God's kingdom or his way of doing things. The kingdom is much bigger than the church which is there to bear witness to it and collaborate in it.

3. The offering of prayer

We have already noted the Anglican characteristic of expressing faith through worship. One of the ways that the church witnesses to its belief in the power of the Gospel is by offering services for and with the wider community. There are many occasions when groups or communities need and want to place a particular event or experience within a religious framework. Sometimes the church is called on to help express communal grief. This may happen, for instance, after a major accident, with large-scale loss of life. The opportunity is then open to communicate the validity of faith in God and the perspective of the Gospel, and to allow the community together to show how it feels. It is also the case that the Anglican Church may be able to give form to significant memories for a community. We see this particularly in Remembrance Services in connection with the two World Wars. The Gospel narratives affirm the importance of memory and also show how different it can be when the memory is of a God who is not trapped in the past but is active in the present.

It is arguable that all church services are public events, held in public buildings and available to anyone who wants to participate. It is, however, often the case that people who rarely go to church may feel awkward about attending an ordinary Sunday service where they suspect they will not know anyone or the customs of the place. It is important that there are forms and occasions of worship which allow people who have little regular contact with church life to join in and offer their own prayer to God. This can often happen at large gatherings marking significant moments such as a confirmation or an ordination. On these occasions, which may well take place in a cathedral, the congregation will be large and made up of people from many different places. This allows everyone to hear the Good News of God and to worship without the anxiety of being noticed.

4. The invitation to faith

Somebody once quipped that 'Anglicans are very good at being nice to people and hoping that they will guess why.' We may recognise in that something of a challenge, but it would also be fair to say the Anglican witness to the Gospel involves offering people a variety of ways to explore Christian faith and to develop a commitment to Christ. Traditionally this has been through confirmation classes in preparation for an adult assuming responsibility for the promises made at baptism. As fewer people in the Western world are baptised and have contact with church life, churches have become increasingly inventive about ways in which the basic facts of Christian faith can be made available for people's consideration. This may be done through big events, lectures, concerts, theatre, multi-media presentations. Many Anglican churches are also running small discussion groups for people who are enquiring about the faith or taking first steps in putting it into practice.

5. Working with other Christian denominations

Part of the witness to the Gospel is demonstrating a new way of living. It is the Christian conviction that in Christ divisions are overcome and this should be particularly evident in the way Christians relate to each other and work together (see for example John 17:20–21). Sometimes this is expressed in formal agreements between churches. It may be that two or more congregations join together and agree to share one building, their worship, work and witness, and become a Local Ecumenical Partnership. For many Anglicans, co-operation is more informal. It is interesting to observe that in many places different churches grow closest together when they unite in an act of service or in proclaiming the Gospel in their neighbourhood, town or city. Nevertheless, serious commitment to other Christians sooner or later must find more formal expression.

Question
How do you think Anglicans could most effectively help to make God known where you live?

Witness in a region, a nation and beyond

The Gospel of Christ knows no boundaries and does not belong to any one person, group, town, tribe or nation. The Anglican Church has developed many ways of expressing this truth through people and structures. The Gospel addresses the questions and needs of individuals

Bishops are public figures and frequently meet national leaders. Archbishops George Carey and Desmond Tutu meet President Mandela.

and also of whole societies. Indeed the entire world, created by a loving God, is offered forgiveness and new life. Here are some examples of ways in which Anglican Christians have responded to the challenge extended by the Father of all to make him known. They are explained more fully in Chapter 12, 'Orders and officers of the church'.

Bishops

The Anglican Church is an episcopal one. The bishops act as leaders in the church's mission and as a focus for witness to the Gospel. They have many opportunities to teach and explain the Christian faith both within the church and beyond it. They are public figures and may often participate in the secular life of a region or a nation as observers, commentators and advisers.

Bishops will co-operate as a group or college within a particular country which lends weight to their witness and leadership. They also share their leadership throughout the Anglican Communion. This allows the church to receive a more global perspective and a wider understanding of what the Gospel means in diverse cultures. It also allows for mutual encouragement and support. In many parts of the world, witness to the Gospel can be a dangerous activity.

Once every ten years Anglican bishops from around the world meet at what is called the Lambeth Conference. In 1988 the bishops from Africa challenged the whole Anglican Communion to a new commitment to evangelism. This resulted in a call to each Province and diocese throughout the world in co-operation with other

Christians 'to make the closing years of this millennium a "Decade of Evangelism" with a renewed and united emphasis on making Christ known to the people of this world' (Resolution 43). Witness to the Gospel cannot be confined to any one decade and so the Conference also stated that it 'looks to God for a fresh movement of the Spirit in prayer, outgoing love and evangelism in obedience to our Lord's command' (Resolution 44).

Diocesan missioners and evangelists, sector ministers and religious orders

The bishops need teams of people who will help to resource the local churches in that work of witness. In many dioceses there are people, both lay and ordained, whose job is to teach and train Christians to be creative and confident in being able to tell their stories of faith and demonstrate the liveliness and depth of the Gospel.

Many of the religious orders also participate in this kind of ministry. Their members by their existence embody something of the radical call that Christ gives to his disciples to leave everything and follow him.

Those who work outside the diocesan or parish structures are sometimes called sector ministers. For instance, they may work as chaplains to industry or hospitals. They are link ministers or interpreters who try to bridge the gap between the church and secular institutions.

Religious orders, and diocesan evangelists and missioners often meet on a national or international basis. This allows an exchange of information, ideas and resources. It also encourages people to look beyond their immediate circumstances and to learn from the experience of others who are partners in the Gospel.

Questions

1. Who and what have been the significant factors in your discovery of Christ? Tell somebody else about them.
2. How do you think we could learn about witnessing to the Gospel from Christians in other parts of the world?

11

Care and change in our society

Lawrence Osborn

The basis for Christian social action

Practical spirituality

'Of all the commandments, which is the most important?' Jesus' response to this question is well known. Less frequently commented upon is the fact that he replied not with one commandment but two: 'The most important one . . . is this: "Hear, O Israel, the Lord our God, the Lord is one. Love the Lord your God with all your heart and with all your soul and with all your mind and with all your strength." The second is this: "Love your neighbour as yourself." There is no commandment greater than these' (Mark 12:29–31).

In Jesus' teaching these two commandments stand together. Genuine love of God entails practical love of your fellow creatures. Elsewhere Jesus makes it clear that love of neighbour extends far beyond ties of kinship and tribal boundaries. Disregarding the mutual loathing between their peoples, the Good Samaritan of the parable displays practical love for the injured Jew. The punch line with which Jesus silenced his interrogator? 'Go and do likewise' (Luke 10:37). Be prepared to risk your time, your money and even your life in caring for someone who may thank you with a kick in the teeth.

A generation later a similar point was made very emphatically by the author of 1 John. The defining characteristics of the Christian are righteousness and love (1 John 3:10). Conversely, a refusal to love others is evidence of spiritual deadness (1 John 3:14f). Elaborating on what it means to love others, he pointed to Jesus' self-sacrifice: 'And we ought to lay down our lives for our brothers. If anyone has material possessions and sees his brother in need but has not pity on him, how can the love of God be in him? Dear children, let us not love with words or tongue but with actions and in truth' (1 John 3:16b–18).

Thus, from the earliest days, Christianity has insisted upon the closest possible relationship between spirituality and practical love. You cannot have one without the other. Christian spirituality is the heart of Christian social action. Without that heart, our social action is mere activism.

On the other hand, social action is the practical expression of our spirituality. We may say we love God but, if we do not show it in our actions, we are liars. The absence of practical care for others from our spirituality reduces it to a flight from reality into idolatrous pietism or mysticism. It is idolatry because it is love directed towards a false image of God: a God who does not require righteous action in contrast to the God who demands righteous action.

The connection between spirituality and righteous action is a constant of authentic Christianity. Lived examples of the connection are to be found throughout the history of Christianity. Take, for example, Basil of Caesarea. He is chiefly remembered as a theologian but he was also engaged in practical love for his neighbours. During a famine in AD 369, he persuaded several wealthy merchants to donate grain to the poor and organised relief efforts. A few years later, he founded history's first public hospital (again, with support for the poor as his priority). Similar examples could be cited from every Christian tradition. And, as we shall see, the Anglican tradition is no exception.

The scope of social action?

Practical love is clearly an integral part of normal Christian practice. What is less clear is its scope. The passages cited above speak of love for your neighbour or for your brother. While the parable of the Good Samaritan extends this beyond its natural limits, it remains quite localised. The love of which Jesus and John speak might be interpreted as a practical response to the perceived needs of those we encounter in our daily lives.

Other examples of Jesus' teaching about care for others seem to confirm this impression. In the parable of the sheep and the goats, he commends those of whom it could be said, 'I was hungry and you gave me something to eat, I was thirsty and you gave me something to drink, I

A volunteer makes a friend at the Holy Cross Centre, Kings Cross, London.

was a stranger and you invited me in, I needed clothes and you clothed me, I was sick and you looked after me, I was in prison and you came to visit me' (Matthew 25:35f). These are tangible acts of love for concrete individuals.

Is Christian social action really nothing more than meeting the perceived needs of the individuals we meet? If so, Marxist critics may be forgiven for accusing us of tackling the symptoms but ignoring the underlying causes; of offering a mere palliative when, in reality, radical restructuring of the social order is needed.

Of course, Christianity has its own vision of an alternative social order. We look forward to the coming of the reign of God, the kingdom of heaven. More than that, the Church is called to be a pilot plant for that kingdom, a seed bed for the promised divine transformation of creation. The love we are called to exhibit is the norm for that alternative order.

Tackling the underlying causes of poverty, oppression and disease was simply beyond the capabilities of the first generations of Christians. The early Church drew its membership mostly from those on the margins of power. By all accounts, Paul's comment to the Corinthian church remained true for several generations: 'Not many of you were wise by human standards; not many were influential; not many were of noble birth' (1 Corinthians 1:26). Instead of directly tackling the social order of their day, they had to be content with the subversive activity of modelling an alternative social order in their personal lives.

However, the question of our responsibility for the wider social order does arise when Christians find themselves in positions of influence. The example of Basil of Caesarea is significant precisely because he was operating shortly after Christianity had been adopted as the official religion of the Roman Empire. This recently won influence allowed him to organise care for the poor on a scale which would have been beyond his capacity as an individual.

Judging by his example and that of many Christians of later centuries, Jesus' call for practical love of our neighbours was seen as a basic minimum rather than a limit. In other words, it was not interpreted as 'You need only love your neighbour' but as, 'Whatever your circumstances, you can at least love your neighbour.'

As we shall see, practical love for neighbours, responding to perceived needs in one's locality, has often been the starting point for much more extensive social reform.

Care for the outcasts

Josephine Butler (1828–1906)
The wife of a Canon of Winchester Cathedral, Josephine Butler reminds us that social reform was not the exclusive province of those on the fringes of the Church. On the contrary, she pursued an active and international interest in social reform from the very heart of the Anglican establishment.

The particular focus of her activity was prostitution. Not content with reaching out in love to individual prostitutes, she launched a successful attack on the institutional undergirding of prostitution. Her activities at the systemic level included campaigning against the Contagious Diseases Act (a euphemistically named act of parliament regulating prostitution in Britain). Subsequently she was a prime mover in the formation of the International Federation for the Abolition of the State Regulation of Vice.

Her activities illustrate the difficulty in maintaining that Christians should keep out of politics. Her concern for prostitutes could not be satisfied with easing the distress of a few individuals. She recognised that there were larger issues and, as opportunity arose, she addressed herself to those larger issues.

Josephine Butler is of interest for another reason: the clear way in which her social concern flowed from her spirituality. Undergirding her work was a life of almost continuous prayer. In this, her model was the Dominican Tertiary St Catherine of Siena (who had dedicated her life to contemplative prayer, service of the sick and the poor, and evangelism).

Areas of concern

Anglicans have been actively involved in the entire spectrum of social concern. In the parable of the sheep and the goats, Jesus taught us to befriend the alien. Taken together with the Old Testament's teaching on social justice, this suggests a command to love those on the margins of our society. Christians of all eras have followed the example of Jesus in showing practical love for the outcasts and the marginalised, and Anglicans are no exception. Of course, the identity of the outcasts will vary from culture to culture. For Josephine Butler and Victorian England, they were prostitutes. In other situations, they may be persecuted minorities or oppressed majorities. They may be the victims of neglect (e.g. Anglican individuals and organisations such as the Church of England's Children's Society have played leading roles in raising the status of children). From biblical times, lepers have been seen as a test case of Christian love. Today many Christians (including Anglicans) are deeply engaged in supporting and campaigning for AIDS victims.

Mention of leprosy and AIDS moves us from care for the outcast to care for the sick. As I have already noted, public hospitals were a Christian innovation and care for the sick has been a continuous theme of Christian social action over the centuries. Many Anglicans have found their vocation in the caring professions. Sometimes they have made major contributions to the development of health care.

In the same breath as he speaks of visiting the sick, Jesus teaches us to visit those who are in prison. The Orthodox Church interprets this as 'ransoming captives': one of the chief corporal works of mercy. Again Anglicans have not been backward in visiting prisoners, campaigning for prison reform (as opportunity arose) and seeking the release of those unjustly imprisoned. One of the most celebrated examples in our own day is surely Terry Waite, whose active concern for captives led to his own imprisonment.

Finally there is the relief of poverty and hunger. Again we find Anglicans working alongside Christians of other churches (e.g. through Christian Aid) in combating these evils. And, again, we see dissatisfaction with mere palliatives leading to active engagement in campaigning for structural changes. By extension, we may include campaigning for improved working conditions and against the exploitation of workers.

Terry Waite (b. 1939), the Archbishop of Canterbury's special envoy, was released in 1991 after spending 1,763 days in captivity as a hostage.

Anglicans in education

Hannah More was one Anglican woman actively involved in the development of popular education. Historically, Christians of all traditions have seen the fight against ignorance as an integral part of social concern. Indeed, prior to the modern era, the churches were the main providers of education in those countries that we usually think of as Christian.

The Anglican Church has been no exception to this tendency. Many of the leading independent schools in England began as Anglican charities and those historical connections are still taken seriously. At one time it was commonplace for the staff of such schools to be clergymen. Indeed, until relatively recently, being the headmaster of a leading independent school was an acknowledged path to preferment (e.g. in 1869 Frederick Temple, then headmaster of Rugby, was appointed Bishop of Exeter). For many of these schools, confirmation into the Church of England remains an integral part of

A caring Anglican

Hannah More (1745–1833)

The daughter of a Bristol schoolmaster, Hannah More was a gifted dramatist and soon found herself much in demand in London high society. Disenchanted with its frivolity and self-indulgence, she turned to Christianity, coming under the influence of John Newton and members of the Clapham Sect.

She became a model of personal piety, devoting many hours to prayer, self-examination and spiritual reading. However, in one significant respect, she departed from eighteenth-century stereotypes of the godly woman: she resolutely refused to stay at home and mind her own business! On the contrary, she became deeply committed to the abolition of slavery.

One of her weapons was her access to the rich and the influential. She even took a plan of a slave ship with her when she went to dinner parties!

Her good works were by no means limited to the abolition issue, however. With encouragement from William Wilberforce and drawing on her own background, she established several schools to provide basic education for the rural and mining communities of the Mendips. Besides the inevitable religious education, these schools offered training in practical skills intended to combat poverty. Sadly, but perhaps predictably, they met with opposition from her local bishop. She also turned her attention to educational theory, writing pamphlets criticising the limited educational provision for young women.

She is sometimes presented as a reactionary figure because of her tracts against the French Revolution. However, while she defended the existing social order, she was highly critical of aristocratic paternalism and exploitation. In her words, 'To expect to reform the poor while the opulent are corrupt, is to throw odours into the stream while the springs are poisoned.'

religious education (this has occasionally produced amusing anomalies, e.g. George Macleod, one of the leading Presbyterian clergymen of this century was also a confirmed Anglican because confirmation was the norm for boys at Winchester College).

However, the Church of England has had no less interest in popular education. This aspect of its educational involvement began to be organised as long ago as 1698 when Thomas Bray founded the Society for Promoting Christian Knowledge. Known today primarily for its publishing activities, one of its briefs was the foundation of charity schools.

Just over a century later the National Society for the Education of the Poor in the Principles of the Established Church (popularly known as the National Society) was founded. Together with its free church counterpart, the British and Foreign Schools Society, this became the major agent in promoting popular education prior to the advent of state education in 1870. Working through the dioceses, it created a network of schools throughout England and was at the forefront of developing teacher training.

After 1870 these schools remained outside the state system. It was not until 1902 that some of them began to receive state subsidies. This resulted in ever closer ties with the state system until the relationship was regularised as part of the 1944 Education Act. Subsequently, church schools have been one of two kinds: aided (schools which continue to be controlled by the church but receive financial aid from public funds) and controlled (schools which the state now controls but which retain their historical connections with the church).

Organising social action

Almost inevitably, catalogues of the above sort highlight outstanding individuals: men and women, lay and ordained, who flesh out for us the meaning of practical Christian love.

However, most Christian caring does not make the headlines. It is not about the heroic efforts of unusually gifted people but rather about the small everyday activities of ordinary Christian men and women.

Acting alone, we make little impact on the needs we perceive around us. But, when those small acts of mercy are co-ordinated, when we act together, we may effect significant changes in the life of our community or the wider society. Thus the question of organisation is bound to arise eventually.

Congregational caring

The Bible seems to suggest that, since New Testament times, two social institutions have been basic to the everyday life of the Christian: the family and the local congregation. When it comes to social action, the local congregation is particularly important. This is the level at which most practical caring by Christians is organised. Arguably it remains the most effective way of embodying Christ's love in our communities in spite of the technological advances which have turned the world into a global village.

The support of a congregation enables care to take place on a much larger scale than would be possible if it was left entirely to individuals. Teams of people will perhaps co-operate in visiting the sick or the housebound or the bereaved. The congregational connection may make possible forms of caring activity which would not be open to the individual, e.g. it may provide them with access to a local hospital, hospice, nursing home or prison. Other congregations may decide to use their buildings for other activities such as drop-in centres, soup kitchens, night shelters; or they may provide local action groups with a hospitable open space for discussion, debate and protest.

Institutional action

It is not always possible to meet the needs we see around us by organising on a purely local level. Many of the problems we face in our highly complex culture operate on a much larger scale than the local parish. This raises the question of organisation for social action on a larger-than-congregational level.

To what extent do the diocesan and provincial structures of the Anglican Church provide its members with resources for co-ordinating, supporting and making more effective their practice of Christian love? It has to be said that within the Church of England the extent of such support varies a great deal from diocese to diocese.

The various forms of political action in which Anglicans might be involved will be dealt with later.

Voluntary societies

A third way in which Christians (Anglican or otherwise) have organised their social action has been through the formation of voluntary societies. The rapid growth in such organisations over the past couple of centuries has brought a mixed response from some quarters.

What is their relationship to the church? In some cases this is clearly defined. For example, the Mothers' Union is a self-consciously Anglican organisation dedicated to affirming marriage and family life. However, many Christian voluntary societies are interdenominational. It is sometimes felt that such organisations weaken the church by drawing off expertise that could have been put to similar use within the congregation, diocese or Province.

It has to be admitted that there is some justification for such doubts. The founders of many voluntary societies set up in the heyday of evangelicalism had a minimalist view of the church: it was regarded as our meeting together for worship and the preaching of the Word and little else. People still believed that they lived in a Christian society. Given such a perception of society, the voluntary society seemed a more appropriate way of organising social action than either congregational or diocesan modes of organisation.

On the other hand, such voluntary societies were often an expression of frustration on the part of lay people (and, sometimes, clergy) with the perceived inertia or even obstruction of the institutional voice. Some Anglican views of the Church did lend themselves to a centralised authority structure. On a congregational level, such views could result in the stifling of individual initiatives. David Watson used to use the metaphor of a wine bottle to describe the average Anglican parish: with the vicar as the cork keeping the parishioners firmly in their place. Alternatively, some traditional understandings of the role of the priest tended to render the clergy blind or apathetic towards lay initiatives. Such apathy left the initiator feeling unsupported and frustrated. In such situations, they had little choice but to seek support among the like-minded or to abandon their initiative. If they opted for the former, yet another voluntary society was the result.

However, there is also a strong positive reason for the existence of voluntary societies. Such bodies allow Christians of different traditions to co-operate on matters of common concern. There is no distinctively Anglican way of caring for the sick, the outcast, the prisoner, the homeless, the oppressed. Virtually the whole spectrum of Christian social concern is part of our shared Christian heritage. Only an exclusivism foreign to the true spirit of the Anglican way would insist on carving up Christian social action along denominational lines. It would be nonsensical to start a specifically Anglican hospice in an area already adequately supplied with hospice care because the existing establishment was a Roman Catholic, Methodist or Baptist initiative!

Politics – the Anglican way

Addressing structural questions

As we have seen, there is a tendency for practical Christian love to go beyond palliative measures as opportunities arise for wider action. Actually caring for individuals in unacceptable situations will force us to ask questions about the situation. Genuine Christian love does not content itself with doling out bread and soup to the inhabitants of cardboard city; it forces us to ask uncomfortable questions about why people are forced to exist in such conditions. If there are the means at our disposal to alter those conditions or influence the decision-makers, such action will inevitably become part of our expression of practical Christian love. In other words, the Christian imperative to love your neighbour exerts a strong pressure towards Christian involvement in politics. Thus, politicians who declare that the Church should keep out of politics are being either dishonest (what they really mean is 'the Church is welcome to engage in politics as long as it agrees with me') or heretical.

But there is a variety of different ways in which individual Christians and churches can engage in political activity.

The politics of influence

For centuries the Church of England enjoyed a privileged position in British society. Members of its hierarchy had immediate access to the most senior levels of government. The decision-makers in society were mostly 'English gentlemen' and, therefore, good members of the Church of England. Of course, both the clergy and the decision-makers were drawn from the same small ruling elite.

The Clapham Sect

The Clapham Sect, which flourished at the end of the eighteenth century and beginning of the nineteenth, is an outstanding example of lay-led Anglican social concern. It also highlights the positive aspects of the politics of influence.

It was an informal network or community of influential Anglican evangelicals. Perhaps the best-known figure in the group was William Wilberforce, but other members were no less influential, including former Governors of India and Sierra Leone and a wealthy banker. Eventually Hannah More was to find herself among their number.

Mention of the name Wilberforce immediately brings to mind the one issue that the Clapham Sect is remembered for, the campaign for the abolition of slavery. It is true that they pursued this issue relentlessly for four decades, effecting first a ban on trafficking in slaves and finally the end of the institution itself within the British Empire. However, they were hardly a one-issue group. Indeed the purpose of the sect was not primarily to engage in social reform. On the contrary, its primary function was as a mutual support group: they met to encourage one another in the pursuit of holiness.

Today we might translate holiness as practical spirituality. In contrast to the emigration inwards characteristic of other forms of Christian spirituality in vogue, holiness is both inwardly and outwardly directed. It is love of God (expressed in prayer and worship) and love of one's fellows (expressed in good works).

Even on a purely personal level, the effect of the Clapham Sect on the lives of its members was dramatic. Take, for example, Henry Thornton the banker. In the midst of a busy public life he still found time for three hours of prayer every day. As far as good works were concerned, he habitually gave away two-thirds of his income.

But the good works of ➤

In such circumstances it was perfectly natural for the political activity of the church to be carried on at the level of personal influence. It was the politics of the old school tie, the London club, the old boy network.

Such an approach has certain strengths but also some very real weaknesses. Precisely because it is so personal, it has the potential to influence decision-makers in very significant ways. One is more likely to be persuaded by someone who has been a close friend for the past thirty years than by a total stranger armed only with arguments and a petition.

On the other hand, that strength is also its main weakness. Personal influence succeeds by being very aware of its own limitations. One only exerts influence or seeks a favour if there is a good chance of it being acceptable to the other party. After all, you want to maintain your influence by keeping on good terms with the other person. On a large scale this means that the politics of influence is not a very effective way of bringing about radical changes in the structure of society. It is a very conservative form of politics: maintaining the *status quo* in order to do a limited amount of good.

Another major weakness is its dependence upon a trickle-down approach to social change. It works best in situations where real political power is concentrated in the hands of a few people (e.g. monarchies and nineteenth-century centralised bureaucracies). In such situations, by influencing the decision-makers, you may reasonably expect to cause changes within the wider society. However, in the twentieth century, political power has become much more diffuse and modern Western societies are no longer structured in relatively simple hierarchies. Today some multinational corporations wield greater political and economic influence than some countries. The mass media can influence public opinion far more effectively than bureaucracies or politicians. The channels of influence have become far more complex than they were a few generations ago.

But even before the politics of influence was rendered obsolete (as an instrument of achieving social change) by the massive social and technological changes of this century, the Church was already losing its capacity to influence society in this way. Throughout Western society in the nineteenth century the churches were increasingly marginalised by the social process known as secularisation. People (certainly the people with influence) were as religious as their parents and grandparents. But religion itself was privatised and displaced from everyday decision-making. Christianity became a matter of personal morality rather than public policy.

The politics of the pressure group

The increasing complexity of Western society has seen the emergence of a different style of political activity. Those without direct access to the ears of the decision-makers have discovered that they are not entirely without political influence. By mobilising and influencing public opinion they can exert an indirect influence on government and big business.

Christians of all denominations have been actively involved in the development of pressure groups since the emergence of voluntary societies in the nineteenth century. While some voluntary societies were aimed specifically at forwarding certain good works, others have seen their role as more overtly political from the outset. Josephine Butler's international campaign to bring about legislative change with respect to prostitution is a clear early example of the latter kind.

In recent decades, the Church of England's approach to politics has increasingly been that of the pressure group. Specifically, through its Board of Social Responsibility, it has marshalled its arguments on various contentious public issues and presented a (more or less) united front to the government of the day. Elsewhere in this book, John Habgood has explained how this works out in practice.

The politics of protest

Where does pressure end and protest begin? The influence of the pressure group lies precisely in veiled threats. 'If you don't negotiate, we will go on strike.' 'If you insist on pursuing this policy, so many thousand people may register their protest at the next election by voting for someone who will change the policy.' The point at which personal influence and peaceful pressure fail is often the point at which protest begins.

In a Christian context, this often takes the form of prophetic denunciation. One example was the widespread boycott of South African goods in the campaign against apartheid.

the Clapham Sect went far beyond the merely personal level of alms-giving. They recognised an obligation to use their influence within British society to cause structural changes in the interests of social justice. The abolition of slavery was undoubtedly their finest achievement, but they were vocal in support of other changes. They campaigned in favour of reform in the workplace, supporting the first of the Factory Acts in 1802 and laying the foundations on which a later evangelical Anglican, the Earl of Shaftesbury, was to build. Perhaps surprisingly they also supported moves for ecclesiastical reform (rightly recognising that a privileged church could only preach the Good News of Jesus convincingly if it put its own house in order). As evangelicals one would expect them to support moves to remove legislative discrimination against Nonconformists but they were equally tireless in pursuing Roman Catholic emancipation.

All of this belies the epithet 'The Tory party at prayer' which has so often (and incorrectly) been applied to the Church of England. In fact, the members of the Clapham Sect were staunch supporters of the Whigs (the more liberal of the two political parties of the time).

William Wilberforce (1795–1833) is holding the Slave Trade Abolition Bill.

Elsewhere Anglicans, like other Christians, have found themselves imprisoned, persecuted or martyred for resisting oppressive regimes in the name of justice and God's truth.

Christian socialism and the development of Anglican social theory

At the turn of the nineteenth century, evangelical Anglicans (notably the Clapham Sect) were at the forefront of social action. However they failed to challenge the ideologies underpinning the industrial revolution. Thus they worked tirelessly for reform within the system but failed to see that there were points at which the system itself should be challenged. As the nineteenth century progressed and society changed under the impact of urbanisation and industrialisation, the evangelicals gradually withdrew into the safety of preaching the Gospel. It was left to other parties within the Anglican way to think theologically about social action.

Christian socialism

This emerged in the middle of the nineteenth century as a liberal and catholic response to contemporary society. The movement was founded by an Anglican lay person, J. M. F. Ludlow, but the intellectual leader in the movement was the controversial Anglican theologian Frederick Denison Maurice (1805–72). Following his lead, members of the movement (which included Charles Kingsley of *The Water Babies* fame) saw the Church of England as the conscience of the nation. In this they were not so very far from the views of the Clapham Sect.

However, they went deeper than the evangelical reformers of the previous generation. Maurice could not accept that the evil and injustice created by the social system emerging from the industrial revolution was merely accidental. In his view, a system which resulted in injustice and exploitation must itself be wrong. Specifically he attacked the doctrine of *laissez faire*, arguing that the Christian virtue of co-operation was a sounder basis for a society than the economists' 'virtue' of unregulated competition.

In the light of the evolution of the term 'socialism', the term 'Christian socialism' is perhaps misleading. It suggests an egalitarian radicalism which would have been entirely alien to the nineteenth-century Christian socialists. On the contrary, by today's standards they were class-bound, paternalistic and politically reactionary. They were conscience-stricken members of the ruling elite who were concerned to improve the lot of the lower classes but still without compromising the status of their own class. However, one who, it could be said, lived before his time was John Neville Figgis (1866–1919) who, while seeing the dangers of the omnicompetent state, held up the vision of the Christian state as the community of communities.

It has to be said that the Christian socialists had relatively little immediate impact on society. Their importance lies not so much in any reforms achieved as in the influence they exerted upon subsequent generations of Anglican social thinkers. Maurice passed on his concerns to Westcott and Hort. They, in their turn, inspired the members of the *Lux Mundi* group (a think-tank of liberal Anglo-Catholic scholars named after their seminal 'Studies in the Religion of the Incarnation' published in 1889) notably Charles Gore and Henry Scott Holland. In much the same way, these same concerns were passed on to the next generation of Anglican social thinkers, including R. H. Tawney and Archbishop William Temple.

One constant in their thought is the belief that the Church has the right and duty to interfere in politics and the social order. There is no room for a quasi-Lutheran compartmentalisation of church and state into two kingdoms in Anglican social theology. This, however, does not imply the church's commitment to a particular political party. Rather it is a recognition that every political philosophy (and, therefore, every political party) is distorted by human sinfulness. The Church has a duty both to commend those aspects of government policy which it perceives to be promoting the kingdom of God and to question government policies which fail to do so (or which actively work against the kingdom).

But how are we to perceive whether a particular policy tends towards the kingdom or away from it? We cannot simply read political policy from the pages of Scripture. The typical Anglican answer has been that we work by means of middle axioms. These are general guidelines for public policy which act as a bridge between basic moral

William Temple (1881–1944)

The second son of Frederick Temple, like his father he was destined to become Archbishop of Canterbury. A privileged upbringing did not blind him to the injustices of late Victorian society and, as a young man he developed lasting interests in education and social work. Following in his father's footsteps, he was for a time headmaster of a major independent school (in his case, Repton). However, he was also actively involved in the Workers' Educational Association.

Having become a parish priest in 1914, he was actively involved in pressing for the Church of England to have greater autonomy from the British government. This was partially achieved with the 1919 Enabling Act.

In 1921 he was made Bishop of the industrial diocese of Manchester. Eight years later he became Archbishop of York and, finally, in 1942, he was translated to Canterbury. Throughout this period he was actively involved in the nascent ecumenical movement.

His lively concern for social, economic and international issues ensured that he rapidly became a prominent national figure. Perhaps the greatest triumph of his years of social involvement was the 1941 Malvern Conference. Held during the darkest days of the Second World War, this was an important reassertion of Christian hope. Its purpose was to look forward to the period after the war and create a vision for a new social order informed by the Christian faith. Temple himself did not live to see the outcome of this conference, but many of the post-war social reforms in Britain may be traced, at least in part, to Malvern.

principles derived from Christian theology and the specifics of legislation and party politics.

Catholic radicalism

If the evangelicals were whiggish in tendency and the liberal catholic middle ground of the church was (or became by the turn of this century) moderately socialist, there was also a radically socialist voice among the Anglo-Catholics. Very much a vocal minority within the church, these were often slum priests impatient to see the liberating Gospel of Jesus Christ incarnated in the terrible conditions in which they lived and worked.

Without doubt, the most outspoken of the Catholic radicals was Stewart Headlam (1847–1924), described by E. R. Norman as 'the first really serious socialist, in the modern sense, in the Church'. Headlam delighted to shock. He saw the Eucharist as a prophetic sign against a Mammon-worshipping world and claimed that those who celebrated Communion had to be holy communists.

But this was not mere eccentricity. His shock tactics (which eventually led the Bishop of London to withdraw his licence) were rooted in a carefully thought out theology of liberation based not on Marx but on Anglican incarnationalism. The physical and social reality of Jesus Christ forced him to reject the dualistic spirituality of the age which reduced religion to a purely private affair. As Kenneth Leech points out, 'For Headlam the Christian community had to be involved in areas far wider than the practice of religion. Its aim was nothing less than salvation and peace, *shalom,* and this involved health, education, politics, beauty, and pleasure. These were all vital elements in that striving for fullness of life which was central to the gospel.'

In spite of much opposition, Headlam had an influence far beyond the slums of East London thanks to the Guild of St Matthew. Originally a parish society founded by him in 1877 and committed to a rule of life emphasising eucharistic worship, it soon became the main radically socialist Christian movement in Britain.

Action in a post-modern context

Green activists have come up with the slogan, 'Think globally; act locally.' My account of the basis for Christian social action suggests that we might change the slogan to

'Serve locally; think globally' (in that order). If so, current dramatic changes in the shape of Western culture do not affect the starting point of Christian social action. Whenever I see that my neighbour is cold, hungry, lonely, exploited or persecuted, I am still called to show Christian love in a practical way.

However the widely discussed demise of modernity does require us to 'think globally' about a number of issues. The complex of challenges to what has been the dominant culture of the West for over a century is sometimes given the collective name post-modernity. A detailed discussion of these issues is beyond the scope of this article. Suffice it to say that post-modernity presents a major challenge to the basic moral principles mentioned above.

For example, powerful cultural forces are now at work demolishing the dominant Western attitude to time, i.e. that events may be placed within a linear progressive historical framework. In its place we are left with historical fragments and projections of the present (rather than genuine hopes for the future) located in an extended present. Because our understandings of selfhood and community are dependent upon historical narratives, this change in perspective threatens to erode the basic Christian principles of personhood and fellowship. We see it already in the fragmentation of communities and, on an individual level, in the post-modernists' fascination with schizophrenia.

At present, these issues tend to be the province of various mission agencies. However, Christian social action and Christian mission are no more separable than spirituality and social action. As we begin to tackle how we can most effectively proclaim the Christian Gospel in a post-modern context, we must also examine what it means to live the Gospel in that context.

Questions

1. 'Christian spirituality and social concern are inseparable.' Do you agree?
2. In what ways should the Church be involved in politics?
3. What are the major social issues in our community? How might we address them
   (a) as individuals;
   (b) as a group:
   (c) as church members;
   (d) as members of the community?

Part 4

Appreciating Anglican structures

12

Orders and officers of the church

David Sceats

Clergy

> It is evident unto all men diligently reading holy Scripture and ancient Authors, that from the Apostles' time there have been these Orders of Ministers in Christ's Church; Bishops, Priests and Deacons.

Ever since these opening words of the ordination service in the English Prayer Book were first written in the mid-1500s people have wondered about them. It isn't really evident from the New Testament that there were bishops, priests and deacons in the apostles' time. The New Testament never uses the word 'priest' to describe leaders of Christian congregations. While it does talk about 'bishops' and 'deacons', there seem to have been quite a lot of other kinds of ministers in the church as well. Nevertheless, following this lead from the *Book of Common Prayer*, one of the distinctive things about the worldwide Anglican Church today is the way it organises itself around this 'threefold order' of ministry.

History

In fact, the threefold order is very old. It was the standard pattern of church leadership throughout the Roman Empire by two hundred years after the time of Christ, though there were other, so-called 'minor orders' of ministry as well. At first, when local churches were basically groups of converts from the local Jewish synagogue, they were organised in a similar way: a group of people called 'elders' shared responsibility for leadership. As churches came into being through the conversion of Gentiles in places where there were no synagogues (and therefore no pattern of leadership by elders) the leaders came to be known by the non-religious Greek word *episkopos*, over-

Priest

The Old English words *biscop* (bishop) and *preost* (priest) are derived from the Latin words *episcopus*, originally meaning overseer, (from the Greek, *episkopos*), and *presbyter*, meaning elder, (from the Greek *presbuteros*). Some parts of the Anglican Communion have tried to revive the use of the word 'presbyter' as an alternative to 'priest' (for instance, in the ordination services in the English *Alternative Service Book*, which speaks of 'The Ordination of Priests (also called Presbyters)', and the Canadian *Book of Alternative Services*, which uses the two terms interchangeably). There are sound theological reasons for trying to make such a change, but the word 'priest' is so much a part of Anglican tradition that it seems unlikely that it will now be replaced in general use.

seer. As time passed, the two words came to be used interchangeably. Then it became customary for one member of the group of leaders to take responsibility for organising the others, and he came to be known as the *episkopos,* while the others were referred to as elders (Greek, *presbuteroi,* the word from which the English word 'priest' is derived).

Deacons (from the Greek *diakonos,* a servant) seem to have been an invention of the early Church. They were people who were originally appointed to look after practical aspects of the church's ministry, like the distribution of charity among the poorer members (some scholars think the seven disciples appointed to look after the daily distribution of food in Acts chapter 6 were the first deacons, though the name is not used there). In the early centuries deacons were powerful figures responsible for ordering the liturgical assembly and administering financial support for the poor. Originally those men and women who became deacons probably didn't expect to go on to be presbyters, but gradually the practice grew up of treating the diaconate as a trial period for those who wanted to become priests. It is still the custom in much of the Anglican Communion for the diaconate to be a probationary period (usually of one year) before someone is ordained to the priesthood, but more and more dioceses are now exploring the possibility of reinstating a permanent diaconate.

Bishops

In the early Church bishops were usually responsible for the leadership of the Christian community in one city or area. As the church grew there might be several worshipping congregations, but they were all part of the church in that place. In other words, bishops were originally more like the modern leader of a team of clergy who share responsibility for a group of churches in a town or cluster of villages, than the modern bishop who is the spiritual leader, pastoral director and ecclesiastical chief executive of a diocese. In the more scattered tribal societies north of the Alps bishops came to have responsibility for a wider geographical area.

A significant change took place as a result of the conversion of the Roman Emperors to Christianity. They saw the Church as a way of holding together their diverse and unwieldy Empire, and increasingly treated the clergy as a kind of civil service. Dioceses were originally the political divisions of the Roman Empire, and once the Church had been 'nationalised' it made sense to link the ecclesiastical and secular jurisdictions. So bishops came to be responsible for all the churches of a diocese, and eventually, as this pattern persisted through the Middle Ages, the word 'diocese' came to have an ecclesiastical instead of a secular meaning.

Bishops today

There are still many signs of this historical background in the Church of England, where many dioceses trace their history back to a period when bishops were great barons, leading troops into battle, defending the realm and managing affairs of state. Some English dioceses now comprise many hundreds of parishes and clergy, and some English bishops continue to be members of the House of Lords. In these circumstances there is a danger that the bishop will seem rather remote and inaccessible to the people and clergy of the diocese. The bishop is likely to be as much a figure of national as of local significance, and there will be little personal contact with the members of the church.

This is much less true in other Provinces of the Anglican Communion, where dioceses are usually numerically smaller, and the church is not established. In one Scottish diocese, for instance, there are only seven clergy! In such situations bishops are much more likely to be in a close pastoral relationship with the clergy and even the laity of the diocese. Sometimes, too, they play a more prominent role in the process of clergy appointments than has been the case in many English parishes, where patronage by individuals and other institutions often restricts the bishop's ability to deploy clergy according to a central policy. More recently, even in England, however, the bishop's involvement in clergy appointments has grown, as a result of the practice of suspending the rights of patrons and appointing priests-in-charge on a limited licence instead.

A bishop's ministry

'A bishop is called to lead in serving and caring for the people of God, and to work with them in the oversight of the Church. He has . . . a special responsibility to maintain and further the unity of the church, to uphold its discipline and to guard its faith . . . It is his duty to watch over and pray for all those committed to his charge, and to teach and govern them after the example of the Apostles . . . He is to ordain and to send new ministers, guiding those who serve with him and enabling them to fulfil their ministry . . . to baptize and confirm, to preside at the Holy Communion, and to lead the offering of prayer and praise.'

From 'The Ordination or Consecration of a Bishop', Alternative Service Book, 1980

The work of bishops

In practice the work of a diocesan bishop is likely to be enormously varied and demanding and will often have a profound influence on the vision and direction of the diocese. The bishop will meet regularly with the senior staff of the diocese (other bishops, archdeacons, diocesan administrators, etc.) to formulate policy, discuss and implement priorities, resolve conflicts, address matters of pastoral concern and discipline, consider questions of clergy deployment, diocesan finance, the development of new patterns of ministry and new initiatives in mission. There will probably also be an important personal ministry among the leaders and formers of opinion in the wider community in which the diocese is set. But the bishop will also be expected to spend a lot of time in visiting parishes to conduct confirmation services, install new clergy, consecrate churches, and celebrate special moments in the life of the local church.

One of the prime responsibilities of bishops is the leadership and pastoral care of the clergy. This begins with the selection and training of ordinands. While few diocesan bishops are involved in this in a hands-on way until the ordination service itself, virtually all will appoint advisers and selectors who will undertake this work on their behalf – and most will meet all potential ordinands of the diocese at some point in their selection. Many bishops will themselves take part in the selection process as chairmen of panels at which candidates for ordination are selected. They will often be involved in offering pastoral support to clergy and their families at times of need such as sickness, bereavement or redeployment, and will have an important part to play in situations where pastoral relationships in the local church have become compromised and clergy must be disciplined.

At the same time, the church in the diocese will look to the bishop for inspiration, a sense of vision and direction, and a prophetic ministry that challenges both the church and the wider community with the values of God's kingdom and the message of the Gospel. Through the bishop the diocese will relate to other dioceses (and their bishops) in the Province and in the worldwide Anglican Communion: thus the bishop is a symbol of the unity of the church and of the fact that the diocese is part of its catholic (i.e. worldwide) identity. And in the present media-conscious age the bishop will be a symbol of the church to the world around – the one to whom journalists automatically turn for a statement of 'the church's point

David Hope is now Archbishop of York. Journalists and broadcasters tend to turn to bishops for a statement of 'the church's point of view'.

of view', and who can all too easily become a target of the less admirable tendencies of the press.

Suffragan bishops

This is a demanding brief. It is not surprising that many dioceses in the Anglican Communion have made moves towards collaborative styles of episcopal leadership which make it possible for elements of the bishop's role to be shared, and for people with differing gifts to share in this ministry together. The practice of appointing one or more *suffragan bishops* (from the late Latin *suffraganeus*, assistant, supporting) is widespread. Suffragans assist diocesan bishops in the performance of their duties, and are members with them of the college or house of bishops in the diocese. Some larger dioceses have gone further and have effectively divided themselves up into several mini dioceses or areas, each of which is presided over by an area bishop to whom the diocesan devolves certain powers. In this way episcopacy is participating in the movement towards collaborative styles of ministry which is an increasingly common feature at every level in the Anglican Church.

In some Anglican Provinces an assistant bishop will be appointed with the right to succeed the diocesan bishop when the latter retires; these are called coadjutor bishops. In other Provinces, however, a coadjutor bishop is someone who stands in for the diocesan bishop at times of illness or prolonged absence.

Priests

The great majority of the clergy in the Anglican Communion belong to the order of priests. This includes most of those who match the familiar image of the Anglican minister – the rector or vicar responsible for the leadership of ministry and mission in a parish. But the widespread use of words like 'rector', 'vicar' and 'parish' wherever the Anglican Church is found, obscures the fact that they can mean subtly different things.

Priests and parishes

In England, where the Anglican Church began, a parish is a place. It has an identity and a community, like a village, or town, a city or a suburb. Often the growth of such places has led to them being subdivided into a number of parishes, but the basic idea of the parish as a place is still fundamental. Ask a priest how big the parish is and you will almost certainly get an answer which numbers it in thousands – the size of the population of the geographical parish.

In this context the parish church is the building at which the community of Anglican Christians within the parish meets for worship. There is a sense in which the church 'belongs' to all the people of the parish: anyone can come to it for Sunday worship; its ministry is available for special services like marriages, funerals and baptisms, and many will take advantage of this, even though they seldom or never cross its threshold otherwise. The members of the congregation at the parish church are likely to have a sense of responsibility for mission and ministry to the whole community of the parish. And parish priests will be likely to see themselves as God's representative for that whole community, not just as the spiritual leader of the 'members' of the church.

Elsewhere in the Anglican Communion things will be different. In a sense the parish is still a place: the church will theoretically be organised on a geographical basis into parishes grouped together into deaneries and archdeaconries within the diocese. But this is not what matters. Ask how big the parish is and you will get an answer in tens or hundreds – the size of the worshipping congregation. The church will define itself by its membership, and the word 'parish' will signify the worshipping community of the church, not the wider community of the place. The non-churchgoing people of the place will probably have few expectations of the Anglican Church, which will, in turn, have a subtly different and more individualistic attitude to ministry and mission. Parish priests will see themselves, first and foremost, as the spiritual leaders and pastors of worshipping communities.

Rectors and vicars

Similar differences occur with the use of words like 'rector' and 'vicar'. In England the use of one of these alternative names for a parish priest is the result of an obscure distinction between the right to receive different kinds of tithes (a kind of church tax) in the Middle Ages. The great majority of English parish clergy are, in fact, vicars, and the word 'vicar' is often used in general speech in England for any ordained Anglican minister.

(More recently, where several parishes have been grouped together into what is called a 'Team Ministry', the leader of the clergy team is known as the 'Team Rector', while the other members are 'Team Vicars'.)

In other parts of the Anglican Communion the term 'vicar' may not be used at all – in Scotland and Canada, for instance, all parish priests will be rectors, or, if there are several priests in a parish, some may be associate rectors. In Australia some dioceses call parish priests 'rectors' while others use the term 'vicar', but both mean a clergy person with tenure. The term 'curate' is usually reserved for clergy who are in the apprenticeship phase of their training, in the first few years after their ordination.

Non-stipendiary priests

Rectors and vicars are usually in full-time paid ministry, but they do not have to be, and one increasing development in the Anglican Church that reflects the economic pressures which all its Provinces are facing, is the growth of non-stipendiary (unpaid) patterns of ordained ministry. In South Africa they are known as self-supported as opposed to church-supported ministers.

Another development of this kind is the exploration of what is widely known as Local Ordained Ministry, where someone from within the worshipping community of a parish is ordained to the priesthood, to minister within the parish they belong to (in contrast to the traditional pattern, where priests are normally appointed to parishes from outside). Such local priests are usually only allowed to offer their ministry within the parish that has called them into it.

Ordained ministry

'Priests are called by God to work with the Bishop and with their fellow-priests, as servants and shepherds among the people to whom they are sent. They are to proclaim the word of the Lord, to call their hearers to repentance, and in Christ's name to absolve, and to declare the forgiveness of sins. They are to baptize, and prepare the baptized for Confirmation. They are to preside at the celebration of the Holy Communion. They are to lead their people in prayer and worship, to intercede for them, to bless them in the name of the Lord, and to teach and encourage by word and example. They are to minister to the sick, and prepare the dying for their death.

They are to be messengers, watchmen, and stewards of the Lord; they are to teach and admonish, to feed and provide for the Lord's family, to search for his children in the wilderness of this world's temptations and to guide them through its confusions, so that they may be saved by Christ for ever.'

After 'The Ordination of Deacons and Priests', Alternative Service Book, 1980

Specialised forms of priesthood

The English ordination services describe the work of priests in language that obviously assumes they will be parish clergy. They are 'servants and shepherds among the people to whom they are sent'. They are required to 'remember with thanksgiving that the treasure now to be entrusted to [them] is Christ's own flock . . . the Church and congregation among whom [they] will serve are one with him . . .' But while the majority of Anglican priests serve in parishes, many do not. There is a wide range of specialist ministries of different kinds, almost all of which are undertaken by priests.

Archdeacons

Some of these are senior management posts, like archdeacons (officers of the bishop who are responsible for discipline and administration within a section of the diocese called an archdeaconry). Archdeacons are sometimes closely associated with bishops in their ministry, especially in matters to do with the deployment and pastoral support of clergy and other ministers: in some dioceses with area schemes they are effectively assistants to the area bishops. They generally also have responsibility for supervising the maintenance of church buildings and property. They may work full-time as archdeacons, but in some cases they will also be responsible for pastoral oversight in a parish.

In some parts of the Anglican Communion, on the other hand, a diocese may have one or more executive archdeacons, who assist the bishop, while other priests are given the title of archdeacon as an honorific recognition of long service or seniority.

A digest of deans

There are at least three different kinds of 'dean' in the Anglican Church. In a cathedral, the dean is the senior priest on the staff: the cathedral's equivalent to the rector, or incumbent, in a parish. In England, cathedrals are usually self-governing corporations established by royal charter and managed by a body known as the Chapter. The other members of the Chapter are usually called 'canons'. It is also customary to recognise a priest's long service or seniority in a diocese by making him or her an honorary canon or prebendary.

Quite different is the 'rural' or 'area' dean who is a priest whom the bishop invites to exercise a measure of supervision over and pastoral support for the parishes and clergy of a given area (usually known as a deanery). Within the Anglican structure of synodical government, the deanery is the first synodical level: each deanery has its own synod, of which the rural or area dean is a chairperson, and to which each parish sends representatives. Rural deans usually take responsibility for parishes where there is a clerical vacancy.

The third kind of dean is a member of staff in some university and theological colleges, and need not necessarily even be ordained! It will depend on the statutes of the college concerned.

Revd Catherine Ogle is a mother, a priest at All Hallows' Church, and religious affairs reporter for BBC Radio Leeds.

Sector ministers

In the complex society of the twentieth century an approach to ministry based only on the traditional Anglican parish structure is not flexible enough. There are many situations in which ministry is needed which fall outside the scope of parishes. Chaplaincies in hospitals, prisons, colleges and the armed forces are good examples, in which priests with special responsibility and experience are needed. There are groups within society, such as the profoundly deaf, for example, for whom ministry requires specialist skills and training. And dioceses are increasingly discovering that they need people with specialised skills of other kinds to support and develop the ministry of the church in its parishes – industrial missioners, evangelists, trainers of clergy and lay people, spiritual directors, advisers in education, ecumenism, world mission, youth work, parish development and social concern – the list is potentially as complex as modern society itself.

Not all these 'sector ministers' will be priests, of course. Some are lay people, and others are deacons, especially when they are women in Provinces where only men may be ordained priest. But the church can usually employ clergy in such posts more cheaply than similarly qualified lay people (especially if the post involves 'dual responsibility' for a parish as well as the sector ministry), and clergy are often judged more likely to have the necessary theological training for such work than lay people, though they may be less well qualified in other ways. And in most Provinces, employing clergy usually means employing priests, especially if the job is a dual one, since only a priest can provide the sacramental ministry which the parish side of dual appointment calls for.

Women and priesthood

One of the great subjects of debate among Anglicans in recent years has been whether or not women may be ordained to the order of priests. To the outsider the debate may seem rather extraordinary, generating more heat than light, and dealing with issues which seem incomprehensible or simply irrelevant. To those who are involved it has challenged deeply held theological convictions and led to passionate exchanges and not a little pain.

One Province of the Anglican Communion which recently took the step of ordaining women as priests is Scotland. Not long before, the Church in Wales took the decision not to do so. The first ordinations of women to the priesthood in England took place in April 1994 but the first time women were ordained to the priesthood in the Anglican Communion was on Advent Sunday 1971, in Hong Kong. Canada and Uganda have had women priests for more than ten years, and New Zealand for more than twenty, so the idea is scarcely new.

Some of those who oppose this development point to the fact that Christ was male, and argue that, since it is the function of priests to represent Christ, they too must be male. They appeal to the fact that all Christ's disciples were male, and that it was the universal practice of the worldwide Church until the second half of the twentieth century to restrict priesthood to men. For some people the chief difficulty lies in whether the Anglican Church has the theological (as opposed to legal) authority to make such a change. Others argue that biblical teaching about 'headship' or authority in the church clearly rules out the possibility that a woman might be in a position of ultimate authority.

Those who support the ordination of women believe that what matters about Christ's incarnation was not his gender but his being human. They point out that the very first witnesses of the resurrection were women, and claim that the predominance of men in leadership roles in the New Testament and in church history simply reflects male-dominated social structures which always characterised human society until the introduction of effective birth control. And they can point to a small but very distinguished succession of women who have, from time to time, had enormous influence for good on the church. They argue that including women in the church's ordained leadership will restore to it a dimension of completeness which it has previously lacked. And they point to the widespread sense among women that they have received God's call to this ministry.

Experience in Provinces of the Anglican Communion where women have been ordained priests suggests that the most convincing argument in favour has been the church's experience of receiving their ministry. In effect the problems of all but those most intractably opposed have simply disappeared when women have taken their place as priests alongside men. It is still early in the experience of Anglican parishes in England but the signs are that this pattern is repeating itself. Some people in the Church of England, however, feel that the commendable efforts that have been made to provide compensation and alternative structures of episcopal jurisdiction (so-called 'flying bishops') for those who opposed the General Synod's decision to go ahead have had the effect of allowing the minority to dictate terms to the majority.

Women bishops?

Canada and the USA already have female suffragan bishops. New Zealand has a female diocesan. Clearly,

Penelope Jamieson (Dunedin, New Zealand), was the first woman to be consecrated a diocesan bishop (1990).

opening the priesthood to women leads inevitably to the question of women bishops. The 1988 Lambeth Conference resolved that each Province should respect the right of other Provinces to make up their own mind about female bishops, without this meaning that they accepted the principle involved. Provinces which differ are urged to maintain the highest possible degree of communion with each other, and, even where communion is 'impaired', to maintain courteous and open communications with bishops of both sexes. Where women are ministering as bishops already, there is widespread acceptance of their ministry; but this may be because those who cannot accept it have left the mainstream Anglican Church and formed 'continuing' Provinces or dioceses of their own.

Deacons

By contrast with priests, the traditional role of deacons in the Anglican Church has been very limited. All Anglican clergy are ordained deacon first, and then, normally a year later, they are ordained again as priests; in effect, therefore, being a deacon is a kind of preparatory period before someone becomes a priest. The main practical difference between the two orders is that priests may preside at celebrations of Holy Communion, and pronounce the liturgical absolution and blessing on the congregation, whereas deacons may not.

But deacons are not always priests in preparation. In Provinces of the Anglican Communion where women may not yet be ordained to the priesthood, there will be two kinds of deacon – those who are serving their probationary period before being ordained priest (who will be men) and those who will remain deacons permanently (who will be women). And in some dioceses, (including some where women are ordained to the priesthood) attempts are now being made to create a permanent diaconate for both men and women.

Both these situations raise questions about the difference between deacons and priests. Where women are permanent deacons because they are women, it is often quite difficult, apart from the sacramental actions (presiding, absolving and blessing) that only priests may perform, to distinguish between their ministry and that of their colleagues who are priests. Women deacons may be pastorally responsible for parishes or district churches. They will preach and minister to the sick, and offer all the other ministries that priests offer. To many lay people their ministry looks so much like that of priests that it is hard to understand why they cannot do all the things that priests can do. On the other hand, where dioceses have tried to create a permanent diaconate they have usually done so on the basis that the deacon's ministry ought to be directed 'outwards', in service to the wider community beyond the church, rather than 'inwards' towards the care and nurture of the church itself, as is the case with the ministry of priests.

The future for deacons

It is probably true to say that the Anglican Communion as a whole is less sure about what the ministry of deacons should be than it is about either priests or bishops. Experiments are going on in a number of places at the present time, and it seems likely that there will be changes in the pattern of diaconal ministry in the near future. One of the things which has helped to move the church towards such changes has been the growing movement towards the ordination of women to the priesthood in the Anglican Church. A side effect of this is that it 'releases' the diaconate from being primarily a ministry for women, and enables new thinking and development to take place.

Places

Ordained ministry is not the only organisational pattern in Anglicanism. As I have already explained in writing about clergy, it has always gone hand in hand with a sense of responsibility for places. But this sense of geographical identity works in different ways in different places.

Parishes

The variety is most obvious with the basic Anglican unit, the parish. As I explained when describing the role of priests, all parishes are geographical areas, but the way people experience the meaning of what a parish is varies from province to province. This is because the basic idea was exported from England, where the church is a legal part of the national constitution, and the parish is also a civil administrative area, to places where there was no established church, or where some other faith was recognised as the state religion, and parishes were purely 'private' ecclesiastical arrangements.

Variations on the parish theme
This can lead to interesting variations. In England there is a dense network of parish churches, and Anglican church buildings far outnumber those of all other denominations. There is almost always one within ten miles of wherever you happen to be; as you drive around the countryside you are seldom out of sight of an Anglican church. In Scotland, by contrast, Anglican churches are far less visible; here, it is not the Anglican Church but the Presbyterian Church of Scotland which is the 'church by law established', and the parishes of Scotland are Presbyterian ones; Anglican churches are very much in the minority. Things are different again in the vast spaces of Australia and Canada, where individual parishes are often geographically larger than whole dioceses in England, though their population is likely to be smaller than many English parishes.

Where the Anglican Church has developed in aboriginal communities in countries like New Zealand and Canada, the experience of being a parish among these first-nations people is sometimes closer to that of English Anglicans than to how it is for white Christians in the country concerned. The close-knit social structure of such native peoples leads to a corporate focus of church life, in which the whole community is, in some sense, perceived as (at least potentially) the Church. This contrasts with the more individualistic approach to church membership in white parishes, where the church's mission is more likely to be directed at the needs (both social and spiritual) of individual people, than at the corporate life of the community.

Dioceses and Provinces
In some ways it is the diocese, not the parish, that is at the heart of Anglican organisation. This is because of the way the Anglican Communion sees its bishops. Unlike the Roman Catholic Church, the Anglican Communion is not a single worldwide authority structure (like a pyramid with the pope at the top). It is really a worldwide federation of dioceses. Each diocesan bishop is, in a very real way, autonomous in his (or her) own diocese. Each dio-

cese, therefore, has its own administrative structures, balances its own budget, employs its own staff, ordains its own clergy, and is responsible for its own discipline. It is the responsibility of each bishop to secure the unity of this worldwide federation by acting in solidarity with fellow bishops. Each diocese is divided into a number of parishes, all of which are under the care of the diocesan bishop, often assisted by suffragans. When the bishop appoints clergy to posts within the diocese, that care (the 'cure of souls') is shared with the persons appointed.

Over the centuries this pattern of diocesan and episcopal organisation has been modified in various ways. For example, dioceses have grouped themselves together into Provinces, and one of the bishops has been appointed or elected as archbishop of the Province, with a role of leadership and ministry among the college of bishops. As the practice of synodical church government has spread, so in most countries the Provinces have grouped themselves into a single, nationwide church governed by a General Synod. General Synods usually have powers to make binding decisions for the whole national church. Anglicans are still working at the many questions that arise from trying to graft this representative, 'bottom-up' synodical pattern of government onto a personal, 'top-down', episcopal pattern of authority and leadership. But the basic idea of a federation of bishops, taking counsel together for the leadership of their dioceses, is deep at the heart of what the Anglican way is all about.

Dioceses are usually divided into administrative units of different sizes: archdeaconries and deaneries. I have explained the roles of archdeacons and deans already; archdeaconries and deaneries are simply the geographical areas within which they exercise their responsibilities. Deaneries are also synodical units, with their own synod, which elects members to the diocesan synod.

The Anglican Communion

The worldwide Anglican Church is known as 'the Anglican Communion', a name which reflects its essentially federal nature. Traditionally, the Archbishop of Canterbury presides over the Anglican Communion, but the role is one of influence, not of power, for the Communion has no legislative powers over the Provinces. There is no worldwide Anglican synod, and no bishop of bishops.

Even the Lambeth Conference, which meets every ten years, is only a consultative body, at whose sessions the bishops of the various Provinces take counsel together. It has no legislative powers. Nor does the Anglican Consultative Council, which is the continuing 'committee' of the worldwide Anglican Communion. These are bodies dedicated to the search for a common mind and common policies, but always respecting the right and responsibility of each diocese, under the leadership of its bishop, to take responsibility for its own mission and ministry in its own context.

Other Orders

Alongside the bishops, priests and deacons of the Anglican Communion there are a number of other organisations, communities and structures that, in a variety of ways, give expression to the principle of order. Some of these we shall look at in a moment under the heading of lay ministry, but there are two movements that need separate treatment.

The Church Army

The first is the Church Army, a lay evangelistic order founded in 1882. In some ways its story is not unlike that of the much bigger Salvation Army, though the Church Army has always worked on the principle that its officers are under the authority and within the context of Anglican parishes. Like the Salvation Army, the Church Army moved into social concern from its original, purely evangelistic origins, though it is probably fair to say that evangelism has remained its number one priority. Church Army officers generally serve as stipendiary (i.e. salaried) lay members of parish ministry teams in situations where outreach and church planting (especially among the socially deprived members of the community) are priorities.

The Church Army is active in many of the Provinces of the Anglican Communion providing evangelistic and social ministry. In parts of western Canada the title 'Church Army' is also used among some native American communities for a lay-led midweek charismatic gathering that takes place within the Anglican parish, but this has no connection now with the Church Army as an international Anglican society.

Anglican religious orders

A catholic impetus of prayer and social concern is represented by over one hundred and fifty religious orders (mainly for lay people) throughout the Anglican Communion. The modern history of these religious orders begins in the nineteenth century. The medieval religious orders were all suppressed at the time of the Reformation, and it was only after the revival of catholic theology and spirituality associated with the Oxford Movement in the 1830s that it was possible to re-establish a society of religious in the Church of England. The first such society was the Society of the Holy Trinity, founded in 1845, on the contemplative model of the Roman Catholic Poor Clares. It was followed during the 1850s and 1860s by a whole series of foundations, some of which were for the contemplative life of prayer and meditation, while others were teaching, nursing or caring orders. Religious orders have continued to be founded, not just in England but throughout the Anglican world, up to the present day. In some cases the members of these orders take the monastic vows of obedience, stability and conversion of life, and live in an enclosed community. In most, however, the three religious vows of poverty, chastity and obedience are taken, and the members follow the religious life of prayer and work in the context of a vocation to ministry in the world.

Members of the religious communities work in many

The Dunloe Centre for the homeless in East London.

different aspects of ministry. In particular, with the widespread current interest in spirituality and contemplative prayer, their ministry is increasingly in demand as spiritual directors, retreat conductors and advisers and guides in prayer.

Ministry for all

The ministry

Q. Who are the ministers of the church?

A. The ministers of the church are lay persons, bishops, priests, and deacons.

Q. What is the ministry of the laity?

A. The ministry of lay persons is to represent Christ and his Church; to bear witness to him wherever they may be; and, according to the gifts given them, to carry on Christ's work of reconciliation in the world; and to take their place in the life, worship, and governance of the Church.

The Catechism, The Episcopal Church (USA) 1979

One of the most important developments in worldwide Anglicanism at the present time is the widespread rediscovery of the ministry of all God's people. This represents a major shift in thinking. For centuries the common pattern of the Anglican Church was for the clergy to be seen as 'the Church', and for everyone else to be regarded as the laity (from the Greek, *laos*, a people). Those who were to be ordained were commonly spoken of as 'going into the Church', as though, when they were lay people, they were somehow less 'in the Church' than the clergy. The word 'lay', itself, of course, carries a whole range of shades of meaning, some of which are not very complimentary. It has often been used in the sense of 'non-professional', 'untrained', or 'inexperienced'. This reflects the way in which people used to think about the difference between clergy and 'laity', which was a distortion of what the Church is supposed to be.

In the New Testament, it is the whole Church, including its leaders, who make up the *laos* or people of God. And the whole Church is called to ministry or service. One of the ways in which Anglicans in many parts of the world have experienced renewal in the recent past is in the rediscovery of the truth that baptism is not only a rite of entry but a commissioning to service. All the members of God's people, therefore, are called to serve each other and the world around them.

Churchwarden

One of the oldest expressions of 'lay ministry' is the office of churchwarden, which was legally recognised in England by the thirteenth century. By the fifteenth century two churchwardens were chosen in every parish by all the adult parishioners, at an annual parish meeting, to care for the property of the church and to be guardians of morality. Today, in England, churchwardens are legally responsible for the fabric and contents of churches, for maintaining good order in the church and churchyard, for allocating seats, and for the provision of public worship during periods when there is no incumbent. They are, technically, officers of the bishop, and must account for their stewardship of the church's goods to the archdeacon each year.

Of course, it has been the pattern for a long time for people to take on certain 'jobs' in the life of their parish. People have cleaned the church, arranged the flowers, made the refreshments, distributed the parish magazine, played the organ, mended the priest's vestments. Some have done more obviously 'spiritual' tasks, like teaching in Sunday School or Junior Church, reading lessons or leading the church's prayers of intercession. Some of those 'jobs' have even been enshrined in the church's official structures, and those who do them are seen as 'officers' like churchwardens and Readers. Most of them have been motivated by the desire to 'help the vicar' with what is perceived to be an increasingly heavy workload.

Shared ministry and leadership in the church often starts like this. The priest is still seen as an authority figure who delegates tasks to others because he (it usually is a 'he') cannot perform them all himself. But what is increasingly growing today, wherever Anglicans worship, is the understanding that ministry is not something that belongs to the clergy, who sometimes delegate bits of it to other people. Rather, it is something which is essentially collaborative, for which all the people of God are responsible together.

New patterns of leadership

This has led parishes throughout the Anglican Communion to begin exploring ways in which lay people may share with the clergy not just the doing of 'jobs' but responsibility for leading the ministry and mission of the whole church. Clergy are increasingly being seen as enablers and trainers of the ministry of others, rather than as the people who will do all the ministry themselves. In the process, the Anglican Church has begun to think in new ways about what its mission to God's world is meant to be. It has also begun to explore all sorts of new patterns of leadership in the local church.

Many of these are based on the principle of teamwork, with groups of people sharing responsibility together for leadership and bringing a variety of different gifts to the common task. Some parishes have introduced 'eldership' schemes, with certain lay people being chosen or elected as elders; others have begun to develop 'local ministry teams'; yet others have tried to build on existing patterns of ministry like Readers, churchwardens and vestry or Church Council Standing Committees. In a period of experimentation like the present, it is very difficult to see which directions will be fruitful for the future and which will be blind alleys. What is clear, however, is that the shape of ministry, especially at local church level, is changing before our eyes, and that the role of clergy and other traditional expressions of ministry, will inevitably change with it.

What the future holds for ministry it is impossible to say in detail, but two things are clear: the ministry of the future will have to make room for the Holy Spirit's

Reader

The office of Reader was first introduced by Archbishop Parker in 1561 to provide for ministry in poor parishes 'destitute of incumbents'. Readers, who served mainly in the north of England, were never very numerous, and the order seems to have died out by the middle of the eighteenth century. It was revived in 1866, partly in response to the needs of a dramatically increasing population in the industrial cities, and a shortage of clergy to minister to them. The office soon came to include a variety of different types of lay ministry which had been developing piecemeal in the Victorian church to assist the clergy. These included catechists, teachers, lay preachers and evangelists. The early Readers were pastors, teachers and leaders of worship, especially in unconsecrated buildings and informal situations. They were not permitted to preach when a clergyman was present, and they might not use the pulpit! Today there are over eight thousand Readers in the Church of England, and thousands more in the worldwide Anglican Communion. In England the office of Reader is the only voluntary lay ministry which is nationally accredited, episcopally licensed and governed by canon.

Questions

1. How appropriate for the Christian Church in the twenty-first century is a pattern of ministry whose roots lie in the Middle Ages and whose structure is based on the devolution of power?
2. Were the Anglican Provinces that have ordained women to the priesthood right to do so? What about women bishops? Should the Church of England have permitted female bishops at the same time as female priests? What reasons might there be for not allowing women to be bishops even though they may be priests?
3. The Church will always need clergy, but it may not always be able to pay them. What would be the consequences if Anglican parishes in the future were largely led by self-supporting (non-stipendiary) clergy? Would this be a good development or a bad one?

sovereign activity in bestowing gifts among the people of God, and accept that God's kingdom is not a hierarchy of power but a sharing in service. It will, therefore, be a ministry in which it is recognised that the ordained and non-ordained both have a vital part to play, the loss of either of which would damage the whole. Such ministry will require support that can make available resources, enable leadership, provide communications, build team relationships, exercise discernment; and it will be in lending support of this kind that the ministry of the clergy is likely to find its most natural expression.

13

Church government

Michael Botting

'Fog in Channel – Europe isolated' ran a famous *Punch* cartoon years ago, when England still regarded herself as the centre of the universe. Until fairly recently, a similar isolationist view has been true of the majority of those who regarded themselves as members of the Church of England, especially in rural areas. For such the Anglican Church was embodied in their parish church building and their local vicar. This attitude was illustrated for me when, in the mid-1970s, as vicar of a large city-centre parish, I was aware that church members were far more concerned about the impending appointment of a new curate than they were of a new bishop for the diocese. However synodical government, Alternative Services and a serious curtailment of finance in many places has at last begun to alter this narrow parochial mentality.

This parochialism must not be dismissed out of hand. The primary activities of committed Christians include worship, witness to Jesus as their Lord and Saviour and practical concern for their neighbours. These will all be best achieved locally. There is a real element of truth in the quip in England that many people do not come to church, but at least it is the Church of England they don't come to! Everybody in England lives in a parish and this has the particular advantage that if they want to worship at, say, a popular festival such as Christmas or require a service at a special time in their lives such as baptism or marriage, it is to the parish church or vicarage they come. Should they be in hospital or prison they are likely to be visited by an Anglican chaplain. Indeed there may even be an official Anglican priest as Stores or Industrial Chaplain at their place of work.

For many active parishioners what happens at the local level is really what matters. But just as we expect everybody over 18 to take seriously their right from time to time to vote in national and local elections, and for some to take on a much deeper involvement in civic affairs, so there is a wider involvement that every responsible Anglican needs to take seriously to a greater or lesser degree. To do so means having a basic knowledge of how the Anglican Church is governed, and how local church members are represented in the corridors of power. It is to these matters that the remainder of this chapter is devoted. We shall be mainly concerned with what happens in England, but shall make some reference to inevitable differences elsewhere.

The Crown

Queen Elizabeth II is 'Supreme Governor' of the Church of England, and 'Defender of the Faith'.

When Queen Elizabeth II first opened Parliament as the new monarch in 1952 she promised to uphold the Christian and Protestant faith. In Westminster Abbey on 2nd June 1953 she made the Coronation Oath in response to the Archbishop of Canterbury's question:

> *Archbishop:* Will you to the utmost of your power maintain the Laws of God and the true profession of the Gospel? Will you to the utmost of your power maintain in the United Kingdom the Protestant Reformed Religion established by law? Will you maintain and preserve inviolably the settlement of the Church of England, and the doctrine, worship, discipline and government thereof, as by law established in England? And will you preserve unto the Bishops and Clergy of England, and to the Churches there committed to their charge, all such rights and privileges, as by law do or shall appertain to them or any of them?
> *Queen:* All this I promise to do.

The Queen then made her Solemn Oath, laying her hand on the Holy Gospel in the Great Bible and saying these words:

> The things which I have here before promised, I will perform and keep. So help me God.

The Queen then kissed the Bible and signed the Oath. The effect of the Declaration and Oath is in fact retrospective, seeing that the Queen became both Supreme Governor of the United Kingdom and of the Church of England at the precise moment her father, George VI, died. However her status shows itself in the giving of Royal Assent to legislation that relates to the church and by nominating as bishops those whose names are given to her by the Prime Minister. The Queen's Royal Assent consummates both state and church action.

Crown appointments include:

1. Diocesan and suffragan (sometimes called area) bishops. The latter assist the former and have a specific area for which they are responsible.
2. Deans of most English cathedrals, Europe and Sodor and Man being two exceptions.
3. Royal Peculiars, like Westminster Abbey and St George's Chapel, Windsor, which are outside diocesan oversight and come directly under the personal jurisdiction of the monarch.
4. Incumbents to a number of parish churches, known as 'Crown Livings', and to parochial vacancies that occur due to the appointment of the incumbent to a bishopric.

The Queen's unique relationship with the Church of England is further seen in her attending and inaugurating the General Synod at each quinquennium, issuing Royal Mandates for the consecration of new diocesan bishops and summoning them to the Palace to pay homage. She is further seen annually at the presentation of the Royal Maundy on Maundy Thursday, attending public worship at Sandringham parish church at Christmas and occasionally at royal weddings in Westminster Abbey or St Paul's Cathedral, London.

Cathedral clergy

The dean has ultimate responsibility for a cathedral, assisted by canons residentiary. The equivalent position to dean in the cathedrals of more recent foundation is called a provost. The latter cathedrals are known as 'parish church cathedrals'. This means that, when they were elevated to the rank of cathedral, they retained their parish, their patron and the provost also held the office of incumbent. A canon residentiary is a member of a chapter of priests serving in a cathedral, has incumbent status and is provided with stipend and free accommodation. The Greater Chapter of a cathedral includes a number of honorary canons. They are appointed by the diocesan bishop, and selected because they are regarded as the more senior members of the diocesan clergy. They have a stall in the cathedral chancel.

Royal Maundy

Royal Maundy are specially minted coins distributed by the British sovereign to a selected group of poor people. An equal number of men and women are chosen, the number for each being the same as the number of years the sovereign has been on the throne.

The appointment of bishops

It will be clear from the above paragraphs that technically the Crown appoints the bishops of the Church of England. How does the Queen know whom to choose? Whether it be a diocesan or a suffragan bishop the name is forwarded to the monarch by the Prime Minister. However, the route by which he or she gets names varies somewhat. When a vacancy for a diocesan bishop occurs the Vacancy-in-See Committee is summoned. This Committee is attended by the Prime Minister's Appointments Secretary and the Archbishop's Appointments Secretary. A description of the vacant see is prepared and a statement is drawn up of what is required in the future diocesan. These documents

Vacancy-in-See

There is a Vacancy-in-See Committee in every diocese which consists of some elected members of the clergy and laity together with the suffragan bishop(s), archdeacons, dean/provost of the cathedral, the clerical and lay members of the General Synod, the chairmen of the Houses of Clergy and Laity of the Diocesan Synod. It is always in existence even when there is no vacancy.

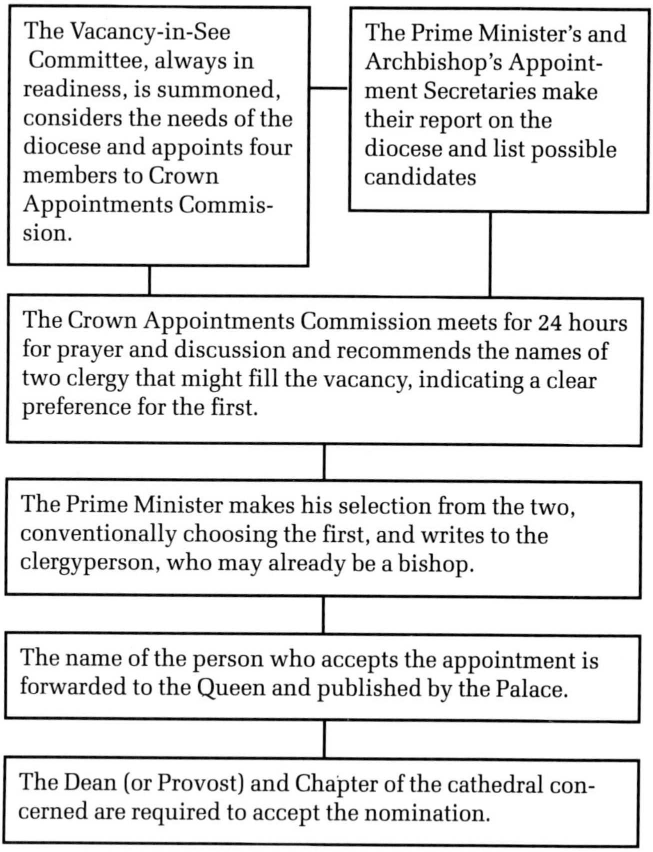

Chart showing the route to an appointment of a diocesan bishop

Upon a See becoming vacant:

The Vacancy-in-See Committee, always in readiness, is summoned, considers the needs of the diocese and appoints four members to Crown Appointments Commission.	The Prime Minister's and Archbishop's Appointment Secretaries make their report on the diocese and list possible candidates

The Crown Appointments Commission meets for 24 hours for prayer and discussion and recommends the names of two clergy that might fill the vacancy, indicating a clear preference for the first.

The Prime Minister makes his selection from the two, conventionally choosing the first, and writes to the clergyperson, who may already be a bishop.

The name of the person who accepts the appointment is forwarded to the Queen and published by the Palace.

The Dean (or Provost) and Chapter of the cathedral concerned are required to accept the nomination.

Note:

The person selected is consecrated a bishop if not already one.

The bishop pays homage to the Monarch and swears allegiance.

The new bishop is enthroned/installed in the cathedral by the Dean/Provost.

The Crown Appointments Commission

The Crown Appointments Commission was established by the General Synod in February 1977 to consider vacancies in diocesan bishoprics in the Provinces of Canterbury and York, and candidates for appointments to them. The members are the Archbishops of Canterbury and York and three members each elected from the Houses of Clergy and Laity of the General Synod. They are assisted by the two non-voting Appointment Secretaries to advise them.

are forwarded to the Crown Appointments Commission.

The Vacancy-in-See Committee also elect by single transferable vote four of their number to represent them on the Crown Appointments Commission and they also discuss with them possible names of those who might be considered for appointment. Meanwhile the two Appointment Secretaries do their own research as to the type of person who should be appointed, by conferring with a wide range of interested parties in the diocese, including a variety of church people, members of other denominations, other faiths and leading citizens. They then make their own report to the Crown Appointments Commission, the members of which can offer names in advance to the Appointment Secretaries, so that CV and other details of the persons named can be provided.

The Commission then meets for twenty-four hours for prayer, worship and discussion, considering first the needs of the diocese and then the names of those who might best fulfil those needs. In due course two names are passed to the Prime Minister with a clear indication of the Commission's preference. It is convention that the Prime Minister always selects the first, but he or she is under no obligation to do so. Although it is thought that on occasion the second name has been chosen, no one knows for certain, and it is always possible that the first person named had refused.

The name of the clergyman who has accepted the nomination is then forwarded to the Queen and the Palace publishes it. The dean (or provost) and greater chapter of the cathedral concerned are required to approve. If not already a bishop the person is duly consecrated (that is ordained a bishop), the chief consecrator normally being the archbishop of the Province in which the vacant diocese is situated. All other bishops, who are able to attend the Consecration, also share in laying hands on the episcopal candidate. As mentioned above the new bishop pays homage to the monarch, kissing hands and swearing allegiance. Finally the new bishop is enthroned or installed by the dean (or provost) in the cathedral.

Suffragan (or assistant) bishop

With regard to the appointment of a suffragan (or assistant) bishop no vacancy-in-see committee or Crown Appointments Commission is involved. The General Synod report 'Senior Church Appointments' summarises the procedure as follows:

'... the diocesan bishop submits a petition with two names of whom the first is his preferred candidate although it is now accepted practice that the second must also be a genuine possibility, in case, for example, the first-named person dies before the appointment is made.

Although he is not required to do so as a matter of law, the diocesan bishop in practice consults the archbishop of the Province beforehand, as well as anyone else he wishes, and when the petition is sent to the Prime Minister it is accompanied by a letter from the archbishop of the Province supporting both names but preferring the first. The Prime Minister has, for at least the last hundred years, advised the sovereign to accept the first-named person (provided he is available for appointment).'

The bishops in the House of Lords

One of the reasons advanced for the Prime Minister to have at least some say in the appointment of bishops is because twenty-six diocesans have a right to take their seats in the House of Lords. They are commonly known as the 'Lords Spiritual'. The Archbishops of Canterbury and York together with the Bishops of London, Durham and Winchester have seats as of right. The twenty-one other seats are filled in order of seniority. The Bishops of Sodor and Man and of Gibraltar in Europe are not eligible.

The special privilege is no easy task, for it brings considerable responsibility. One bishop, shortly expecting to take his seat, asked another, who had taken his some time before, what difference it would make to his work? 'It will just increase your guilt' was the discouraging reply. All bishops are grossly overworked if they are attempting to fulfil their episcopate properly. To have to spend several weeks a year on official duty in the House of Lords, and from time to time to prepare relevant and well-researched speeches, can be very time consuming. Votes following debates on important moral issues or on education, say, can be especially hard on bishops from the northern Province.

By law established

The laws of England are determined by Act of Parliament. The present relationship between Parliament and the Church of England underwent fundamental changes as a result of the Church of England Assembly (Powers) Act 1919, always known as the Enabling Act. This Act affected the government of the church from top to bottom, from the old Church Assembly to Parochial Church Council. In 1920 the Upper House of Convocation (i.e. bishops) and the Lower House (i.e. clergy) of the northern (York) and southern (Canterbury) Provinces were joined with the House of Laity to form a single National Assembly of the Church of England. This body was granted by Parliament powers to draft legislation, insofar as the Church of England was governed by statute. These powers have now passed to the General Synod, which effectively came into existence in 1970, of which more later.

The consequence of the Enabling Act is that the church has total freedom to revise and amend its own laws, save only that they have finally to be forwarded to Parliament as draft Measures, which are then vetted by an Ecclesiastical Committee (originally set up under the Enabling Act). This Committee decides whether it is appropriate for the Measures to be laid before the Lords and Commons, who only have the limited powers to say 'Yes' or 'No'. Assuming the former is given in both Houses the Measures in due course become part of the law of England. With the notable, indeed notorious, exception of the 1927 and 1928 Prayer Books, it is extremely rare for either House to say 'No'. Notable amongst the legislation that Parliament approved was the Pastoral Measure 1968, as a result of which many of its powers were devolved to the church authorities.

The Church of England is unique among the churches of the worldwide Anglican Communion in being ultimately governed by the lay secular authority, namely the Queen in Parliament.

Other Anglican churches

All other churches in the Anglican Communion are synodical or self-governing and self-financing. Their method of appointing bishops is outlined in 'Episcopal Ministry', the report of the Archbishops' Group on the Episcopate 1990 as follows:

> The solution . . . falls into three main categories. In the first, the choice is made by election within the vacant diocese, in which both clergy and laity participate, sometimes voting by houses, sometimes together. Often there is a requirement for a special majority. Invariably the choice of the diocese has to be confirmed – e.g. by the bench of bishops in the Scottish Episcopal church, or by reference to the Standing Committee of the dioceses in New Zealand. A second major category comprises cases where the choice is made on a provincial basis. Thus in Wales, when a diocese becomes vacant, the provincial electoral college assembles, with representation from all six dioceses of the Province, but with the vacant diocese doubling its representation for the occasion. A third main (but smaller) category is of dioceses which stand alone geographically. In such a case, the clergy and laity of the diocese make their choice, which must then be confirmed by the Archbishop of Canterbury. In all three categories there is usually in each case a 'reserve' power, providing for the case where the electoral body is unable to agree (or to obtain the required majority for any one candidate). In such a case the choice usually falls to the House of Bishops of the Province or (in the case of an extraprovincial diocese), to the Archbishop of Canterbury.

Authority in the Church of England

There are a number of centres of authority in the church, which normally provide valuable checks and for healthy administration.

For more than six hundred years Lambeth Palace has been the official residence of the Archbishop of Canterbury. In 1867 the palace was the venue for the first Lambeth Conference attended by 76 bishops.

Lambeth

The official London residence of the Archbishop of Canterbury is Lambeth Palace on the south bank of the River Thames. Next to the monarch he is the first citizen of the land, chief spokesman for the church in the House of Lords and in the English media. Apart from the obvious fact that he is automatically Chairman of the House of Bishops, General Synod and Church Commissioners, his authority lies more in his person than in his actual powers.

Ever since 1867, and approximately every ten years, the incumbent archbishop has called together bishops throughout the Anglican Communion for the Lambeth Conference, originally meeting at Lambeth Palace, later at Church House, Westminster and more recently at Canterbury. The results of the deliberations are more advisory than authoritative, an example being the recommendation, originating with African bishops, that the final ten years of the twentieth century should be declared a Decade of Evangelism.

The bishops

The responsibility of the bishop in the Church of England today, especially the diocesan bishop, is summarised in the Declaration that the archbishop makes to the bishop-elect at Consecration:

> A bishop is called to lead in serving and caring for the people of God and to work with them in the oversight of the Church. As a chief pastor he shares with his fellow

> bishops a special responsibility to maintain and further the unity of the Church, to uphold its discipline, and to guard its faith.
>
> *ASB 1980, p. 388*

Further responsibilities include promoting mission, teaching the Gospel of Christ, ordaining new ministers and having special care for those in need.

Every time a new incumbent is instituted into a parish the bishop shares the Cure of Souls which is 'both yours and mine'. In practice the bishop will leave the new incumbent to do most of the work, only returning to the parish to take confirmations, possibly share in some major anniversary, deal with any serious pastoral problems that may arise, and visit the clergy should they fall ill.

Nowadays the diocesan bishop has a very considerable administrative responsibility, which is shared with the senior staff – suffragan bishops, archdeacons, diocesan secretary etc. Bishops work through a Bishop's Council and Diocesan Standing Committee, which determines the general pastoral, evangelistic and financial work of the diocese and the agenda of the diocesan synod. A substantial amount of the bishop's time is taken up with appointing men and women to positions of special responsibility in the diocese. For example:

Archdeacon, who has particular responsibilities relating to the material and temporal resources of the church. These duties are especially seen at institutions of new incumbents, when the bishop instructs the archdeacon to induct the rector/vicar into the temporalities of the benefice. Every year the archdeacon is required to hold a visitation of the churches in the Archdeaconry to enquire from the churchwardens about the state of all the churches and churchyards and their appurtenances (i.e. property).

Rural (or area) dean, who is normally an incumbent, but also oversees a group of parishes, known as a Deanery. He or she will meet with fellow clergy approximately monthly, to discuss matters of common local concern, church reports, means to collaborative ministry etc. The rural dean will also call together the lay people elected to the deanery synod about four times a year, sharing the oversight of that body with a locally elected lay chairperson.

Benefice

In England the entire country is divided up into Church of England parishes, which normally have a church building where public worship is conducted, marriages solemnised etc. The person authorised to be responsible for these activities is the incumbent, usually known as the rector or vicar, who is provided with a free parsonage house in which he or she and the family must live. This provision is known as a Benefice which is endowed with fixed capital assets. A wide variety of people or institutions have the right of patronage to offer people benefices in their gift, including the Crown, university colleges, patronage trusts and private individuals. The most usual patron in a diocese is the diocesan bishop.

Warden of Readers, who has the general oversight of the training and care of (lay) Readers in the diocese, usually assisted by deputy wardens in each deanery.

Sector ministry posts, whose occupants may be responsible to promote social work, education, more general lay training, etc.

Appointments to benefices, of which the bishop is the patron.

The work relating to ordinations will mostly be shared centrally with the Advisory Board of Ministry, which advises the House of Bishops in this matter, and locally with the Diocesan Director of Ordinands, who is the bishop's officer. All diocesan bishops also have to share in the membership of various central church boards.

Synodical government

In 1969 the Synodical Government Measure No. 1 was passed, ushering in a new era in the government of the Church of England. The new General Synod opened offically on Wednesday, 4th November 1970 with a memorable service of Holy Communion in Westminster Abbey in the presence of the Queen, the Lord Chancellor, the Prime Minister and others. This was followed by the inaugural session in Church House next door, where the Queen, accompanied by the Duke of Edinburgh, addressed the Synod. The powers of the Synod simply follow those of the former Church Assembly as far as the state is concerned, but it has brought the Houses of Bishops, clergy and laity together into a much closer and integrated way. All elections are by the single transferable vote, by far the fairest form of proportional representation and particularly recommended by the Electoral Reform Society.

The House of Bishops consists of all 44 diocesans together with nine suffragan or assistant bishops elected from their own number. The House of Clergy consists mainly of elected representatives from each diocese by the clergy holding a full licence in the diocese, exact numbers being in proportion to the numbers of clergy in each diocese. They are called proctors. Each diocese is also represented by at least one archdeacon. To this number is added 15 deans or provosts of cathedrals elected from their own number and representative of the Services, prison chaplains, universities and religious

ANNUAL PAROCHIAL CHURCH MEETING *elects*

(a) **PAROCHIAL CHURCH COUNCIL**

House of clergy
Incumbent and other licensed clergy (not elected)
Ex-officio Synod members
Co-opted members

House of laity
A specified number of representatives (elected by the Annual Parochial Church Meeting)
Licensed lay workers (ex-officio)
The churchwardens (ex-officio)
Ex-officio Synod members
Readers
Co-opted members

(b) **DEANERY SYNOD**

House of clergy
All incumbents and other licensed clergy *elect* (not elected)
Members of General Synod and Diocesan Synod (ex-officio)
One retired member of the clergy
Co-opted members

House of laity
A specified number of parochial representatives (elected by the Annual Parochial Church Meeting) *elects*
Licensed lay workers
Ex-officio Synod members
Co-opted members

(c) **DIOCESAN SYNOD**

House of bishops
The Diocesan Bishop
Suffragan or assistant bishop (not elected)

House of clergy
A specified number of representatives (elected by the Deanery Synod house of clergy)
Ex-officio members – dean or provost, archdeacons, proctors in Convocation, the chancellor (if clerical), the chairman of the Board of Finance (if clerical)
Up to five co-opted members
The bishop may nominate up to ten additional members

House of laity
A specified number of representatives (elected by the Deanery Synod house of laity)
Ex-officio members – the chancellor (if lay), the chairman of the Board of Finance (if lay), the members of General Synod
Up to five co-opted members

(d) **GENERAL SYNOD**

House of bishops
(The Upper House*)
All diocesan bishops (not elected)
A number of suffragan or assistant bishops *(elected)*

House of clergy
(The Lower House*)
The proctors (elected by the Deanery Synod house of clergy)

* Convocations

House of laity
A specified number of representatives (elected by the Deanery Synod house of laity)
Ex-officio members (if lay)
The Dean of the Arches & Auditor
Vicar-General of the Province of Canterbury
Vicar-General of the Province of York
The three Church Estates Commissioners
Chairman of the Central Board of Finance
Up to five co-opted members

Church officers

The Dean of Arches, Auditor and Vicars-general are officers responsible for the Ecclesiastical Courts, dealing with the law as it especially applies to the Church of England. Church Estates Commissioners (appointed by Parliament) and the Chairman of the Central Board of Finance are especially responsible for Church of England finances.

communities, making approximately a total of 250.

The House of Laity consists of laity elected by the members of deanery synods, exact numbers being in proportion to numbers on the electoral rolls of each diocese. To this number is added several ex-officio members, namely the Dean of Arches and Auditor, the Vicars-general of the two Provinces, the three Church Estates Commissioners and the chairman of the Central Board of Finance, making approximately a total of 250.

No clergyman or lay person is obliged to stand for General Synod. Those who choose to do so may send out election addresses to the electorate of their Houses, postage paid for by their dioceses. General Synods are elected for a period of five years and, until 1994, met for three groups of sessions in February, July and November, either in London or York. Since 1994 there has been an attempt to reduce the number of groups of sessions to two per year. The dioceses pay all their General Synod members' travelling and accommodation expenses.

Should a General Synod vacancy occur within two years of the main election the top of the list of those who failed to be elected automatically fills the vacancy. Later than that there normally has to be a by-election.

Members of the Synod may stand for election to the Church Commissioners (see below) and to the various boards of the Synod, such as Education, Mission and Social Responsibility. Members automatically become ex-officio members of their diocesan and deanery synod and their Parochial Church Council (PCC).

The agenda of Synod sessions is set by the Standing Committee and covers theological, liturgical, missionary, legislative and financial business. Diocesan synods and private members may propose motions. Frequently debates are on reports previously commissioned by the Synod. The initial debate on the report is on a motion that the Synod will receive it. Assuming it does, the Synod then has to debate what action should be taken. This can mean that it is passed down to lower synods, dioceses or deaneries for their observations by a specified date.

The advent of synodical government has meant that the diocesan conferences of the past became diocesan synods and ruri-decanal conferences became deanery synods. In each case the laity have become more involved. The business of these synods is much the same as the conferences they have replaced, except, as mentioned above, they may from time to time have to debate General Synod business, but they may also send business up to higher synods for debate.

Sometimes it does not work as well as intended. For example, in 1988 the important report 'Children in the Way?' (National Society/Church House Publishing) from the General Synod Board of Education, about the Christian nurture of children, was sent to deaneries, with very specific questions to be answered. In at least one deanery synod, to my personal knowledge, the voting was meaningless. Hardly anyone seemed to have read even a summary of the report, much less the report itself, reflecting a lack of responsible participation.

The 'Enabling Act' of 1919 referred to earlier in this chapter, which brought the Church Assembly into existence, was also responsible for the obligatory creation of Parochial Church Councils. Previously the only obligatory parochial statutory meeting was the annual 'vestry' meeting which, jointly with the incumbent, chose the churchwardens. This still exists and the churchwardens are ex-officio members of the PCC.

In order to elect a Parochial Church Council this necessarily meant that every parish was obliged to have an Electoral Roll. Since the coming of synodical government electoral rolls have to be revised annually for the Annual Church Meeting of the parish, and every six years have to be totally revised and everyone in the parish that is baptised, and wishes to be a member, has to re-apply.

The main function of the PCC is to share with the incumbent in the pastoral, liturgical, evangelistic and financial affairs of the parish, coupled with responsibility for the fabric of the church building and ancillary buildings in the parish. The importance of this level of church government is implied in the opening paragraphs of this chapter. But synodical government has given PCC members a little more responsibility, because those they elect to the deanery synod are those who, in turn, elect to the General Synod.

Church electoral roll

A lay person shall be entitled to have his/her name entered on the roll of a parish if he/she is baptised, of sixteen years or upwards, has signed an application form for enrolment and declares him/herself either:
(a) to be a member of the Church of England or of a Church in communion therewith resident in the parish; or
(b) to be such a member and, not being resident in the parish, to have habitually attended public worship in the parish during a period of six months prior to enrolment; or
(c) to be a member in good standing of a church which subscribes to the doctrine of the Holy Trinity (not being a church in communion with the Church of England) and also prepared to declare him/herself to be a member of the Church of England having habitually attended public worship in the parish during a period of six months prior to enrolment.

The Church Commissioners

One might question whether the Commissioners should technically be called an authority, but it simply has to be acknowledged that 'He that pays the piper calls the tune'.

The stipend

A stipend is a fixed or regular payment made to clergy to enable them to carry out their work and maintain their family without having to have alternative employment. In effect it is their salary. The income tax authorities certainly regard it as such!

Not infrequently in General Synod debates, when there is a call for a report or a commission, the question is asked 'Who pays?' As a result of the Church Commissioners Measure 1947 the Commissioners came into existence on 1st April 1948, uniting the old Ecclesiastical Commissioners and Queen Anne's Bounty. They are really a Parliamentary Trust, holding a large part of the historic resources of the Church of England. From these resources the bishops' and clergy stipends and pensions have been paid.

Because income has not kept pace with required expenditure, it seems increasingly likely that the Commissioners may only be able to afford bishops' stipends, their remaining assets contributing towards pensions for clergy and licensed lay workers.

Church Canon Law

Following the report 'The Canon Law of the Church of England' published in 1947, Canon Law underwent considerable revision especially associated with Archbishop Fisher's period at Canterbury. The Canons Ecclesiastical issued by the Convocations of York in 1964 and 1969 were published in 1969; although Canons do not go through Parliament, they receive the Royal Assent and have the force of law.

The Introduction by Archbishops Michael Ramsey and Donald Coggan states that, with the exception of two Canons, the former Canons dating back to 1603 and those made subsequently, but prior to 1947, have been repealed. No longer are clergy obliged to wear nightcaps in bed!

One of the two unrepealed Canons dealt with the seal of the confessional, that is that information confided to a priest must not be revealed to anyone under any circumstances. The new Canons are in seven sections and deal with matters relating to the Church of England generally, the conduct of public worship, the responsibilities of those in Holy Orders, the Order of Deaconesses, the duties of lay officers, matters relating to church buildings, and the Ecclesiastical Courts. It is apparent that the Canons now need constantly to be kept under review and possible revision.

The voluntary principle

To have a fuller understanding of how the life of the Church of England functions one cannot only look to the official bodies which has been our main concern so far. As in national affairs in Britain in general, so in the church in particular, there are the voluntary agencies. Space does not allow great detail, except to draw readers' attention to the major areas covered and name the more important.

Educational

The National Society for Promoting Religious Education was founded in 1811 and was chiefly responsible for setting up, in co-operation with local clergy and others, the nationwide network of church schools in England and Wales. The Society now works very closely with the General Synod Board of Education.

Missionary

The Society for Promoting Christian Knowledge (SPCK) is the oldest Anglican missionary society. Founded in 1698 it seeks to support the work of the Church worldwide through the production and distribution of Christian literature and other communication resources.

The United Society for the Propagation of the Gospel (USPG) was formed in 1965, but basically consisted of the Society for the Propagation of the Gospel, which has been in existence since 1701, together with various other missionary societies concerned with various parts of the world, primarily in Africa and Asia. It tends to be supported by the catholic wing of the Church of England.

The Church Mission Society (CMS), which was founded in 1799, also mainly covers Africa and Asia. The Church's Ministry among Jewish People (CMJ) dates from 1809. The South American Missionary Society (SAMS) was founded in 1844 and its name defines its area of concern. Crosslinks, formerly the Bible Churchmen's Missionary Society, was founded in 1922 and covers parts of Europe as well as Africa and Asia. All these societies tend to be supported in the main by the evangelical wing of the Church of England.

The Church Army, founded by Preb. Wilson Carlile in 1882, now consists of some four hundred trained evangelists, men and women, lay and ordained, who work throughout the Anglican Communion.

The Church Pastoral Aid Society (CPAS) founded in 1838 by Lord Shaftesbury, claims to be the the oldest home missionary society, producing educational materials for all ages, especially youth. It provides help for parishes through trained evangelists and by giving grants in inner-city areas. It holds the patronage of quite a number of parishes and helps to supply other patrons with information of clergy requiring livings and curacies.

Patronage Trusts

Every parish church in England has a patron. Reference has already been made in this chapter to the patronage held by the Crown, diocesan bishops and CPAS. Some patronage is in the gift of private individuals, others owned by university colleges and some by Patronage Trusts, which are listed in the *Church of England Year Book*. With the exception of the Society for the Maintenance of the Faith, which aims to promote catholic teaching and practice, all the others tend to be of evangelical sympathy. Under present regulations no parish has to accept an incumbent that has not been approved by the Parish Representatives, who it has appointed. Most, if not all, Patronage Trusts work closely with the bishops of the dioceses in which the vacant parishes are situated.

Questions

1. What do you think full participation in the life of the Anglican Church should involve? (Baptism, confirmation, membership of an electoral roll, or something more?)
2. What are the advantages and disadvantages of an established church in spreading the Gospel?

14

Church buildings

Richard & Sarah Burton

If someone were to ask you, 'What is your local church like?', would you think of the building or the people? You might want to say that the Church is the people and the buildings are only there to provide shelter for the worshippers. While this is quite correct it is not the whole picture. Over the years church buildings have been used to express what Christians have thought about the Church, and worship, and God.

The chances are that if you belong to the Anglican Church then you worship in a building which is older and grander than most other local buildings. At the very least this has helped to give you your identity as a Christian. Perhaps you find yourself explaining something like, 'I worship at St Saviour's, it is that ornate medieval church on the market square.' The building has also to some extent determined how you worship and it could even have influenced your understanding of God. That, in part, was what it was supposed to do.

Your church building may well be an asset in local mission. It is a focus of the activity of the local church and stands as a symbol to the values of the Christian community which the wider community can easily identify. But the downside to this equation is that your building costs you dear in energy and money just to keep it standing in good repair. Is it worth it?

Keynote question

Our churches have been influenced by Christians whose worship and mission were in many ways different from the way we see the work of the Church today. To what extent are the buildings we have inherited compatible with the life and witness of the Church today?

The historical development of church buildings

The design of church buildings is influenced by the architectural style and achievements of the day, the use to which the building is to be put and the ideas it is intended to reflect, and practical considerations such as financial and material resources available.

The earliest churches met in homes or in secret meeting

Buildings and the Mission of the Church

Pope Gregory the Great sent Augustine to take the Gospel to England in 596. In a letter to Augustine dated 601 Gregory sets out how buildings can be used in mission: 'The heathen temples of these people need not be destroyed, only the idols which are found in them . . . If the temples are well built it is a good idea to detach them from the service of the devil and adapt them for the worship of the true God.' Perhaps in our own day we have adopted a similar strategy. In recent years one of the most effective forms of mission has been 'church planting'. New congregations are planted in some surprising buildings such as pubs, sports centres and schools. Are Christians today saying that the Gospel is as effective at redeeming the heart of our modern society as it was at redeeming the land of the Saxons?

places like the Catacombs. The first purpose-built church buildings took the form of the Roman basilica. This was the architectural form used throughout the Roman Empire for important public buildings. It consisted of a rectangular hall with two rows of longitudinal pillars, creating side aisles, and a semi-circular apse at one end. In these basilican churches the clergy were seated around the apse, facing the congregation across the altar, which stood on the line dividing the apse from the rest of the building.

Anglo-Saxon (600–1066)

Augustine's first cathedral at Canterbury, and the early tenth-century cathedral at Wells were built in the basilican style. However, the majority of churches in Britain were fairly small, consisting simply of a rectangular nave with an apse or a small rectangular chancel. Most were built of local materials as transport was difficult and costly. Many were timber-built as the Anglo-Saxons were skilful at working in wood. They were less skilled at stonework and where stone was used it was unshaped or shaped roughly with an axe. Naves were narrow, as the builders were unable to roof wider buildings, and they were high in comparison to their width. Chancels were short. Towers, which were common by the tenth century, also appeared tall in comparison to their small base area. Many remnants of these towers can be seen today where the rest of the building is of later date. Other features of the period were small, narrow windows and doorways usually rounded at the top (some rose to triangular points). By the beginning of the seventh century it had become customary for the apse or chancel to be positioned at the east end of the building so that worshippers faced Jerusalem and the rising sun symbolic of the new life of Christ's resurrection.

Norman (1066–1200)

The Norman conquerors initiated a new era in church building, with a revival in religious activity and closer association with Rome. Their architectural style drew its inspiration from the buildings of their native land. Their first concern was with major church buildings and a number of cathedrals were started in the Norman style, including Durham, Canterbury, Lincoln and St Albans as

Durham Cathedral:
Above: general view.
Below: the Norman nave.

well as monastic foundations. They then set about providing every village with a place of worship. Consequently most medieval churches are Norman in origin.

Buildings were of rough stonework, which meant that the walls needed to be thick in order to be strong enough. The usual plan was a nave and chancel, sometimes with a choir in between. Towers were usually built at the west end. In some larger churches and cathedrals a central tower was constructed over the choir. Transepts were lateral extensions added north and south of the choir, or the east end of the nave, which were essential in providing adequate support for the tower. They also gave the building a symbolic cruciform shape.

In larger buildings aisles were built on either side of the nave, separated from it by a row of arches on circular piers. It then became necessary to raise the nave walls above the level of these arcades to provide a clerestory containing windows, as the aisle windows alone gave insufficient light in the nave.

Norman architecture is characterised by round arches in arcades, chancel arches, doorways and windows. These were heavily decorated with bold, crude designs such as 'chevron' and 'beakhead'. In doorways a semicircular tympanum filled the space between the arch and

Medieval cathedrals

This plan shows the typical layout of a medieval cathedral (Durham). The choir, which was usually immediately to the east of the crossing, contained carved wooden stalls for the monks or canons. It was separated from the nave by a stone screen. At the east end was the sanctuary with a free-standing altar. This was sometimes separated from the choir by a further screen. Beyond the altar stood the Retro choir containing the shrine of the patron saint. The cloisters were a covered arcade, usually surrounding an open court, which gave access to different parts of the cathedral precincts. The chapter house with access from the cloisters was built for meetings of the cathedral chapter.

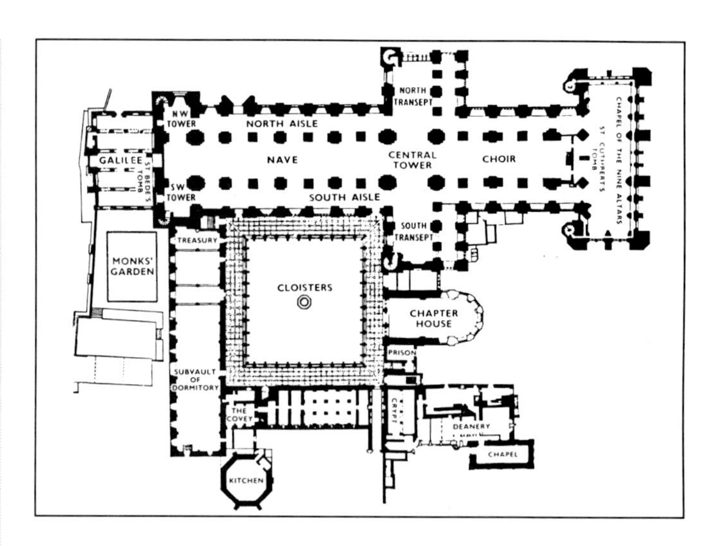

the square lintel. This was decorated with patterns or pictures with a religious theme. The sculptors took their inspiration from a mixture of everyday life, residual pagan ideas and Christian symbolism.

Gothic (1200–1540)

In the Middle Ages there was an emphasis on the separation of the clergy from the laity. The existing chancel arch was often enlarged and a large wooden screen placed across the new archway to separate the chancel from the nave. Commonly, a wooden tympanum filled the top of the new arch. At the top of the screen stood the rood, a crucifix with the figures of Mary and John on either side and the tympanum was painted as a background to this. Chancels were lengthened and given square east ends where previously they had been semi-circular. The altar was set at the east end of the chancel.

Private masses became common, necessitating the provision of chapels to contain additional altars within the church. The original altar then became known as the High Altar. Chantry chapels were built by guilds or individuals so that masses would be said for them when they were dead. Fonts were placed inside the south door or at the west end of the church so that they were near to the entrance. This symbolised the infant's entry into the life of the church at baptism.

The thirteenth century saw the introduction of a new style of church architecture based on pointed arches, known as Gothic. This was first seen in 1140 with the building of the Abbey of St Denis in France. The arch shape was that formed by the overlap of two circular arches. This effect had been seen in the preceding years as a decorative feature. The new use of the pointed arch may have been influenced by Moorish architecture or may have been a structural development. The Gothic builders built in solid stone creating stronger structures which were consequently able to use taller, narrower pillars and contain larger windows with less wall between. Stone ceilings (stone vaulting), which had been developed by the Normans, were popular as they reduced the risk of fire. These were, however, costly and so smaller or less wealthy churches had wooden ceilings (in York Minster the vaulted ceiling was built of wood). Buttresses had to be built to support the weight of the stone vaulting.

Gothic architecture is divided into three periods: Early English, Decorated and Perpendicular.

Early English (1200–1300)

The strength of the Church in the thirteenth century was reflected in the quantity of building which took place. The wealth of the Church enabled major projects to be undertaken. Salisbury Cathedral was built in just forty years and in rural areas money from the wool trade contributed to many fine churches. Much of the work involved rebuilding or enlarging of existing structures.

Early English windows were narrow with steeply pointed arches (lancet). At first these were separate; later several lancets were grouped to form a single window. Small round windows were sometimes set above the lancet groups; the patterns of stonework surrounding these is called tracery. Clustered columns became popular; these consisted of a central pillar surrounded by a number of narrower shafts. Gargoyles were introduced at this time to conceal the lead pipes which drained water from behind parapets.

Decorated (1300–1350)

In the fourteenth century churches were frequently used for secular purposes such as plays, markets and legal transactions. Porch walls became village notice-boards and parish records were stored in the buildings.

Churches continued to be altered and enlarged with an emphasis on widening and opening out. The arches of the

Cathedrals

A cathedral is a church which houses the bishop's throne (Latin: *cathedra*). To be seated is a sign of the bishop's authority as a teacher and reflects the authority of Jesus who taught in the same way (Matthew 5:1). The cathedral is the mother church of a diocese. People come to cathedrals on pilgrimage; in Durham, for instance, to pray at the shrine of St Cuthbert. They have become gathering places for major community and church occasions. Many people who do not normally worship in church visit them as tourists.

Cathedrals are some of the most spectacular buildings of Western civilisation. They are an essential element of a nation's heritage and symbols of spiritual vision and values, but they are also costly to maintain. Some attract such large numbers of visitors that the sheer volume of people passing through causes damage to the fabric and creates such bustle and noise that they cannot easily be seen as places of prayer. It is becoming common practice to charge an entrance fee, at least to certain parts of the building; but does this contribute to the idea that cathedrals are some kind of religious museum? Can they be places of prayer and Christian witness in the modern world or are they to be simply monuments to the glorious achievements of past ages?

Typical windows of the three Gothic periods.

The Book of Common Prayer influenced church design

Cranmer's First *Book of Common Prayer* was introduced in 1549. This led to re-ordering of church interiors to conform with new guidelines for public worship. There was a new emphasis on the proclamation of the Word which required that clergy lead services from positions where they could be heard by all present. It was also intended that all communicants should gather together around the communion table.

period were wider and less pointed. Window tracery became increasingly intricate. The Decorated style is seen at its best in the octagonal chapter houses built for the conduct of cathedral business.

Perpendicular (1350–1540)

Churches of this period were financed by the parish and there was an emphasis on colour and comfort. Seating became common in the form of wooden benches which were often intricately carved. Walls, screens, roofs and glass were all painted, resulting in a profusion of colour.

Throughout the period arches became progressively lower, culminating in the classic Tudor arch. Simple regular (rectilinear) tracery sprang from long perpendicular stone ribs (from which the period derives its name).

Renaissance and Classical (1540–1830)

At the Reformation the church underwent a period of upheaval, during which church building came to a halt. Under Henry VIII came the Dissolution of the Monasteries. There was more interest in putting money into domestic buildings than into the church. In parish churches royal arms were displayed (compulsory after 1660) and bells were silenced or pulled down.

The Reformers began to effect radical changes during the reign of Edward VI. There was a move to replace all stone altars with wooden communion tables. These were set in the choir or the chancel but sometimes at the east end of the nave. When in the chancel they were generally placed long-wise so that all the communicants could gather round more easily. In some churches screens were removed so that no part of the building was divided off from the rest. Features which were considered 'superstitious' were destroyed. Roods were taken down, effigies and carvings were removed or defaced, and wall paintings were covered with plaster and whitewash. Chantry chapels were no longer permitted.

Under the rule of Elizabeth I a compromise was achieved between former church practice and the reforming zeal of the Puritans. Rood lofts and their attendant figures were taken down but screens were retained or replaced, thus conserving the separation between chancel and nave. The use of the building was, however, radically different from that of the Middle Ages. Clergy and laity gathered together around the table, in the chancel, for the Eucharist. Clergy were encouraged to lead services from their accustomed positions so long as they could be heard clearly. Usually the offices were read from a reading desk placed at the east end of the nave (or in the centre of the nave in larger churches). In effect there were two separate worship areas within the one building; the nave, where Morning and Evening Prayers were said and the chancel where the celebration of the Eucharist took place. The Commandments were displayed at the east end and other biblical texts were written on the walls to provide both instruction and decoration. Painted glass was allowed to remain and bells were rung again.

Gothic influence persisted in the Classical period but new direction in architectural development was derived from the Italian Renaissance. The characteristics of Classical architecture were round columns (or square ones, called pilasters) with decorative tops (capitals) and horizontal bands of decoration above (entablatures), also round arches and triangular facades (pediments).

During the Civil War and the ten years of the Commonwealth, churches underwent further destruction at the hands of the Puritans.

In 1660 the monarchy was restored and a new era of church architecture began with the work of Sir Christopher Wren.

The new churches of the Classical period were usually built to the 'auditory' plan. This meant that the building was a single open worship area, so that worshippers could easily hear both preaching and services. However, within this there were still three distinct areas: the font remained at the west end for baptism, the central area focused on the pulpit and reading desk for preaching and the offices, and the altar was set at the east end for Communion. This arrangement was not intended to diminish the importance of the altar in relation to the pulpit. Each area had a different function but was of equal importance. Most of these new churches were built in towns.

In the villages a local squire might put up a church in the same style as his house but otherwise most building involved alteration of existing churches. Increased congregational space was achieved by widening naves or adding galleries supported on Classical pillars, so that the people would not be too far away from the preacher.

The Laudian Reforms

In the first half of the seventeenth century concerns were voiced about the current positioning of altars. Altars standing unprotected in the centre of the chancel or in the nave were liable to abuse. Churches were used not only for worship but also as schools and parish halls and thoughtless and irreverent use was sometimes made of the Lord's Table. Also, the method of administering Communion, with the people kneeling around the table and the priest taking the sacrament to them, wherever they were kneeling, could result in irreverence and disorder. Where a large number were present the people were liable to press against the altar and accidents and disorder were likely as the priest endeavoured to move round to all the various communicants. William Laud (1573–1645), the Dean of Gloucester, headed a movement to have altars restored to the east end of the chancel with a rail running right across the chancel in front of them. Others hoped for less radical solutions such as railing off the altar where it stood. However, Laud became Archbishop of Canterbury in 1633 and with the support of Charles I set about ensuring that all altars were replaced at the east end of the chancel and railed off in the manner which he and his supporters had prescribed.

St Paul's Cathedral, London.

These galleries were often used to house the musicians. The importance of the altar was emphasised by painting the ceiling and walls in the chancel. The east wall was always decorated, sometimes with an intricately carved back-piece to the altar which is called a reredos.

Imposing two- or three-decker pulpits, consisting of pulpit, reading pew and clerk's pew, were a common feature of the period. These were usually painted white and were placed centrally, so that the preacher could be seen and heard as well as possible. High-backed box pews with hinged doors were popular and these were set at a variety of angles in order to focus upon the preacher, or simply to fit in where they might. Families had their own pews and the squire's discreetly positioned family pew was fitted out for comfort, sometimes with a private entrance and complete with fireplace. The overall effect engendered a feeling of belonging. The system was, however, subject to abuse as the rich took the best places and little room was made for the poor.

Sir Christopher Wren (1632–1723)

In 1666 the Great Fire of London provided Sir Christopher Wren with a unique opportunity to develop his interpretation of the new style. 87 churches were destroyed and it was decided to build 53 new churches on former sites. Wren's churches took account of the centrality of preaching in Reformation worship and were spacious, open buildings. They were rectangular in shape and internally divided by classical pillars with deep pedestals arranged in the form of a Greek cross, square or oval. These supported ceilings of ornate plasterwork above decorated entablatures. The buildings culminated in vaults or domes. They had towers, some with spires, which combined Gothic and Renaissance features. Altars were surrounded by carved and painted altar pieces. Pulpits were richly decorated. Wren's towers and spires dominated the London skyline and artfully focused the eye towards the climax of his architectural achievement: St Paul's Cathedral.

Victorian (Gothic revival) (1830–1900)

The influence of Gothic architecture had never disappeared and at the end of the eighteenth century it became more popular again, particularly as a decorative feature. The Victorians, however, initiated the Gothic revival which was an attempt to return to the architecture of the medieval period.

The leader of the Gothic revival in England was Augustus Pugin (1812–52). He believed that the morals of society influenced architectural development. He proclaimed that Christianity was at its purest in the fourteenth century and that consequently the architecture of this period was the most Christian in concept. This point of view coincided with the aims of the Oxford Movement to return to pre-Reformation practices in worship. Pugin subsequently converted to Roman Catholicism but his ideas were developed by the Camden Society, a group set up in Cambridge in 1839 to study the historical development of church architecture. The most favoured architectural style was Decorated, which was considered to represent the high point of Gothic architecture.

The Camden Society also had very firm ideas about the conduct of worship and the ordering of church interiors. Long chancels were preferred but these were usually separated from the nave not by a screen as in the medieval period but by steps leading to a raised chancel. At the east end the altar was raised further above a second set of steps. Facing stalls were placed in the chancel or choir to accommodate the clergy as this was considered a more suitable place for the reading of the offices. The innovation of having a surpliced choir, who sat in the chancel stalls with the clergy, soon became common practice. Organs were also introduced in the vicinity of the chancel. Galleries became redundant and were usually taken down. Large central pulpits were removed and smaller ones were positioned at the north side of the chancel steps. At the south side of the steps stood a lectern, frequently shaped as an eagle, from where the lessons were read. The pews were low and open and all faced the altar. The west end was considered the best place for the font.

The Victorians opened up churches and cathedrals so that the eye was drawn straight to the altar as the focal point of the church. This was a different use of the building from that of the medieval period. Their aim was to produce devotion in worship by creating a sense of mystery and reverence and by the use of symbolism. It was considered better for the congregation to be passive witnesses of worship conducted reverently by the clergy and choir than for them to take an active part in the liturgy. This was in direct opposition to all the attempts made in the previous three hundred years to achieve corporate worship as intended at the Reformation and laid out in the *Book of Common Prayer*.

Churches throughout the Anglican Communion were influenced by these ideas; thus, for example, St Andrew's Cathedral, Sydney, Australia (1837), was originally designed with nave and aisles modelled on those of St Mary's Church, Oxford and a steeple modelled on the tower of Magdalen College, Oxford; and the present St George's Cathedral, Cape Town, South Africa (1897), was modelled on thirteenth-century French Gothic.

The Victorian bequest

The enthusiasm created by the ideas of the Camden Society was a driving force which probably changed the face of the Anglican Church far more than we realise today. Greatly increased town populations gave ample scope for building new churches and major restoration of old buildings also took place. Although the intention in this work was to return to medieval architecture the Victorians imposed their own ideas and produced in effect a new style of church building. Such firm ideas were developed on the correct ordering of buildings and worship that churches became much more uniform. The Victorians have bequeathed to us the idea that there is a right way to do all things in Anglican worship.

Glossary

Nave: The main part of the church where people sit or stand for worship.
Choir: The part of the church containing seats for the clergy and the choir.
Sanctuary: The part of the church containing the altar.
Chancel: Originally the sanctuary, later became the area consisting of sanctuary and choir.
Apse: A semi-circular or polygonal recess at the termination of part of the building.
Aisle: An extension on the north or south side of the nave and separated from it by a row of columns.
Transept: North or south arm of a cruciform church.
Tracery: The intersecting stone rib-work in the upper part of a Gothic window.
Clerestory: The part of the building which rises above the height of the aisle roofs and contains windows to admit light to the central parts of the building.
Altar: The word used for the eucharistic table until the Reformation when the term Lord's Table or Board was preferred. The term altar has continued in use to the present day.
Font: A receptacle for the water used in baptism.
Pulpit: An elevated stand for the preacher.
Lectern: A bookstand to support liturgical books.

A distinctive feature of Victorian Gothic was the use of combinations of natural colours in decoration (polychromy) introduced by William Butterfield. Different coloured stones, marbles, bricks and tiles were arranged to create ornate designs.

Church buildings in the twentieth century

During the 1930s a large number of churches were built to meet the needs of new housing estates. Following the Second World War there was further demand for new buildings both as a result of bomb damage and because of the continuing development of new housing areas, particularly in the suburbs. These were built in a variety of architectural styles; many looked back to former styles such as Classical, Gothic or Romanesque, some were built in contemporary style. However, most were drab and uninspiring and the vast majority used the Victorian plan for internal ordering.

During this period church building in Europe was developing in response both to contemporary architectural design and to the requirements of the new liturgical movement. A new emphasis on the Church as the Body of Christ and the importance of every-member ministry resulted in a renewed desire to have the worshipping community gathered together around the communion table.

In the new churches a single altar is set within the body of the building. In order to retain a sense of reverence and mystery the table is usually raised and the sanctuary area marked out in some way. Some new churches have not included pulpits but a pulpit or reading desk is generally considered necessary, both for practical reasons and to provide a visual symbol of the importance of the Word alongside the sacrament. This, along with modern thought on spatial relationships, has led to new experimentation in grouping altar and pulpit and sometimes font as well. General preference is for a pulpit within the sanctuary but not right next to the altar. Placing the font in the sanctuary emphasises the importance of the sacrament as well as allowing baptism to take place in the face of the congregation. However, other arrangements permit alternative symbolism. A font at the entrance of the church emphasises that entry to the church is through baptism. Some churches have favoured separate

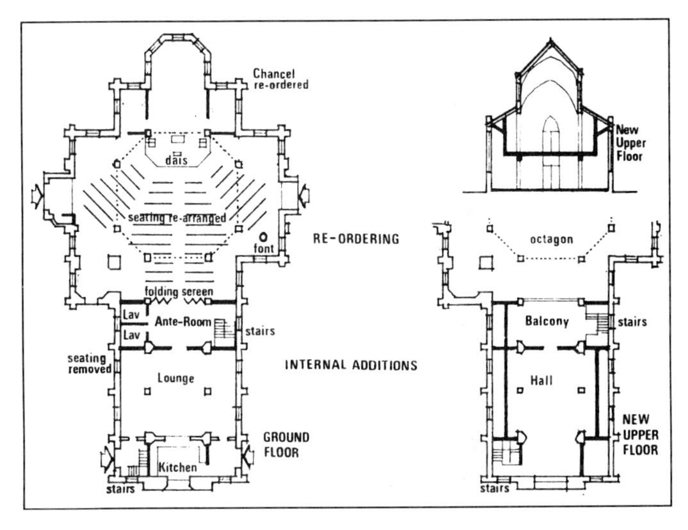

Christ Church, Highbury, with its re-ordered interior designed to make it an everyday church.

baptisteries. Steps down to the font speak of dying and rising to new life in Christ.

The new nave, presently being built to complete St Mary's Cathedral in Auckland is designed to resemble a Maori 'whare' (meeting house) opening on to a Marae (gathering place). The new nave is intended to accommodate worship for all denominations.

Many existing buildings have, in recent years, been re-ordered to a greater or lesser extent to take account of developments in the liturgy. In its simplest form this has involved moving the altar forward from the east wall so that the President can face the congregation. However, more thorough re-orderings have involved bringing the altar to the east end of the nave and rearranging the seating, particularly that of choir and clergy. Some churches have returned to the practice of seating the choir at the west end of the nave; others have kept them in the chancel but facing west or have seated them to one side (south or north) of the altar. Those who draw their inspiration from basilican worship seat the clergy at the east end, facing the congregation across the altar.

In recent years, increasing use of the creative arts in worship has led to the need to provide space for drama and dance to take place and seating for orchestras or music groups. Colourful banners with Christian themes have become a popular form of church decoration.

Sometimes circumstances have made it impossible for Anglicans to build churches. In Lima, Peru, some Anglicans in new towns worship in a space marked out by a

The full-time church building

Many congregations are looking at ways of making better use of their buildings as maintenance of a large building for only a few hours' use each week appears to be a poor use of resources. Churches are, therefore, being reordered not only with liturgical use in mind, but with the intention of fulfilling as many of the needs of the church and the local community as possible. In this way the building can be used not only on a Sunday for worship but every day of the week for Bible studies, youth groups, committees, concerts, toddler groups, lunches, keep-fit classes, etc. This might mean putting in toilets and a kitchen, or redeveloping an area for offices and smaller meetings. It might even mean putting a whole new floor in to utilise the existing space in the best way possible.

Are church buildings worth the cost?

In Tadcaster, a small country town in Yorkshire, the church has had to find over £125,000 to repair the church fabric in less than a decade. The church is the architectural jewel of the town and has been a place of Christian worship for over eight hundred years. Recently a loose pinnacle has been noticed on the tower. This is one of eight pinnacles on the tower alone but will cost over £10,000 to repair. The question must be raised in everyone's mind: Is it worth it? Should the building consume such a large proportion of the church's resources?

simple wattle fence. Likewise, in Sudan where political unrest and religious persecution have caused people to leave their homes in the towns and take refuge in the bush, congregations have created open-air worship areas. The Dinka people of Ba'el Gazal, in Southern Sudan, have built a new cathedral in the bush using traditional building techniques. It is a low, cruciform, aisled church built with mud walls and a thatched roof and with simple log seating.

Redundant buildings

Decline in local population or in church attendance can mean that churches are no longer viable. It may then be necessary to close the church, in which case what should be done with the building?

Some churches are handed over to the Redundant Churches Commission which keeps the fabric in good repair but the building remains unused by a worshipping community. Other churches are turned to more secular uses. Churches have become information or resource centres, museums, offices, flats, cafes or sports centres.

Symbols of the sacred

The sight of a country church set amongst beautiful scenery is a reminder of God's presence and activity in the world which can bring an immediate sense of reverence and awe. Churches can be powerful symbols of the sacred. In a busy secular world they stand as pointers to a different quality of life and love. But symbols are complex and can change.

Have you ever thought of the occasional visitor to a church service? She sits on hard bench seats, looks at carved woodwork and stonework she has only seen the like of before in large stately homes. All this may well speak of immense wealth and status. Churches do not easily speak of the simplicity and vulnerability of the Gospel. Many hark back to Prince Bishops and the Church exercising immense authority in the land. In spite of all this many Christians have wanted to build for permanence; why?

Church buildings can give a sense of identity and focus to the local community. A building can express the aims and purpose of the Church: its understanding of God and worship, sacraments and mission. It also reflects the community's confidence in its message and its hopes for the future.

For Anglicans, buildings are reminders of our rich heritage and an expression of our hope for the future. They say something about our desire and delight in worship as well as our aims in mission to bring the grace of God into our bruised and confused world. Our regular worship in places of beauty forms and informs our minds more than we have perhaps realised.

Questions

1. When a visitor attends your church what do you think he or she might feel about the building?
2. How is your church building a help or hindrance to your mission in your local community?
3. What furniture (altar, pulpit, etc.) do you consider to be essential in an Anglican church?
4. Do you think your church building is fully utilised? If not, how could you realistically change it so that it could be better used?

Part 5

The way ahead

15

The Anglican future

Ian Bunting

A selector asked the potential priest, 'What do you really like about the Anglican Church?' She replied: 'Its breadth.' 'And what do you dislike?' was the next question. 'Its breadth.' Our strengths are often the complement of our weaknesses. The same is true of the Anglican Church.

It depends of course how we view Anglican breadth. Some have described the Anglican way as a 'third way', a middle way between Catholic and Protestant, between Rome and Geneva. Some others have seen the church more like a tree. The branches spread out from a single trunk which is well rooted in the soil of God's love in creating the world, preserving it and redeeming it. This reflects the picture Jesus gives us of himself as the true vine and his disciples as the branches (John 15:5). So when we talk about the Anglican Church being comprehensive we are not talking about all Anglicans being alike. We are wanting to affirm the strengths of each branch bonded to the trunk without eliminating the differences. Ours has always been, and will go on being, a unity in diversity. The Anglican future is likely to have five clear characteristics. We may think of them as a threat or an opportunity.

1. A rich variety

The differences which Jesus recognised in his followers and Paul identified in the early churches are potential strengths as much as weaknesses. In the final homecoming of God's people to the city of God John has in view different leaders and different nations converging through the same open gates (Revelation 21:24–6).

Contrary to what we sometimes think, there have always been differences in the church. Britain was never an exception. So, for example, Celtic Christians in the north had an approach to the faith which differed from that of the Roman missionaries in the south. It was always much more than a seemingly trivial argument about what was the right date to celebrate Easter that divided them. Our Celtic forebears had an intuitive and earthy approach to their preaching and healing mission which took them out of their monasteries to where people lived. The Roman missionaries, on the other hand, worked to a clear strategy of mission which focused on adapting the faith within the prevailing culture. They aimed to establish a structured church around centres of faith and worship, in which existing natural communities would be nurtured. They had different models of mission but the same Gospel.

Today, throughout the Anglican Communion, we find a similar diversity of approach but with it the desire to express our common bond and purpose. Anglicans are good at adapting to the circumstances in which the churches find themselves; our modern creatively used church buildings and flexible patterns of worship offer good evidence of this. Nevertheless they have a character or identity which they also communicate. It is still a commitment to comprehensiveness. As the British Empire gave way to the commonwealth of nations, so autonomous Anglican Provinces with different styles of church life have recognised each other as belonging to the same family of faith. More than that, they respect what God is doing within each branch as an expression of the shared journey along the Anglican way.

Sometimes the differences among Anglicans have been sharp. For instance, the arguments between Anglicans about churchmanship issues a hundred years ago which took them into the English law courts still leave a residue of suspicion and mistrust. Although, as we can see in this book, important contributions have come from the differing corners of the church, some issues have threatened to divide us. For example, the action of some Provinces in ordaining women to the priesthood where others have refused has bequeathed to a few a legacy of bitterness which tempts them to look for fellowship elsewhere. It is, however, inescapable that those who remain Anglicans are going to have to work out their relationship to women priests and, soon, bishops. Women are going to be integrated into the leadership of the church. In the future, Anglicans will have to discover a sometimes painful unity in diversity. As with disagreements over churchmanship and the ordination of women so with other issues, around sexuality for instance, Anglicans will be struggling to maintain respect for difference of opinion within the fellowship of faith.

Because we are a practical rather than a confessional church (like the Roman Catholic and some Protestant churches) Anglicans do not find it hard to adapt to the culture in which we find ourselves. From the days when the Thirty-nine Articles were authorised we have, in the terms of Article 34 of the *Book of Common Prayer*, refused to impose uniformity of tradition or ceremony on churches in other lands, times or cultures. So long as nothing is ordained which is contrary to the Word of God, national churches are at liberty to order their own affairs so as to build up the Church where they are. So, for example, the Lambeth Conference (1988) welcomed the presence of bishops from the Church of South India, the Church of North India, the Church of Bangladesh and the Church of Pakistan, 'acknowledging that their presence reminds us that our commitment as Anglicans is to the wider unity of the Church'. In this book, therefore, we have seen how much there is for the older Anglican churches to learn from their sisters and brothers in the developing world.

As a consequence, we may expect in the future to see a rich variety of expressions of the Anglican way. But we are held together like the different branches of a tree in the common source of our life in Christ. This is expressed in a core of dogma or religious truth divinely revealed and defined by the church in its historic creeds. There will be an ongoing debate within Anglican churches about the extent to which individual churches or Provinces have enshrined the common inheritance and vision. But, putting our variety within the framework of a shared conviction of what we believe about God, the strength of a comprehensive church vastly outweighs its weakness. The kaleidoscope of God's created order and the many facets of God's redemptive purpose encourage us to think of diversity as a strength not a weakness.

Of the traditions of the church

'It is not necessary that traditions and ceremonies be in all places one, or utterly alike; for at all times they have been divers, and may be changed according to the diversities of countries, times and men's manners, so that nothing be ordained against God's Word.'
(Article 34, The Book of Common Prayer)

2. Christ at the centre

Jesus came preaching the kingdom of God (Mark 1:15). The New Testament makes it clear that Jesus is the King of the kingdom. The Anglican Church is a Christocentric church; that is, we find our unity in Christ, to whom the Scriptures and the historic creeds bear witness. We are not a church in which the the official church leaders are the sole authoritative interpreters of the truth. In the Roman Catholic Church by contrast the leadership, called the 'Magisterium' and represented by the bishops led by the pope in apostolic succession from the apostles and Peter, are the final authority. Nor are we a confessional church wedded to some doctrinal formula agreed at a fixed point in time which determines how we interpret the Christian faith today. For example, some Reformed churches still look to the Westminster Confession in that way. The Thirty-nine Articles, which form one of our Anglican foundation documents, are different. Certainly they contain a core of essential Christian teaching founded in the Scriptures. But there are other matters which may be determined by the 'common authority' of the church so long as they are not 'repugnant to the Word of God' (Article 34). The Anglican Church finds this a useful basis on which to continue in dialogue with a wide range of other Christian churches with respect and appreciation of their differences.

This means that there can be a unity in essentials and liberty in non-essentials. But it is this liberty, or breadth, which some feel is a weakness in the Anglican way. It begs the question: What is and is not essential? However, we do not allow ourselves to be driven to distraction by the limited number of absolute Anglican convictions. These are found in the the three historic creeds (Article 8). Instead, we positively celebrate the fully Christ-centred practice of the Anglican way which determines how we get to know God and make God known.

First and foremost, we do this in *worship.* Archbishop Michael Ramsey once said we do our theology 'to the sound of church bells'. It was a way of saying that Anglican worship forms what we believe. 'If you want to know what we believe,' he said, 'come and pray with us.' When people argue too lightly that the Anglican liturgy is no longer a bond that unites us they fail to see how, nevertheless, it has a shape, language, style and form which is recognisable almost anywhere we meet it in the world. Anglican worship has a family likeness. For instance, it is infused with Scripture. Again, it is unapologetically Trinitarian in character and inescapably Christ-centred. So, without spelling out precisely what we are to believe about particular Christian truths, we are channelled in our thinking. Anglican worship directs our thinking about God, salvation, life, worship, the world, the church, behaviour, and everything else. We set it all within the framework of our worship. This includes the witness of the Scriptures to the providence of God, the lordship of Jesus Christ as Saviour and the presence of God's Holy Spirit with us.

Secondly, the *Book of Common Prayer* gives a comprehensive vision to the *mission* of the church in all the circumstances of people's lives and experiences. All our praying, in the Prayer Book even for rain, at sea, or in war, is through Jesus Christ our Lord. Christians are often tempted to separate the spiritual from the material world. We may avoid some hard questions if we look for spiritual, or other-worldly, interpretations to some of the promises of the Bible. But our Anglican faith upholds both the providence of God in the everyday events of life and the presence of God with us now. The incarnation of Christ, God revealed in the human life of Jesus of Nazareth, assures us of it. We say at the Eucharist, 'His Spirit is with us.' We may not disengage our Christian faith from any of life's challenges, be they local or global, spiritual, material, moral, political, social or economic. Late in the twentieth century, for example, the influential Church of England report 'Faith in the City' (1985), set down a benchmark in this respect. It addressed church and nation and called upon both to tackle injustice and deprivation in the cities of Britain.

Sometimes the newer Anglican liturgies reflect the same kind of global and social consciousness. For instance, the American Episcopal Church sensed our more recent environmental awareness in one of its eucharistic prayers offering praise for 'the vast expanse of interstellar space, galaxies, suns, the planets in their courses and this fragile earth, our island home'.

If our liturgy has shaped and echoed our practical theology, it has also determined our pastoral care. It still does. The *Book of Common Prayer*, and its successors in the

The marks of Anglican worship

'We believe that some of the marks which should be safeguarded for those who wish to stand in any recognizable continuity with historic Anglican tradition are:

- a clear structure for worship
- an emphasis on reading the word of God and in using psalms
- liturgical words repeated by the congregation, some of which, like the creed, would be known by heart
- using a collect, the Lord's Prayer, and some responsive forms in prayer
- a recognition of the centrality of the Eucharist
- a concern for form, dignity, and economy of words.'

from 'Patterns for Worship', London, Church House Publishing 1995, p. 5

The Satkaar Project, Leamington Spa. It is important for Christians to meet people of other faiths and to pay attention to them.

Inter-faith dialogue

This Conference commends dialogue with people of other faiths as part of Christian discipleship and mission, with the understanding that:
(1) dialogue begins when people meet each other;
(2) dialogue depends on mutual understanding, mutual respect and mutual trust;
(3) dialogue makes it possible to share in service to the community;
(4) dialogue becomes a medium of authentic witness.
Acknowledging that such dialogue, which is not a substitute for evangelism, may be a contribution in helping people of different faiths to make common cause in resolving issues of peacemaking, social justice and religious liberty, we further commend each province to initiate such dialogue in partnership with other Christian Churches where appropriate.'

Lambeth Resolution 20 of 1988

Anglican Communion worldwide, provides a comprehensive ministry to people. But it does not judge whether they are all personally committed disciples of Christ. With faith and within a proclamation of the Gospel it offers the church's ministry from the womb to the tomb.

Thirdly, Anglican *spirituality* is essentially Christ-centred. This may seem an obvious point to make. However, it has been reported that Prince Charles has a preference for being known, when he is king, as defender of faith rather than 'Defender of the Faith', like all the kings and queens of England since Henry VIII. To many, some Anglicans among them, in the multi-faith world of today it seems to make sense. Moreover it is true that, thanks to rapid communications, we find ourselves in frequent conversation with people of many faiths and of none. Yet the Anglican Church has launched itself into a future of evangelism, at the heart of which is the Good News of Jesus Christ (see Lambeth Resolution 43 of 1988). No one imagines that this is an easy option, because evangelism implies the ultimate truth as we find it in Christ. It does, however, resonate with our Anglican confidence in the truth of the Christian Gospel as the ground of ultimate hope. At the same time the call for dialogue with those of other faiths shows that we respect other peoples and their point of view.

3. Practical Christianity

The Anglican way is practical: it is not pragmatic or speculative. A pragmatic church operates on the basis of responding to things as they happen. A speculative church lives by theory and conjecture. Practical Christianity takes action and thinks about what it is doing in relation to what it believes. It is the way of faith and obedience. It is practical and Christ-centred. Someone has said, 'We are more likely to act our way into a new way of thinking than think our way into a new way of acting.' It sums up a thoroughly Anglican approach. Some Christians in other traditions find us exasperating in this respect. It is, however, the way we tackle our mission. For example, it is the way we teach the faith, order our church life, and respond to the pressures which weigh upon us. It is not unreflective action; in fact it is a constant attempt to adapt and relate our faith and life to the culture in which we find ourselves but without compromising its central core.

First, traditionally, Anglicans have taught the faith by means of the public reading of the Scriptures, and instruction in the scriptural faith by means of sermons and catechisms. The Lambeth Conference (1988) believed this continues to be of the first importance in the work of revising Anglican Prayer Books (Resolution 18: The Anglican Communion: Identity and authority). In the past, confirmation candidates were expected to learn the Prayer Book catechism by heart. This practice has fallen out of general use. However, catechisms, and they vary from Province to Province, continue to provide a framework for instruction in the faith. They are basic. Like the chapters of this book, they cover belief, behaviour and what it means to belong to the Church. One of the consequences of no longer teaching the catechism by rote is that Anglicans are not always able to articulate central truths as confidently as their parents and teachers. Of course it must always be more than the simple repetition of words. But the catechism tries to put Anglican faith in a nutshell. Possibly, future revisions will include our Lord's two commandments (Matthew 22:37–9) and the Beatitudes (Matthew 5:3–10). But to be able to repeat the Creed, the Ten Commandments and the Lord's Prayer, together with a simple explanation of the two Gospel sacraments of baptism and Holy Communion is to lay a practical foundation for Christian living and believing. Further Christian teaching in sermons and in other settings can build upon it.

Second, we order our church life by means of canon law which, in England, has sections covering themes such as the character of the church, its worship, ministry, church buildings and their use, and church government. While the details will interest few lay people, they establish a structure for our church faith and practice which, importantly, is binding on the clergy. The Greek word for canon means 'a straight rule or bar'. Each Province has its own canons. In England, canons are approved by General Synod before being publicly issued to the church (promulged) at General and Diocesan Synods. These days canon law undergoes constant revision. For example, it has been necessary to agree canons which permit the ordination of both women priests and those who have been divorced and remarried. But this illustrates the practical and flexible approach of the Anglican churches to the arrangements of church life. As we know, the debate about such issues is often painful and protracted, but the end result is that there is a process in place for implementing change in Anglican practice. We have what Article 34 describes as the 'common authority' of the church to do so.

Although some Anglicans have argued that changes like those we have mentioned have serious doctrinal implications which synods are not competent to decide, the great majority have held a different point of view. Canon law gives us a careful way to proceed, admittedly by a lengthy process of debate and decision. Anglican churches make changes incrementally, a small amount at a time. Slow perhaps, but it displays a characteristically Anglican principle of working. We try to integrate Scripture, the received tradition of the church, and the wisdom of the Holy Spirit at work among us. At the end of the process, we express our decision in a canon. When we get impatient with the pace of change, it is worth reminding ourselves of the timescale of our decision-making within the vast span of Christian history. We may then be able to see things in a more healthy perspective.

Third, like all other churches, Anglicans have to come to terms with the pressures of the age which weigh upon them. Some of these pressures have a sharp practical edge to them. For instance, Anglican churches worldwide have had to learn how to pursue their mission under severe financial constraint. Most Anglican churches rely almost entirely upon the giving of their present worshippers. Unlike the Church of England they have little inherited wealth to cushion them from the chill financial climate in which they find themselves. It is here they may have much to teach the Church of England which can no longer survive on the beneficence of the dead.

In the past, Church of England clergy stipends (a stipend is an allowance rather than a salary) were to enable them to be available for ministry in the parishes of the land. The money often came from the generosity of past generations of Christians who provided for both the upkeep of church buildings and the livelihood of the clergy. Most Anglicans know that this provision is no longer adequate for either task. As with other Provinces, the Anglicans in England are facing increasing calls to give generously to the mission of the church and its maintenance. We have much to learn from other Anglicans as we decide how to move forward in our day.

For example, in South Africa, Anglicans have faced the need for more ministers for many years and have come up with a practical cost-effective strategy which is designed not for retreat but advance. They have discerned two different sorts of ordained ministers appropriate for the church's mission today: apostolic ministers who are usually deployable and church-supported when it comes to finance, and community ministers who are usually locally focused and self-supporting (non-stipendiary). The church of the Province of South Africa ordains priests to both forms of ministry. So it continues the Anglican determination to be so far as possible a church for everybody within the constraints of reduced financial resources. Here then is one example of a valued Anglican approach from which other Anglican churches may learn and make adaptations according to their own circumstances.

The multiplication of other forms of ministry, Readers and pastoral assistants for example, is another practical expression of the same concern. But, as the title of one Anglican report in 1985 aptly put it, 'All Are Called'. The Anglican Church of the future will be one which listens more carefully to Christian people (laity) who are in the front line of Christian witness in the world. We will become a church less dominated by clergy, but one in which clergy and laity work together collaboratively within the life of the church and in the world around, of which the church is part.

4. A church for everybody

The purpose of the Church
'The Christian Church is the only co-operative society that exists for the benefit of its non-members.'
William Temple

When we say that the Anglican Church wants to continue to be a church for everybody, it could sound patronising. Certainly, the Church of England in the past was both patronising and paternalistic. But that need not be so today. What we mean is that Anglicans have a concern for everyone, not just those who call themselves Anglicans, or come to church, or even consider themselves Christian. This lies at the heart of the parish principle. Equally, looking at it from a different perspective, Anglicans want to express their interest in and commitment to all peoples everywhere. This is the global dimension to the Anglican Church which is expressed in the principle of episcopacy. So the Anglican Church is both parish based and episcopal. The parish principle keeps us locally focused in our mission and ministry. The bishops remind us that we are catholic; that is, universal in our connections and outlook.

This dual focus is an important contribution we have to offer within the partnership of all Christian churches. For example, in the Western world we live in a leisure culture which infuses the life of the Church as other institutions in our society. Pleasure becomes an end in itself. We

A church for everybody.

recognise how we are individualised by the moral relativism of our age. We see how old moral guideposts have moved and each person has to establish their own standards and values for a happy life. But it grates against the standards and values rooted in a community by the Christian tradition which Anglicans have inherited and still want to uphold. The same is true of the autonomous individualism which urges upon us our self-sufficiency and competence to deal with all the challenges life throws up against us.

Anglicans by contrast believe that we are not simply lone Christians, Anglican or otherwise, but people bonded by God to others in a relationship of mutual dependence and interdependence, our common humanity, for which we must take responsibility. Anglicans believe in the depth and breadth of God's love in Christ to which the Scriptures bear witness. We are impelled to look beyond our own immediate local or family priorities. We are part of a wider community of which the Anglican Communion is a symbol.

The *parish principle* emphasises that we are committed to people both in the communities in which we reside and the communities of common concern in which we live our lives. These communities are not always the same, as they were for most folk in the past. In our mobile modern culture, we not only find many natural groupings on the basis of neighbourhood but also equally natural communities or networks cemented by common concern, for example a gathering of the deaf or people of the same ethnic origin. In short, we find a multitude of formal and informal communities of people who share the same needs, priorities and interests. Our hope and aim is, if possible, to provide a presence and witness in each, which is appropriate to each, or enculturated within each. This will display an Anglican appreciation of the Jesus Christ who put flesh on the bones of God's love. We want to sow a seed of his kingdom which will, like the mustard seed in Jesus' story, grow into a great tree (Matthew 13:31,32).

Bishops are very important for Anglicans. They are symbols of our commitment to the universal concern of God for the world, and the catholic or universal nature of the Church. For much of the last hundred years the uninterrupted succession of bishops (apostolic succession)

A prophetic church

'A society which has reached the point of confessing no principle but that of rivalry, no maxim but that of "Every man for himself", may in its dying agonies ask help of the Gospel – but assuredly too late.'

F. D. Maurice (1805–72) in a sermon entitled 'The Law of Christ the Law of Humanity' (1858)

An Anglican and Lutheran understanding of bishops

'We acknowledge that the episcopal office is valued and maintained in all our churches as a visible sign expressing and serving the Church's unity and continuity in apostolic life, mission and ministry.'

from The Porvoo Common Statement (1993) following Conversations between twelve churches, four British Anglican and eight Nordic Lutheran Churches, which took place between 1989 and 1992

has been an Anglican essential in contemplating unity with other churches. However, Anglicans have entered into conversations with non-episcopal churches, and episcopal churches which have a different history and view of bishops. If, as a consequence of these discussions, unions come about, some of the sticking points on the historic episcopate will be modified, while still recognising its importance.

Episcopacy, like the parish or local principle, will continue to express Anglican commitment to everyone individually and collectively. Bishops, however, fulfil the purpose in a different theatre of operations. For one thing, they are the public face of the church in a nation. Anglicans think of them as guardians of the faith and trustees of our inheritance. They are teachers. They maintain links with other bishops in the Anglican Communion. Generally, they are accorded respect within the leadership circles of the nations in which they serve the Anglican Church, even including secular nations like the United States of America. People listen to them with attention. As Christians they bear their witness in the public arena as they face national and global challenges. Often, as with economic and political issues, on the ground, in the parishes, these deeply affect people who find themselves powerless to make any effective response on their own account.

For example, Anglicans have always had a respect for the political institutions of the nations. This is not simply an historical accident. We have valued the biblical injunction to submit to the authorities in power (Romans 13:1, 1 Peter 2:13,14) and to pray for sovereigns and all in high office (1 Timothy 2:2). With Augustine, we have recognised that in this life the earthly city and its flawed structures of authority is inextricably interwoven with the City of God and its flawless rule of love. Anglican Christians acknowledge the inevitable discrepancy between the two. But, like the prophet Jeremiah, they work for the peace of the one while looking for the establishment of the other (Jeremiah 29:7). It is not, therefore, an uncritical respect. It was Archbishop Desmond Tutu in South Africa, for example, who sharply commented on the difficulty of Christians in praying for reconciliation: 'How can I embrace you my brother when you are standing on my head?' Throughout this book there are examples where, in speaking out in areas of national interest, the Anglican churches, usually in the person of their bishops, have attracted suspicion, scorn and sometimes active persecution. People in authority have felt threatened by what the bishops have said and done. Especially in recent years, the bishops have seen it as their responsibility to make a Christian stand for the oppressed and voiceless within a nation.

If, however, we are to be a church for everybody it follows that there is also an imperative to proclaim what we believe. It was the African bishops in 1988 who prodded the Lambeth Conference to launch upon a Decade of Evangelism. They were reminding Anglicans of the Christ-centred nature of their faith. In the face of increasing secularisation and militant fundamentalisms, Anglicans cannot be allowed to forget it. For instance, interfaith worship services might suggest Christ-centredness is not important. It is. Jesus Christ is Saviour for all. To this truth, a church for all is committed.

Decade of Evangelism

'This Conference, recognising that evangelism is the primary task given to the Church, asks each province and diocese of the Anglican Communion, in co-operation with other Christians, to make the closing years of this millennium a "Decade of Evangelism" with a renewed and united emphasis on making Christ known to the people of his world.'

Lambeth Resolution 43 of 1988

No one imagines that it will be easy to evangelise the modern world. But then it never was easy. It was not easy to evangelise England. But we can learn from the way some of the early evangelists went about it. They achieved it by preaching the Gospel so as to include what was good in the prevailing culture on the one hand, and by indigenous church planting on the other.

In 597 Pope Gregory, for instance, gave Augustine of Canterbury a vision and a task. The vision was nothing less than the conversion of the whole nation. It was to be accomplished through a clear strategy of mission based upon the principle of adaptation. The other historic principle which will continue to appeal to Anglicans is indigenous church planting. Dating from about 635, it derives more from the Celtic tradition with its emphasis on holiness, spontaneity and the infectious lifestyle of winsome Christians.

5. Ecumenical and international

We have already suggested another dimension which will mark our Anglican churches in years to come, deriving from the episcopal nature of our church. The Anglican future promises to be ecumenical in sympathy and international in scope. This has already begun. In fact it began in the sixteenth century with Anglicans offering hospitality and fellowship to Christians from other lands and churches, a tradition which has continued ever since. The diversity accepted in Article 34 naturally leads to a generous spirit. During the twentieth century in particular Anglicans have always been prominent in the developing ecumenical movement. The resolutions of successive Lambeth Conferences bear witness to the breadth and seriousness of this ecumenical concern, and how far we have outgrown the blinkered vision of the days of the British Empire. Almost certainly, one consequence for the Church of England will be an adjustment to the 'established' nature of the church. Doubtless the debate about the benefits or otherwise of this arrangement for the spread of the Gospel in England will continue. Certainly the relationship of church and state will change. In the light of Anglican ecumenical and international awareness this could be an advantage.

We have never been happy with denominationalism and especially with the thought that we might be just another denomination, as Anglicans are in the United States for instance. A denominational allegiance has the possible virtue of expressing some strong convictions, but at a cost. As Anglicans, we have a commitment rather to the catholicity or universal character of the Church. So, for example, in England new talks with the Methodists are now in progress, and in Europe and Scandinavia with Lutheran churches. Our strategy of Christian mission restrains us from drawing boundaries which are too firmly defined. Ours are porous. We are not associational churches attracting only the like minded. Ours is to be a witness to the whole community.

Themes for the Lambeth Conference 1998

1. Being truly human.
2. Holding and sharing the Faith.
3. Living as Anglicans in a pluralist world.
4. Seeking full visible unity.

Therefore, we prefer to think of ourselves as inclusive, not exclusive. We do not think that means we have no sense of our identity. Identity and inclusiveness are not mutually exclusive within the Anglican way. You can see the way it works out in a rural church where there are no other denominational churches meeting in the vicinity. Members who come from other Christian traditions, Methodists or Roman Catholics for instance, are warmly welcome not only to attend but receive Communion with us at the Lord's Table. They share in the everyday witness and work of the church. We try to hold together different Christian strands in a common bond which roots us in our shared Christian inheritance in the Scriptures and the centuries-old traditions of the church. Of course, we hope that those who want to stay in fellowship with us will join us not only in worship but in appreciation of our unique Anglican contribution within the partnership of all the Christian churches.

The future is rich in promise and full of opportunity. That brings us back to where this chapter started – with the picture of many branches depending on the life flowing through one trunk from roots which are well bedded in the soil of God's self-revelation. We may expect the Anglican future to be such a unity in diversity; not a weak assembly of disparate branches in artificial harmony. We pray for that unity which God wills for his Church; with nothing less ultimately in view than the visible unity of God's kingdom present on earth as it is in heaven.

Questions

1. What controversial issues will stretch the unity of the Anglican Church in the future, and how do you think they will be resolved?
2. What is your view of the decision of the Anglican Church both to evangelise and to enter into dialogue with those of other faiths?
3. How good are Anglicans you know at adapting to the surrounding culture, without compromising the core of Christian truth?

16

Praying with the church

Anglican prayers, ancient and modern

Anglicans all over the world share a number of prayers (or collects) which are rooted in our history. Whether in the words of the *Book of Common Prayer* or a modern version such as the *Alternative Service Book* (1980), many like to learn them by heart. We end with a selection.

A General Thanksgiving

Book of Common Prayer:

Almighty God, Father of all mercies, we thine unworthy servants do give thee most humble and hearty thanks for all thy goodness and loving-kindness to us, and to all men. We bless thee for our creation, preservation, and all the blessings of this life; but above all, for thine inestimable love in the redemption of the world by our Lord Jesus Christ; for the means of grace, and for the hope of glory. And, we beseech thee, give us that due sense of all thy mercies, that our hearts may be unfeignedly thankful, and that we shew forth thy praise, not only with our lips, but in our lives; by giving up ourselves to thy service, and by walking before thee in holiness and righteousness all our days; through Jesus Christ our Lord, to whom with thee and the Holy Ghost be all honour and glory, world without end. *Amen.*

Alternative Service Book:

Almighty God, Father of all mercies,
we your unworthy servants give you most humble and hearty thanks
for all your goodness and loving kindness
to us and to all men.
We bless you for our creation, preservation, and all the blessings of this life;
but above all for your immeasurable love
in the redemption of the world by our Lord Jesus Christ,
for the means of grace, and for the hope of glory.
And give us, we pray, such a sense of all your mercies
that our hearts may be unfeignedly thankful,
and that we show forth your praise,
not only with our lips but in our lives,
by giving up ourselves to your service,
and by walking before you in holiness and righteousness all our days;
through Jesus Christ our Lord,
to whom, with you and the Holy Spirit, be all honour and glory,
for ever and ever. *Amen.*

The Collect for Purity

Book of Common Prayer:
Almighty God, unto whom all hearts be open, all desires known, and from whom no secrets are hid; Cleanse the thoughts of our hearts by the inspiration of thy Holy Spirit, that we may perfectly love thee, and worthily magnify thy holy Name; through Christ our Lord. *Amen.*

Alternative Service Book:
Almighty God,
to whom all hearts are open,
all desires known,
and from whom no secrets are hidden:
cleanse the thoughts of our hearts
by the inspiration of your Holy Spirit,
that we may perfectly love you,
and worthily magnify your holy name;
through Christ our Lord. *Amen.*

The Prayer of Humble Access

Book of Common Prayer:
We do not presume to come to this thy Table, O merciful Lord, trusting in our own righteousness, but in thy manifold and great mercies. We are not worthy so much as to gather up the crumbs under thy Table. But thou art the same Lord, whose property is always to have mercy: Grant us therefore, gracious Lord, so to eat the flesh of thy dear Son Jesus Christ, and to drink his blood, that our sinful bodies may be made clean by his body, and our souls washed through his most precious blood, and that we may evermore dwell in him, and he in us. *Amen.*

Alternative Service Book:
We do not presume
to come to this your table, merciful Lord,
trusting in our own righteousness,
but in your manifold and great mercies.
We are not worthy
so much as to gather up the crumbs under your table.
But you are the same Lord
whose nature is always to have mercy.
Grant us therefore, gracious Lord,
so to eat the flesh of your dear son Jesus Christ
and to drink his blood,
that we may evermore dwell in him
and he in us. *Amen.*

Morning Prayer: Third Collect, for Grace

Book of Common Prayer:
O Lord, our heavenly Father, Almighty and everlasting God, who hast safely brought us to the beginning of this day; Defend us in the same with thy mighty power; and grant that this day we fall into no sin, neither run into any kind of danger; but that all our doings may be ordered by thy governance, to do always that is righteous in thy sight; through Jesus Christ our Lord. *Amen.*

Alternative Service Book:
Almighty and everlasting Father,
we thank you that you have brought us safely
to the beginning of this day.
Keep us from falling into sin
or running into danger;
order us in all our doings;
and guide us to do always
what is right in your eyes;
through Jesus Christ our Lord. *Amen.*

Evening Collect

Book of Common Prayer:
Lighten our darkness, we beseech thee, O Lord; and by thy great mercy defend us from all perils and dangers of this night; for the love of thy only Son, our Saviour, Jesus Christ. *Amen.*

Alternative Service Book:
Lighten our darkness, Lord, we pray;
and in your mercy defend us
from all perils and dangers of this night;
for the love of your only Son,
our Saviour Jesus Christ. *Amen.*

Collect for the 19th Sunday after Trinity

Book of Common Prayer:
O God, forasmuch as without thee we are not able to please thee; Mercifully grant, that thy Holy Spirit may in all things direct and rule our hearts; through Jesus Christ our Lord. *Amen.*

Alternative Service Book (5th Sunday after Pentecost):
Almighty God,
without you we are not able to please you.
Mercifully grant that your Holy Spirit
may in all things direct and rule our hearts;
through Jesus Christ our Lord. *Amen.*

A Collect or Prayer for all Conditions of Men

Book of Common Prayer:
O God, the Creator and Preserver of all mankind, we humbly beseech thee for all sorts and conditions of men; that thou wouldest be pleased to make thy ways known unto them, thy saving health unto all nations. More especially, we pray for the good estate of the Catholick Church; that it may be so guided and governed by thy good Spirit, that all who profess and call themselves Christians may be led into the way of truth, and hold the faith in unity of spirit, in the bond of peace, and in righteousness of life. Finally, we commend to thy fatherly goodness all those, who are any ways afflicted, or distressed, in mind, body, or estate; that it may please thee to comfort and relieve them, according to their several necessities, giving them patience under their sufferings, and a happy issue out of all their afflictions. And this we beg for Jesus Christ his sake. *Amen.*

A General Intercession

Alternative Service Book:
O God, the creator and preserver of all mankind, we pray for men of every race, and in every kind of need: make your ways known on earth, your saving power among all nations. (Especially we pray for . . .)
Lord, in your mercy
hear our prayer.
We pray for your Church throughout the world: guide and govern us by your Holy Spirit, that all who profess and call themselves Christians may be led into the way of truth, and hold the faith in unity of spirit, in the bond of peace, and in righteousness of life. (Especially we pray for . . .)
Lord, in your mercy
hear our prayer.
We commend to your fatherly goodness all who are anxious or distressed in mind or body; comfort and relieve them in their need; give them patience in their sufferings, and bring good out of their troubles. (Especially we pray for . . .)
Merciful Father,
accept these prayers
for the sake of your Son,
our Saviour Jesus Christ. Amen.

The Blessing after Communion

The peace of God, which passes all understanding, keep your hearts and minds in the knowledge and love of God, and of his Son Jesus Christ our Lord; and the blessing of God almighty, the Father, the Son, and the Holy Spirit, be among you, and remain with you always. *Amen.*

Further reading

Introducing the Anglican way

Extension Studies Module on Anglicanism: St John's College, Nottingham, NG9 3DS, 1996.
Ramsey, Michael: *The Anglican Spirit,* ed. Dale Coleman, SPCK, 1991.
Stephenson, Alan M. G.: *Anglicanism and the Lambeth Conferences*, SPCK, 1978.
Stevenson, Kenneth, & Spinks, Bryan: *The Identity of Anglican Worship*, Harrisburg: Moorhouse, 1994.
Sykes, Stephen, & Booty, John: *The Study of Anglicanism*, SPCK, and Minneapolis: Fortress Press, 1988.

The history of the Anglican Church

Chadwick, Owen: *Michael Ramsey,* Oxford University Press, 1990.
Hastings, Adrian: *A History of English Christianity 1920–1990*, HarperCollins, 1990.
Iremonger, F. A.: *William Temple*, Oxford University Press, 1948.
Neill, Stephen: *Anglicanism*, Penguin Books, 1958, and Mowbray, 1977.
Neill, Stephen: *A History of Christian Missions*, Penguin Books, 1964.

Historical texts

Bede: *A History of the English Church and People*, Penguin, 1955.
Coleman, Roger (ed.): *Resolutions of the Twelve Lambeth Conferences 1867–1988*, Toronto: Anglican Book Centre, 1992.
Hooker, Richard: *Of the Laws of Ecclesiastical Polity*, J. M. Dent, 1907.

Contemporary Anglican faith and practice

Anglican Communion Office, Anglican Communion Secretariat, Partnership House, 157 Waterloo Road, London SE1 8UT:
The Anglican Communion, A Guide, 1991.
The Anglican Communion, A Handbook, 1994.
Anglican Consultative Council, Anglican Communion Secretariat, Partnership House, 157 Waterloo Road, London SE1 8UT:
Anglican World (periodical).
Anglican Cycle of Prayer (annual), Cincinnati: Forward Movement Publications and London: Church House Publishing, London, SW1P 3NZ.
Bunting, Ian (ed.): *Closer to God*, Practical Help on your Spiritual Journey, Scripture Union, 1995.
Grove booklets: Spirituality, Worship, Pastoral, Evangelism and Ethics Series (quarterly), Grove Books: Cambridge, CB3 9HU.
Meakin, Tony: *A Basic Church Dictionary and Compendium*, Norwich: The Canterbury Press, 1995.

Acknowledgments

The authors would like to thank the following for permission to reproduce photographs, illustrations and extracts:

The Anglican Church of Australia, pages 42, 51, 53.
The Anglican Communion News Service/James Rosenthal, page 49.
The Anglican Communion Office, page 139.
Anglican World/John Lake, page 81.
Anglican World/James Rosenthal, pages 16, 17, 64, 111, 120, 159, 165, 182, 206; also, front cover photos (excluding top right, by Ian Bunting).
Barnabys Picture Library, page 222.
The British Library, page 131.
The Canterbury Press Norwich, page 209: diagram from Tony Meakin's *A Basic Church Dictionary and Compendium* (The Canterbury Press, 1990).
The Central Board of Finance of the Church of England, page 86: extract from *Patterns for Worship*, Commended Edition (Church House Publishing, 1995, *p. 241*).
The Church Mission Society, pages 27, 38, 82, 129, 238.
The Church Mission Society/Andy Hutchinson, page 103.
Church Society/Lambeth Palace Library, pages 25, 44.
The Church Times, page 187.
The Church Times/Gideon Mendel, page 38.
The Church Urban Fund, page 155.
The Church Urban Fund/Stefano Cagnoni, page 148.
The Church Urban Fund/Sam Tanner, pages 163, 195, 234.
Terry Culkin, page 89.
Taffy Davies, pages 3, 19, 67, 125, 177, 227, 229, 243.
The Dean and Chapter of Durham, pages 217, 218.
Episcopal News Service, page 189.
Episcopal News Service/Herb Pilcher, page 106.
The Evening Standard, page 37.
HarperCollins, page 96.
The Julian Centre, Norwich, page 135.
Keith Ellis Collection, page 200; also, cover photo of General Synod.
The Leprosy Mission, Peterborough PE2 5GZ/Lens Ideas, page 102.
The Mansell Collection, pages 30, 71, 171.
The Mansell Collection/National Portrait Gallery, page 91.
The Mothers' Union/Pat Harris, page 153.
The National Portrait Gallery, page 73.
Papua New Guinea Church Partnership/C. Luxton, page 57.
The Sunday Express, page 58.
Maurice Taylor, Architect, page 225.

Index

Page numbers in italics refer to captions of illustrations

Act of Supremacy 73, 77
Act of Toleration 1689 74
adaptation of worship 89, 95–6, 230, 241
Africa:
 growth in Anglican Communion 145
 new religious movements 34–5
 prayers from 140–1
Age of Reason 80
AIDS 39, 40, 164
all-age worship 95
All Souls, Langham Place *111*
Allen, Roland 57
Alternative Service Book 1980 89, 94, 96, 132, 141
 on bishops 181
 Holy Communion in 97
 on marriage 152
 prayers from 244–6
 on ordained ministry 185
Andrewes, Bishop Lancelot 135
Anglican Catholics 57, 58
Anglican Church:
 authority 205–8
 a broad church 21–3
 character 18, 21–32
 a church for everyone 238–41
 common language 22
 early history 43
 and ecumenical movement 18, 80
 family likeness 22
 future 229–43
 generosity of spirit 154
 history after Elizabeth I 79–81
 nature 18, 21–32
 origin and history 69–81
 sharing faith 145–51
 spectrum 21–3, 113–14
 variety 229–31
Anglican churches, government 205
Anglican Church of Australia 45, 123
Anglican Church of Canada 122–3
Anglican Communion 78–9, 193–4
 definition 54, 55
 common ground 123–4
 origin 54–5
 provisionality 61–2, 124
 range and problems 122–3
 size and scope 144
Anglican Consultative Council 65, 144, 194
Anglican principle and system 61
Anglican worship 82–96, 233
Anglo-Catholic worship 110–11, *111*, 114–15, 115–17, 122
 mission services 95
 prayer 134, 138–9
 social activism 174
Anglo-Saxon churches 216
Anselm, Archbishop of Canterbury 135
anti-clericalism 71
apartheid 35, 139
apostolic succession 115, 117
archbishops 193
archdeacons 186, 207
area deans *see* rural deans
Articles of Religion *see* Thirty-nine articles
assembly, for Holy Communion 107
Assyrian Church of the East 59
atonement 29, 92
Auden, W. H. 136
Augustine, St of Canterbury 16, 69, 216, 241
Australia, Anglican Church of:
 constitution 45
 Prayer Book 96
 churchmanship 123
Authorised Version 131
 see also Bible
authority:
 in Anglican Church 205–8
 and Anglo-Catholics 117

balance, in mission of Anglican Church 150
baptism 26, 49, 85, 91, 101, 102–5, *103*, 151–2
    of believers 103, 152
    and children 26, 104
Baptists 152
Basil of Caesarea 162, 164
Becket, Archbishop Thomas 36
Bede, Venerable 43, 69, 130
belief, Anglican 42–52
    core 45–7
    expression of 50–1
    sustaining 48–50
belonging, circles of 147
Benedicite 30
benefices, appointments to 208
Benson, R. M. 139
Bible 131, *131*
    English 71, 72
    and Evangelicals 118
    study 14
    versions 131–2
bishops
    appointment 201–3
    authority 206–8
    historic episcopate 24, 239–41
    House of Lords 35, 36, 181, 203–4
    selection 35
    tasks 31, 159–60, 180–3
    term 179
    women 189–90
Board of Social Responsibility 37–8, 171
Book of Common Prayer (*BCP*) 23, 25–6, *25*, 45, 50, 72, 77
    archaism in 90
    baptism in 103
    and 'ceremonies' 93
    Cranmer's 91–2, 132, 135, 220
    influence on architecture 220
    and 'natives' 55
    prayers from 244–6
    sacrament defined 100
    1662 edition *44*, 133
    traditions not uniform 231
boycotts 171
Bray, Thomas 166
Breaking of Bread 107
    see mainly Holy Communion
Browning, Robert, quoted 121
Burma 145
Butler, Josephine 164, 171
Butterfield, William 224
Calvin, John 43
Camden Society 223
Canada, Anglican Church of 96, 122–3
    women priests 188
canons (laws) 81, 86–7, 212, 236
canons (people) 186
Canterbury 16
care, function of the church 148–9, 161–4
Carey, George, Archbishop of Canterbury *16*, *159*
Caroline Divines 80
catechisms 235
cathedral clergy 201
cathedrals 129–31, 219
Catholic Radicalism 174
catholic tradition of Anglican Church 15–16, 21, 57, 58
catholicity, pole of Anglicanism 61, 63, 238–41
Celebrating Common Prayer 133
Celtic Christianity 69–70, 230
Celtic Mission 70, 230, 241
chaplaincies 187
charismatic movement 16, 113–14, 119–20, 128, 138
Charles, Prince of Wales 234
Chau, Ernest *42*
Chicago-Lambeth Quadrilateral 24, 59–61
Chinese Anglicans *42*
Christian Aid 165
Christian Socialism 36, 139, 172–4
Christian Unions 138
Christianity:
    as official religion 34
    and social order 39
Church:
    authority of 47
    as the sacrament of Christ 101
    and society 33–41
    sustainer of faith 48
    in the world 33–5
    and worship 86–7
    year 89–90, 141
Church Army *148*, 194, 213–14
Church Assembly 94
    see also General Synod
church buildings 127–8, 215–26
    historical development 215–24
    twentieth-century 224–6
Church Commissioners 210, 211–12
church government 199–214
Church Mission(ary) Society (CMS) 56, 59, 137, 213

Church of England *see mainly* Anglican Church
Church of England Assembly (Powers) Act 1919 204, 211
Church of England Board for Social Responsibility 37–8, 171
Church of North India 60
Church of South India 60
church officers 210
Church Pastoral Aid Society (CPAS) 214
church planting 156, 216
churches 129–31, 225
  symbols of the sacred 226
  see also church buildings
churchmanship 110–24
Church's Ministry Among Jewish People (CMJ) 213
churchwardens 196, 211
Clapham Sect 137, 170–1, 172
classical style, church architecture 220–2
clergy 179–91
  appointments 50, 208
  history 179–80
Cloud of Unknowing, quoted 135
coadjutor bishops 183
Collect for Purity 84
college, for training Anglican leaders 66
colonies 55, 56, 79
Communion *see* Holy Communion
communion table from Zaire *129*
community 48, 49–50
Community of the Resurrection 139
compline, revived 133
confession 52, 138
confessional churches 232
confirmation 26–7, 49, 91, 105–6, *106*, 151–2
congregations, and social care 167
conservatives in Anglican Church 21
Constantine, Emperor 34
contraception, artificial methods 39
convergence by churches on Word and Sacrament 100–1
Coronation Oath 200
Cosin, Bishop John 135
Counter-Reformation 54
Coverdale's Bible 72
Cranmer, Archbishop Thomas 72–3, 91–4, *91*, 132, 133, 135
Creation story 89–90
creeds 28, 87, 104, 232
critical solidarity 35–7
'Crisis at Christmas' shelter *38*
Crosslinks (Bible Churchman's Missionary Society) 59, 213
Crown and church 200–1
Crown Appointments Commission 202–3
Crown livings 201
cultural context of Anglicans 63–4, 144–5
curates 185
Cyprian, Saint 62

Daily Office 92, 132
deacons 179, 180, 190–1
deaneries 186
deans 186, 201
death and life, sacramental aspect 101
death *see also* funerals
Decade of Evangelism 144, 160, 206, 241
Declaration of Assent 45
Decorated style, architecture 219–20
deism 80
denominationalism 242
dioceses 192–3
  creation 146
dissent 36
divorce 153, 236
Dix, Dom Gregory 95, 108
doctrine:
  of the Church of England 86–7
  teaching the Anglican way 28–30
  and worship 77–8, 86–7
Donne, John 136
Dunloe Centre for the Homeless *195*
Durham Cathedral *217–8*
duty, Christian 142

Early English style, architecture 219
East African revival 137
ecclesiology, in Anglican church 59–61
ecumenical movement 60–1, 80–1, 158, 241–3
education 165–6, 155–6
  and voluntary organisations 213
Edward VI 72–3
'eldership' schemes 197
electoral rolls, parish 211
Eliot, T. S. 136
Elizabeth I, Queen 73, *74*, 76
  verse quoted 27
Elizabeth II *200*, 200–201
Enabling Act *see* Church of England Assembly (Powers) Act 1919
engagement, of the church in society 50–1, 233
episcopacy *see* bishops
Episcopal Church in the United States of America 39, 45, 96, 196, 233

Essenes 33
Established Church 35, 204–5, 242
Ethiopian Orthodox Church 59
Eucharist 107
    see mainly Holy Communion
eucharistic theology 27
evangelical revival 80
evangelical tradition 14, 111–12, 114, 117–19
    prayer in 134, 137–8
evangelism 14, 28, 56–7
    and Lambeth Conference 1988 144, 159–60, 206, 234, 241
evil, delivery from 120

failure, by Anglicans 52
faith, invitation to 158
'Faith in the City' report 38, 233
family services 95
Farrer, Austin 140
Figgis, John Neville 173
finance 35, 237
Fisher, Archbishop Geoffrey (Lord Fisher) 81, 212
fonts 104
Frere, Bishop Walter 94–5
funeral service 90–1
funerals 153–4

General Synods *49*, 94, 193, 204, 208–12
    Boards of 210
glossary of ecclesiastical architectural terms 224
God:
    encounter with 84–7
    knowledge of 47–8
    and liberals 122
    nature 46
    and Thirty-Nine Articles 45–7
godparents (sponsors) 103
The Good News Bible 131
good works and justification 29
Gospel, Jesus Christ as 143–4
gothic churches 218–20
gothic revival churches 222
government of the church 199–214
grace, in sacraments 100
Graham, Dr Billy 138
Great Bible 1539 71–2, 131
Gregory, Pope 216, 241
Guild of St Matthew 174

Hackett, John 132
Headlam, Stewart 174
healing, the Word as 98
    the church's ministry 149
Henry VIII 72, 74
Herbert, George 30, *30*, 132, 136
    quoted 65, 132
Herft, Bishop Roger 149
Highbury, Christ Church *225*
Holy Communion 26, 27, 85, 101, 106–9
    and Anglo-Catholics 139
    and children 105
    and Cranmer 92
    diversity 63–6
    form of service 107–8
    and music 109
    term 107
    themes 108
Holy Cross Centre *163*
Holy Spirit 46, 47
    and charismatic movement 119–20, *120*
homosexuality 40
Hooker, Richard 43, 49, 52, 77–8, 139
    on scripture 108
Hope, David, Archbishop of York *182*
Hopkins, Gerard Manley, quoted 115
house church movement 63
House of Bishops 208
House of Clergy 208
House of Laity 210
House of Lords, and bishops 35, 36, 181, 203–4
Huddleston, Archbishop Trevor 139, *139*
human rights abuse 40
humanity:
    as sacrament 102
    in worship 87–91
Huntington, William Reed 59–60, 61
hymns 94, 111, 117

incarnation 27, 29, 46–7, 115–16, 135
incarnation of Jesus Christ 44, 98, 115–16
Indian Syrian Church 59
influence, politics of 169–71
institutions, and social care 167
instruments of communion 60
interdenominationalism, and voluntary societies 168
interfaith dialogue 234
involvement in local life 156–7
Iran 145
Ireland, Church of:
    new prayer book 96
    reformation and after 75–6
isolationism 199

James I and VI 74–5
Jamieson, Bishop Penelope *189*
Japanese Anglicans *27*
Jerusalem Bible 132
Jesus Christ:
  centrality 31, 40–1, 84, 232–4
  to Evangelicals 118
  as Gospel 143
  incarnation 33, 46–7
  to liberals 121
  primordial sacrament 101
  and social action 161, 164
Julian of Norwich 135, *135*
Justin Martyr 107

Keble, John 117, 138
Ken, Bishop Thomas 135, 136
Kennedy, Studdert 139–40
Kenyan blessing 95
Keswick Convention 137
Knox, John 74
Koinonia 107

laity 196
  lay patronage 77
  role in church 49–50, 196–8, 209–11
Lambeth Conferences 40, 194
  and evangelism 159–60
  origin and history 60, 206
  and provisionality of Anglican Communion 61–2
  social issues 39–40
  variety of languages used 65–6
  1888 24, 60
  1930 62
  1978 149
  1988 241
  1998 themes 242
Lambeth Palace *206*
language used in Anglican gatherings 65–6
Latin America:
  base communities 63
  Christianity 35, 39
Laud, Archbishop William 75, 135
  reforms 221
Law, William 135
laws 204–5
lay patrons *see* laity
leaders, training 66
leadership 64, 197–8
lepers *102*, 164
Lewis, C. S. 140
liberal tradition 15
Liberal Catholic worship 114
'liberal churchmanship' 112–13, 115, 120–2
liberation theologians 35
Lightfoot, Bishop J. B., quoted 48
Lima document, and baptism 80, 103
Lindisfarne Gospels 72, *131*
liturgical movement 95
liturgy 50, 65, 133, 232–4
local ecumenical partnerships 80, 158
local ordained ministry 185
locality, and the Anglican Church 61, 63, 145–6, 238–9
Lollards 71
Lords Spiritual 203–4
Lord's Supper 107
  see mainly Holy Communion
love, in the commandments 161–2
love of God 30
'loyal dissent' 58
Luther, Martin 42
Lutheran churches:
  and bishops 240
  unity with 62, 80, 242
Luwum, Archbishop Janani *38*, 39, 137, 150
Lux Mundi group 173

Making Women Visible 96
Mandela, President Nelson *159*
manuals and primers 133
Mar Thoma Syrian Church 59
marriage 152–3
Mary I 73, 77
Mascall, Prof. Eric 15
Mass 107
  see mainly Holy Communion
Maundy money 201
Maurice, F. D. 36, 139, 172
  quoted 239
medieval cathedrals 218
meditation, rediscovery 128
Meiderlin, Peter 146
Meissen Declaration 80–1
Methodism 63, 242
middle axioms 38, 173
middle way 78, 139, 229
ministry 31
  Anglican 48–9
  of all church members 118, 196–8
  in the future 237–8
mission:
  by Anglo-Catholics 116
  comprehensive 233
  and evangelicals 119

mission: *(cont.)*
five marks of 144
and models of the church 147
and the Reformation 53–4
services 95
world 143–60
Missionary Church 62–3
missionary societies 55, 119, 122, 149
missionary work 128, 213–14
missioners 160
missions of assistance 58–9
moderation 44
monasteries 70, 77
moral teaching 29
More, Hannah 165–6
Mothers' Union 153, *153*, 168
multinational corporations 170
music, and Holy Communion 109
mystics 135

National Society for Promoting Religious Education 166, 213
New English Bible 131
New Zealand, Anglican Church in Aotearoa, New Zealand and Polynesia:
Aukland Cathedral 225
Diocesan Bishop *189*
Prayer Book 91, 96
Women Priests 188
Newman, Cardinal John Henry 138
Newton, John 137
Niebuhr, Reinhold 39
non-jurors 58, 75
non-stipendiary priests 185, 237
Norman churches 216–18
nuclear weapons 40

O'Donnovan, O. M. T., quoted 44
Ogle, Revd Catherine *187*
openness 44, 51–2, 146, 148
ordained ministry 185
Ordering of Bishops, Priests and Deacons (Ordinal) 23, 24–5, 28, 45
orders and officers 179–98
orders 194–6
Orthodox churches 59
other denominations, working with 158
outcasts, care for 164
Oxford Movement 27, 57, 80, 115, 138, 195, 222–3

Papua New Guinea *57*
parish churches 184
see also church buildings
parishes 63, 183–4, 191–2, 239
system 146
Parliament, approval of Book of Common Prayer 94
parochial church councils 211
parochial church meetings 209
parochialism 199
Paschal mystery 23
Pastoral Measure 1968 204
pastoral rites (occasional offices) 90–1, 151–4
patronage 77, 208
patronage trusts 214
Patterns for Worship 86–7, 89, 92, 95, 233
Paul, St 34
Paul VI, Pope, *Humanae Vitae* 39
perpendicular style 220
pilgrim way 141–2
places, and the church 191–4
politics, and Anglican Church 169–72, 240–1
polygamy 40
poor, sacrament of 102
Pope 42
Porvoo Declaration 81, 240
post-modern context 174–5
poverty 40, 165
practical Christianity 235–8
practical spirituality 161–2
prayer 127–42
and Holy Communion 108
in local community 157
varieties 134
in worship 84–5
prayer books 132–4
new versions 96, 235
see also Book of Common Prayer
prayers:
African 140–1
rhythm of 141–2
selection of 244–6
preachers 98
prebendaries 186
Presbyterian Church 43
presence, in the community 155–6
pressure groups 171
priests 183–9
specialised forms 185–8
team 179
Prime Minister, and appointment of bishops 201–2, 203
printing, central to reforms 93–4

prisoners, love for 165
proctors 208
prostitution 164, 171
protest, politics of 171–2
Protestant churches 42–3
providence and incarnation 43–4
provinces 193
provosts 201
psalms 25, 89, 92
Pugin, A. W. N. 222–3
Puritans, in Anglican Church 21

radical churchmanship 114
radio and television, services on 134
Ramsey, Archbishop Michael (Lord Ramsey) *58*, 133–4, *140*
  quoted 50, 51, 232
readers 197
reason 25, 48, 114, 120–1
received tradition *see* tradition
reconciliation 30
rectors 184–5
redemption, and Evangelicals 119
Redemptoris Missio 143
redundant churches 226
reformation 36, 43, 48, 52, 70–1
  and Evangelicals 117
  and mission 53–4
Reformed churches 43
religious community, and Anglo-Catholics 116
religious orders 195–6
renaissance style of architecture 220–2
renunciation, in baptism 104
retreat 128
rhythm of church year in calendar 141–2
rites of passage 90–1, 151–4
Roman Catholic Church 42, 54, 73, 80, 232
Romans, and Christianity 69, 164, 180–1, 230
Royal Maundy 201
royal peculiars 201
royal supremacy 76–7
Runcie, Archbishop Robert (Lord Runcie) 38
rural deans (area deans) 186, 207

sacramental theology 26–8
sacraments 48–9, 99–102
  and Anglo-Catholics 116
  and Book of Common Prayer 26
  defined 99–100
  number of 101–2
  as ritual 101
  in worship 85
sacrifice 29
St Paul's Cathedral, London 222
salvation 24, 47
Saravia, Adrianus 55
Satkaar project, Leamington Spa 234
schools, and Anglican Communion 165–6
Scotland, The Scottish Episcopal Church:
  Prayer Book 96
  Reformation in 74–5
  women priests 188
scripture:
  Anglican view 24–5, 43
  basis for worship 114–15
  and Holy Communion 107–8
  as sacrament 101
  source for knowledge of God 47–8
  in worship 85, 92
sector ministers 160, 187–8, 208
sects, defined 34
Sermon on the Mount 48
A Service of the Word 95
Shaftesbury, Anthony Ashley Cooper, Lord 36
sick, care of 164–5
Sign of the Cross, and baptism 104
Simeon, Charles 137
slavery, abolition 170
social action 161–9, 174
  organising 166–9
social concerns 149–50, 233
society:
  care and change in 161–75
  and change 149–50
Society for the Maintenance of the Faith 214
Society for the Promotion of Christian Knowledge (SPCK) 79, 166, 213
Society for the Propagation of the Gospel (now USPG) 79, 213
Society of St Francis 133
Society of St John the Evangelist 116, 139
solidarity 35–7
South Africa, The Church of the Province of:
  the Church's witness 35, 39
  duties of a Christian 142
  types of ministers 237
South American Missionary Society (SAMS) 213
South Asia, churches 57
speaking in tongues 119
spirituality 234
  and charismatic movement 119–20
  practical expression 127
spoken word 98
state and church 43
stations of the cross 139

stipends 212, 237
Stott, John 138
Sudan, Yambio Cathedral *82*
suffragan bishops 183, 203
Sursum Corda 93
Sydney, Australia *51*, *53*
synodical government 208–12

tabernacle *89*
Tadcaster parish church 225
Tanzania, refugee camp *103*
Taylor, Jeremy 135–6
Te Deum Laudamus 29, 30
team ministries 185, 197
technological advance 40
Temple, Archbishop William 36, 37, *37*, 39, 139, 149, 173
  quoted 238
terrorism 40
Thirty-Nine Articles 23, 26, 45, 77, 117, 232
  in Ireland 76
  in Scotland 75
Thomas, R.S. 136
Thornton, Henry 170
thurifer and boatboy, Papua New Guinea *57*
Tractarian movement, world mission 57–8
  see also Oxford Movement
tradition 48, 93, 114, 231
  value of received tradition 49
Trinity, nature 28–9, 46
Tutu, Archbishop Desmond 39, *64*, 139, 150, *159*
  quoted 40, 240
Twentieth-century churches 224–6
Tyndale, William 71, 72, 131

Uganda, women priests 188
Underhill, Evelyn 140
uniformity not imposed 114–15, 231
unity, the Anglican purpose 30–2
Universities' Mission to Central Africa 57

Vacancy-in-See Committee 201–2
Vatican Council, 2nd 1963 95–6
Venn, Henry 56–7, 137
vernacular liturgies 65
vestry meetings 211
vicars 184–5
Victorian churches 222–4
Vietnamese congregation *51*
visible word 99
voluntary principle 56, 213–14
voluntary societies, and social care 168–9

Waite, Terry 165, *165*
Wales, The Church in:
  Anglican church 21
  and Reformation 76
  and women priests 188
war and peace 40
wardens of readers 208
water, and baptism 104
Watson, David 138, 168
Watts, Isaac 119
Wesley, Charles and John 137
Whichcote, Benjamin 139
Whitby, Synod of 70
Wilberforce, William 36, 170, *171*
witness:
  through caring 148–9
  model for 144
  region, nation etc 158–60
  wider community 154–8
women:
  bishops 189–90
  deacons 190–1
  ordination *81*, 117, 230–1
  priesthood 188–9
Word 97–9
  forms 98–9
  and sacrament 48–9, 97–109
world church 60
World Council of Churches:
  Conference on Church and Society 40
  Lima Document 80
world mission 56–7
worldwide communion 53–66
worship:
  corporate activity 83–4
  current and future developments 95–7, 233
  and doctrine 77–8, 86–7
  encounter with God 84–7
  faith through 150–1
  historical developments 91–5
  humanity celebrated 87–91
  nature 232–3
  principles 83–91
  and theology 50
  varieties in Anglican churches 82
Worship and Doctrine Measure 1974 86–7, 94
Wren, Sir Christopher 222
written word 98
  see also scripture
Wyclif, John 71, 72

Zaire *129*